Elementary Bioinformatics

Elementary Bioinformatics

Imtiyaz Alam Khan

M.Sc., PGADB
Bioinformatics tutor, Microbiologist.
Ex-Lecturer, Dept. of Biotechnology,
Rai University, Hyderabad.

PharmaMed Press
An imprint of Pharma Book Syndicate

A unit of BSP Books Pvt. Ltd.

4-4-316, Giriraj Lane,
Sultan Bazar, Hyderabad - 500 095.

Published by :

PharmaMed Press
An imprint of Pharma Book Syndicate

A unit of BSP Books Pvt. Ltd.

4-4-316, Giriraj Lane, Sultan Bazar, Hyderabad - 500 095.
Phone: 040-23445605, 23445688; Fax: 91+40-23445611
E-mail: info@pharmamedpress.com

ISBN : 978-93-52300-09-9 (HB)

Preface

This book presents good coverage of Bioinformatics concepts, concise coverage of multiple sequence alignment practicals, gene identification practicals, domain identification practicals. More illustrations have been included in most of the chapters to emphasize the importance of topics under study. This particular edition is prepared to facilitate students, academicians and research workers. Genetic Engineering which is a part of Bioinformatics, is also explained very clearly. This book is designed keeping in view of all Universitie's Syllabus; basically meant for JNTU B.Tech Students. Anybody interested in learning basic Bioinformatics can use it.

This book will serve well as a supplement to either a formal Bioinfomatics Course or an integrated curriculum. We hope that senior students, graduates, postgraduates, academicians and researchers will use this book as a reference for Bioinformatics information.

TO THE READER

"Elementary Bioinformatics" is a very handy book, which is helpful in understanding Bioinformatics from its grass root levels. As we all know, bioinformatics is a highly emerging field. It is now in its primordial state and within few years it will reach climax. Understanding Bioinformatics at this level that too in a very conceptual, concise and vivid manner is what the requirement of present scenario. Every topic is explained very clearly, especially sequence alignment, multiple sequence alignments, phylogenetics predictions, gene predictions and so on.. After reading them the reader will get clear concept of those topics. Few practicals are also included in order to make them comfortable with online Bioinformatics tools.

"Elementary Bioinformatics" is designed to provide a logical framework for organizing, learning, reviving and applying the conceptual and factual information required.

Acknowledgement

I am extremely thankful to Azher Khan, Asst. Prof., Dept of Computer Science DCET for his contributory work on Internet - Elementary Commands and Protocols in Chapter 1 of this book.

Contents

1 Internet

2 Sequence Analysis
(Introduction to Bioinformatics/Sequence Analysis)

3   Calculation of Sequence Alignments

4 Computational Biology
(Biological Database Management System)

5 Computational Biology :
Information Retrieval From Databases

6   Phylogenetic Analysis

7   Phylogenetic Prediction

8   Genetic Engineering

9   DNA Sequencing

10   Genome Mapping

11   Gene Identification

1

Internet

1.1 Scope of Bioinformatics

Bioinformatics has emerged as a distinct discipline that straddles the interface between the traditional biological sciences and the computer sciences and advance computational methodologies. It is rapidly becoming a powerful new approach to understanding life, and it may well reverse the reductionist paradigm that has held sway in molecular biology ever since Erwin Schrodinger turned on a generation of physicists to biology with the publication of "What is life ? more than 50 years ago.

The new discipline of bioinformatics promises to provide the tools needed to attack the complexity of conducting holistic biological research, "because of this complexities, biology will eventually become the most computational science, surpassing physics," said Delici, who predicts that within the next 10 to 15 years bioinformatics will become the integral part of biology.

Modern day biotech and drug discovery industry has witnessed the development of high through put automated equipment, which enables amassing of data faster than it can be analyzed and the utilized. Pharmaceutical research will clearly be the one major benefactor of development in bioinformatics. 100 of new drug targets have been identified by using computational techniques, which involves searching for genes similar to known protein encoding genes. In the future, virtual toxicology screening may be the first setup in predicting the effects of new chemical or complex metabolic pathways. In addition, bioinformatics will likely provide the methodology, to make highly accurate predictions about protein tertiary structure based on amino acid sequences and a viable means to design drugs based on computer simulation of the docking of small molecules to the predicted protein architecture.

According to figures from Framingham mass based market analysis firm IDC Bio-IT market will reach $38 billion in 2006. The market includes pharmaceutical, healthcare research and biotechnology companies, as well as Govt. linked institutions. A number of recent work force studies have shown that there is a high current and unmet demand for people trained to various levels of expertise in bioinformatics, serve the upcoming biotech and biopharmaceutical industry which has observed significant growth in genomic era.

1.2 Introduction (Elementary Commands and Protocols)

The Internet has become an important tool for biological and biomedical research scientists. Using the Internet, it is possible to perform a number of kinds of analysis on research data and to search for and obtain information. Over the last several years, the number of tools and the amount of information relevant to biologists available on the Internet has grown and the ease of use of these tools has grown as well. As a result of both of these trends, the value of Internet resources for biologists now significantly outweighs the costs in time and money of using it. The overall goal of this chapter is to help biologists use the Internet effectively and to illustrate to computer scientists, how biologists are currently using the Internet.

This chapter has three specific goals :

1. To provide background information which will help demystify computer network usage.
2. To provide an introduction to the resources available to biologists over the Internet in sufficient detail to allow the students in this course to explore and learn how to use these resources on their own.
3. To provide practical instruction to these students on using the specific network resources needed during the remainder of the course.

It is assumed that the students can use a Web Browser (e.g. Internet Explorer or Netscape Navigator) to access the contents of the course.

1.3 How Different Internet Services are Used

As noted above, different Internet services are characterized by client software, server software, a set of capabilities they agree upon (e.g. text, pictures in the GIF format, etc.), a protocol by which they communicate (i.e. how the data is encoded in a stream of bytes), and a port on which the client contacts the server to begin communication. The distinction between different services can be blurred because different services can perform similar functions, because different services can share capabilities, and because of the existence of multifunction clients (and servers). Specifically, many modern Web clients are highly multifunctional, being gopher, ftp, e-mail and net news clients in addition to being Web clients. Finally, note that although this chapter deals with services delivered via the Internet, some of these same services can be delivered via other, very different kinds of networks, Internets, or dedicated connections.

What is presented here is a very superficial overview of a few of the available Internet services.

1.4 Telnet

Telnet is one of the oldest of the network services and perhaps the easiest to understand. Telnet allows one computer to "log on" to another computer as if it were a terminal. Once logged on, you frequently will have all the privileges of a local user; you can run programs, create and delete files. This is probably the most common way that users with accounts will use a computer.

Although "full service logins" as is described above are perhaps the most common use of the telnet protocol, in fact as much control as the host's system administrator desires may be imposed on a telnet connection. Thus, a telnet service may be advertised with a public login name and password. Login with this name, however, is likely to be restricted to a limited number of commands. The National Institutes of Health in the United States used, at one point, such a telnet login to disseminate information as to the membership of study sections. Such specialized telnet services have become much less common since the rise in popularity of the Web.

A telnet session can negotiate a range of different protocols, but this almost always includes ASCII text. Because many protocols for other services (e.g. SMTP, HTTP) are encoded as ASCII text, a telnet client can sometimes be used to connect to a server for these other protocols. Most people will use a telnet client the first time connecting to a MOO, and some people will continue to use telnet as their client, although most of us find dedicated clients to be significantly more convenient. Similarly, it is possible to connect to a Web server with a telnet client if you understand the syntax of HTTP. This is almost never done to use a Web server, but is occasionally done when debugging.

From a practical point of view, every telnet host will be different, and thus you will need to learn about each one as you have occasion to use it.

1.5 Ftp

Telnet is useful for interactive computer access, but is much less useful for transferring files. Ftp is an older service designed specifically for file transfer. Originally like telnet, it was intended for account owners. However, as it became apparent that it was useful to make files available to the world at large without giving all those wanting the files an account, the variant of "anonymous ftp" developed. In this variant, logging in with a "magic" user name (most commonly "anonymous" or "ftp") eliminates the requirement for a password.

In 1996, "To a large extent, use of the World Wide Web has rendered (direct) ftp access obsolete." Although there was and is some truth to that statement (especially given that files on an ftp server can be retrieved by a Web client), the need for ftp clients has not vanished. Some users will choose to avoid them, preferring the simplicity of dealing with a single piece of software, but within their domain ftp clients are more versatile than Web browsers, in some cases one has more control with an Ftp client, and for simple file transfer they are quicker and more convenient.

Once logged on via ftp, access to the host filesystem is accomplished by a series of commands. On a UNIX ftp client, the commands are unix-like; *cd* to Change Directory and *ls* to List the files in that directory. To transfer files, you execute either *get* a file from the host computer or *put* a file onto it (where allowed). *These commands do not depend on the host computer running UNIX!* These are ftp commands, some of which happen to be similar to UNIX commands. A client may choose to hide these commands; a client with a graphical user interface (GUI), for example, might not have typed commands at all, but buttons.

One pair of ftp commands which is especially important to understand are *binary* and *ASCII*. Ftp transfers occur in ASCII (text) mode by default. In ASCII mode, the file received may not be identical to the one on the host, as ftp may make changes in the file during transfer, to allow for differences in how different operating systems handle text. For example, UNIX terminates lines with the linefeed character (ASCII 10 decimal), the Macintosh operating system with a carriage return (ASCII 13 decimal) and MS-DOS uses one of each. These differences are corrected for during an ASCII transfer. This is highly desirable for text files, but catastrophic for binary files like program object code and pictures. Thus, before *get*ting such a file, it is important to issue the *binary* command. This instructs ftp to transfer files unmodified.

1.6 E-mail

Both ftp and telnet are interactive, more or less real-time programs. Sometimes it is useful, however, to communicate with another computer, or more commonly, a user on another computer, by leaving them a message, which they can read and respond to at their convenience. This is done over the Internet by using e-mail.

E-mail is a generic term for a variety of processes which can use different protocols and network technology, and which, in many cases uses a more complex client/server model than many of the other protocols discussed in this chapter. At present, most e-mail is transmitted by SMTP (Simple Mail Transfer Protocol) via TCP/IP over the Internet. SMTP transmits e-mail on port 25 between two dedicated, full time servers. Although the assumption is that both SMTP servers will be generally available, should the receiving server not be reachable when the transmitting server needs to send e-mail, the e-mail message will be held and the transmission will be retried several times over a period of days until a successful transmission occurs or until the maximum retry time has been exceeded, at which point an error message will be returned to the sender. Importantly, should the initial attempts at sending e-mail fail, the sending server will frequently e-mail a warning to the user while continuing to attempt delivery. Such warnings can be safely ignored.

The SMTP programs discussed above are typically symmetrical (e.g. the program can alternatively serve as client or server), and are complex. Typically, you will not interact with these programs directly. Rather, dedicated client software is used to compose, send, receive, and read e-mail, and it is that software which communicates with the SMTP server. If you send and receive e-mail via a computer that is always on and always connected to a network reachable by your mail server (e.g. a Unix workstation), then incoming mail is saved to a mail spool file on your computer from where your client software retrieves it, and outgoing e-mail is passed to the SMTP server. Examples of client software running on Unix workstations are mail, mailx, mush, elm, mutt, and pine. Also, as is discussed below, web browsers sometimes can be used as e-mail clients.

If you send and receive e-mail via a computer that is not always on and/or not always connected to the network (e.g. a Mac or a Windows computer), sending e-mail proceeds as above, but receiving e-mail is different, in that the SMTP server cannot necessarily get incoming e-mail onto your computer's file system. In that case, a different protocol is used, most commonly POP3 (aka POP). (IMAP is a newer protocol for accomplishing the same task about which you may hear more in the future.) The SMTP server stores your e-mail on a remote host and your local client retrieves it from a POP3 server when you check for mail. Typically, a POP3 account will be provided by whoever provides your Internet access. Thus, to install an e-mail client on a Mac or Windows computer, you typically have to provide the domain name and/or IP address of the SMTP and POP3 servers (frequently the same) and the user name and password for the POP3 account.

The use of e-mail has been expanded in a number of ways. One of the simplest and earliest was to extend it to automatically deal with groups of readers. This is accomplished by having mail delivered to an address, which corresponds to a program rather than a user. That program in turn resends that message to all the members of the group of readers. Another e-mail address, corresponding to a different but related program, can allow users to issue commands, e.g. to add or remove themselves from the group. Two of the most common of such software packages are Listserver and Majordomo. Although you do not need a sophisticated knowledge of Majordomo to participate in the course, you should at least learn how to unsubscribe from lists when you are no longer interested in them.

List server software has a number of problems. First, remembering the commands and e-mail addresses (one for each group to which you belong and one for the list server to issue commands) is difficult. Second, these list servers are completely dependent upon and very picky about e-mail addresses. At some universities, a user's e-mail address is different depending on how they log onto the system, and these addresses change with some regularity. This will usually not introduce problems for *receiving* mail from a list server as your system will probably resolve these changing names automatically, but produces recurring problems *sending* mail to a list server, as the list server may require that your posting comes from *precisely* the same address as is present in the subscription list. Third, because list servers use the e-mail system, messages from a list server group are intermixed with your private e-mail and with messages from all the other list servers you subscribe to. Fourth, the e-mail program you are likely to be using to read the intermixed mess of messages lack many commands which are extremely useful for efficiently following a group that even the most primitive Usenet software will have. It might be thought that Usenet software would make list servers obsolete in the same way that www ought to make ftp absolete. Why this has not occurred will be discussed in the next section.

A similar e-mail extension uses "mailservers"; programs which receive e-mail and automatically generate a response. (Most list servers have a limited form of this capability.) Mail servers can provide services that one might expect to perform using ftp or the Web. The way this is done is that e-mail is sent to a program on the host computer rather than to a user and this program responds to information in the *Subject* or *Body* of the e-mail message. For example, it is possible to retrieve sequences from Genbank or to use blast to search genbank using mail servers. Use of mail servers have some advantages that have mandated their continued use. Because they are mail based, they are asynchronous. A user can make a request at their convenience, and then go on to other tasks while waiting for their request to be fulfilled.

On the server end, requests can be queued to be filled as the host machine has the resources to do so. With the growth of the Web, hybrid servers have appeared where you request a document via the Web but where the document is delivered to you via e-mail. This is useful if the document is large and/or if its generation takes a long time. This is, for example, an option on NCBI's BLAST server.

The biggest disadvantage of mail servers is that communication with them requires a very precise syntax in the e-mail message. Further, there are no standards for this syntax and thus each different mail server has a different syntax for us to learn. This is an enormous advantage of the hybrid Web/e-mail servers described above. As of this writing, however, the homework requires that you learn at least a basic subset of the commands for the retrieve server.

Basic e-mail is a text-only service. This would limit the usefulness of mail servers; it would prevent them from returning pictures or programs, for example. Originally, this problem was solved by encoding such binary files as ASCII text and placing that text in the body of the e-mail message. On a Unix system, this could have used the program uuencode (and the companion program uudecode to reverse the process). It was then the responsibility of the user to cleanly remove the encoded material from the e-mail message and to use decoding software to convert it back to a binary file. More recently, e-mail was formally extended to handle "complex" messages using the MIME (Multipurpose Internet Mail Extension) protocol. Using a MIME-compatible mail client, one can "attach" arbitrary files to an e-mail message, and with luck, the person receiving these e-mail messages will have a client that understands the MIME attachment you sent and their client will handle the attachment appropriately; most commonly by saving it as a copy of the file to their file system. Unfortunately, this process frequently fails. In the simplest case, the recipient has an old e-mail client that doesn't understand MIME at all. This is relatively easy to deal with, in that this simply defaults to the "old" system; the "attached" file is present as a clearly delimited, encoded block of text (which looks like gibberish) in the body of the e-mail message; a knowledgeable user can infer the nature of the contents and the method of encoding from the e-mail message and (given the correct software) recover the contents. More problematic are transfers that "almost" work; where the recipient has a client that understands MIME, but where the sender uses a

MIME type or an encoding method that the recipient's client doesn't understand. In this case the attachment can be garbled or lost altogether. Incompatible encoding methods are, in my experience, a frequent problem. Common encoding methods include uuencode, bin hex, base64, with some mail clients using proprietary methods. The only solution to this problem is to pre-negotiate formats between sender and recipient.

Finally, in an attempt to allow for formatting (boldface, italics, colored text, etc.) of e-mail messages, a number of "rich text" extensions have developed. For example, if you use your Web client as an e-mail client, it may allow you to format your messages using HTML. These are completely non-standard and will only work if sender and recipient have clients, which agree on a particular extension.

1.7 Using the Web

Words and Pictures. Hyperlinks between and within documents. Movies and Music. Online shopping, database access, and even basic attempts at virtual reality. Is there anything the Web cannot do?

The Web describes information using Hypertext Markup Language (HTML) and transmits it using Hypertext Transfer Protocol (HTTP). The current common name, The Web, is a contraction of its original name, the Word Wide Web, also abbreviated as WWW or W3. A Web browser performs multiple tasks. First, any Web browser is an HTTP client; it knows how to transfer data using the HTTP protocol. Second, any Web browser also knows how to interpret and display HTML, the content markup language used on the Web. Different browsers have different display capabilities and display the same HTML code in different ways (which is why HTML is referred to as a content markup language instead of a page description language) but all of them can understand (parse) HTML and do something reasonable with it.

Some of the differences in the way different Web browsers display the same Web page come from different design decisions ("what font should be used for <H1> text?") and some of it comes from the fact that different Web clients have different capabilities. Some of these differences, such as the ability to display various kinds of still or moving images as part of the Web page or to run programs written in Java, Active X, or JavaScript, represent extensions to HTML. These extra capabilities may be built into the browser or may be added by "plug-ins"; software extensions which give the browser new functionality. Finally, the behavior of a Web browser can frequently changed by configuring its preferences; if you find the default font too small, that can often be increased.

Many new computer users assume that the Web and the Internet are synonymous. However, many protocols other than HTTP flow over the Internet. In part, the new user is confused by the fact that, in addition to supporting extensions to HTML, many popular web browsers have support for other protocols such as e-mail (SMTP, POP, IMAP), newsgroups, ftp, and gopher for example. What this really means is that the particular piece of software (e.g. Netscape Communicator) is more than just a Web client, it is also an e-mail client, an FTP client and a Gopher client. Finally, HTTP does not have to be transmitted over the Internet, and HTML doesn't have to be transmitted via HTTP. Web technology has become a common interface tool for communication between computers on a local network (sometimes called an Intranet). Because Web clients are also a limited FTP client, many people choose so to use them. In the case where a Web page contains a link to an FTP server, simply selecting the link downloads the file. If, however, you are given the following instructions to retrieve a file:

"The file is available by anonymous ftp.

Ftp to ftp.bcm.tmc.edu

And retrieve mbcr/pub/file.txt"

...You could accomplish this with your www client by pointing your client to this URL:

ftp://ftp.bcm.tmc.edu/mbcr/pub/file.txt

1.8 Problems on the Web

One of the major problems currently afflicting the Web is that of incompatibility. This is particularly unfortunate and ironic in that one of the goals of the original Web development was seamless integration of information resources across the Internet. One common symptom of this problem is a browser logo and a statement like "Best Viewed with Netscape 4.5". One attempt at solving this problem is the campaign for platform independent Websites.

Another recurring problem is that of security. Keep in touch with the author of your browser and upgrade to new versions as seems warranted.

1. Consider turning off support for Java in your browser.
2. Above all, be cautious, alert, and informed.

1.9   Some Practical Considerations for Using The Web

1. It has become increasingly possible to spend money on the Web. Nonetheless, **with one exception**,: it is unlikely that you will spend money by accident. The exception is an important and unfortunate one; if you work for a non-profit institution (company) located outside of Switzerland, according to Geneva Bioinformatics, the owners of SwissProt, you must pay a substantial licensing fee (thousands of dollars a year) for any use of this database. For example, while using the otherwise free service Entrez you might innocently link to and download a SwissProt sequence file. According to Geneva Bioinformatics, you have just become liable for an annual licensing fee, and there is no way you could have known that. Thus, if you are working for a for-profit organization, you should either carefully avoid SwissProt, or else pay the licensing fee. Other than that, you will find that many resources on the Web are free, and those that are not, inform you clearly and carefully before obligating you to pay.

2. "Although the Internet is becoming increasingly important to biologists, it is still not a sufficient resource for keeping up with biology...With access to a good (or even adequate) science library, you could do without the Internet." This is changing. Reasonable people might now differ as to whether the library or the Web is now more important, but most would probably agree that both are now virtually essential for the working biologist. To be clear, *physical* access to a library is becoming less essential, but belonging to an organization *affiliated* with a library remains important. Most research is still published in conventional journals. What has changed is that a complete copy (full text and figures) of more and more journals have become available via the web.

However, most of these are only available to subscribers. Most working biologists cannot afford personal subscriptions to all of the journals they need to read. However, if your library subscribes to a journal, that usually entitles you to view, download, and print articles from the journal's website. I'm certainly not suggesting that libraries and librarians are unimportant. Information Science is an increasingly important discipline, but I think most librarians and users of libraries can agree that the role of libraries and librarians in science is changing rapidly and it is difficult to predict where it is going.

3. Network resources are not as reliable as one would like. If you select a resource and receive only an error message, the fault is likely to be with the server. It is even the case that if you reach the server and don't receive the results you expect (e.g. search for a common term and get nothing in return) this might be due to the fact that the server is misbehaving rather than you doing the search incorrectly. And finally, what has become an increasing problem is that WebPages will either move, be edited to significantly change their meaning, or become temporarily or permanently unavailable.

4. Compared to the well-developed conventions for referencing data from the paper literature, conventions for acknowledging of Internet resources in a thesis or paper are in utter chaos. Surfing the net for a few months will uncover a number of competing standards for how to accomplish this. For resources available on the web, a URL is my reference of choice. However, given the previous point, I have become cautious about publishing references to digital resources at all.

5. Just because it is on a computer doesn't mean it is correct. This sounds like a banal truism, but it is startling how good the beauty of computer output can make bad data look. Genbank is loaded with author errors (both in the sequence and comments sections) and probably contains some archivist-introduced errors as well. The same is true of Medline. Any study, which assumes perfection in such data, will produce an incorrect result.

1.10   Finding Web Resources

The Web is vast and disorganized, and the overwhelming majority of what is there is irrelevant to you. Further, the Web changes constantly; new resources appear, old resources become outdated or disappear and the paths and techniques used to access resources change. The bad news is that there is no perfect way of finding the resources that might be useful to you. The good news is that you don't need a perfect way; finding even half the useful resources on the Web is well worth while, and a lot better than ignoring the Web altogether.

I find the following approaches the most useful for identifying biological resources on the web:

1.11   Search Engines

There are several websites from which you can launch searches. You type in words that you expect to find on the Web page you are looking for, and it will return to you a list of pages on the Web that contain those words. The services that I keep links to are:

(i) Google

One of the finest search services. Provides a much shorter, more focused list of sites than most other services. This is currently the first search I try.

(ii) Alta Vista

This used to be my first choice. Very complete, very powerful search facilities. I switched to Google because Alta Vista frequently generates an unusually large list of sites.

Others

Different search services give different results. If one of the above two search services doesn't find what I am looking for, I try one of the following:

o Infoseek

o HotBot

o Yahoo

(iii) Natural Links

The original dream of hypertext was that natural relationships between topics would be linked. Within the realm of biology, this dream is increasingly coming true. Although such links are not nearly as complete, or as easy to use as one might like, they are improving and already are extremely useful. If one accesses Medline via Entrez, for example, one can (sometimes) link from the bibliographic citation retrieved from Medline to a full text copy of the article on the publisher's website. Similarly, one can link from OMIM to the HUGO gene nomenclature site to Gene Cards to Tumor Gene Database. Such links are not always labeled in the most obvious ways or located on a page or within a site exactly where you would expect them so, for the present, it is important to explore a site creatively in order to find all the valuable links that might be there.

2

Sequence Analysis (Introduction to Bioinformatics / Sequence Analysis)

2.1 Concept of DNA Protein Sequence Alignment and their Importance

After obtaining DNA sequences or Protein Sequence, first thing is to compare those sequences with known sequences. Comparison is done at the level of constituent amino acid residues/nucleotides, in order to find out conserved variable sequence patterns between the new and the known sequences. Presence of conserved residues especially those relevant to Protein function would enable one to guess about the nature of the Protein. In order to find out the conserved residues the residues of one of the sequence are directly mapped on to the residues of the other sequence. The process of mapping is called sequence alignment.

2.2 String

A string is any DNA or protein sequence, which contains the characters A, G, C, T in case of DNA and amino acids, like O, S, R, W, in case of proteins. Strings alignments can be understood clearly form the Fig. 2.1(a) and (b).

For example the Fig. 2.1 (a) illustrates an alignment of two DNA Sequences (strings). Note this alignment has been obtained by merely sliding the second sequence on the first sequence until a maximum number of Nucleotides matches is found. Fig. 2.1 (b) illustrates another alignment where a Gap has been introduced in the second sequence in order to increase the number of matching Nucleotides (6 Matches).

The two of the alignments illustrated in Figures 2.1 (a) and 2.1 (b) are respectively called Ungapped and Gapped Alignments. It can be seen that gapped alignment gives better mapping of Nucleotides than the Ungapped alignment.

Fig 2.1 (a) Sequence A   GGTGGAC   Fig 2.1 (b) GGTGGAC
              Sequence B   AAAGGTGAC   AAAGGTG AC

While working out alignment of two sequences, Gaps are often introduce to maximize the number of matches. From evolutionary point of view a gap represents either a deletion or an insertion of Nucleotides/ Residue depending on which of the two sequences we are considering. From Fig. 2.1 (b) we could infer that sequence B has a deletion (G) With respect to sequence A or sequence A has an insertion (G) with respect to sequence B. In addition to insertions and deletions (Most commonly called INDELS) there can be unmatched sequences at the terminal regions (for Example sequence AAA in Figures 2.1 (a) and 2.1 (b) such sequences are often called sequence Over Hangs or simply Overhangs.

In the previous example we saw that the two sequences have a few matching nucleotides and therefore we can say that those sequences are similar to each other. One may also say that the two sequences are homologues meaning they have a common evolutionary history (that is to say they have a common ancestor). However we need to have additional information to justify their evolutionary relationship such as conservation of structurally and functionally important nucleotides.

People often interchangeably use the words homology and similarity. We would like to emphasize that the words homology and similarity are distinct and represents two different concepts. Sequence similarity does not always confer homology. Homology stems from the only fact that the two sequences under consideration have common ancestor and that they may be functionally similar. Two sequences are either homologous or no homologous. But similarity can be expressed by means of scores. For example Sequence X and Sequence Y are 50% similar to each other.

So far we have discussed a case where two sequences are aligned. It is also possible to simultaneously align more than two sequences. The alignment involving two sequences is known as pair wise sequence alignment and the alignment involving more than two sequences is known as multiple sequences alignment.

Sequence alignment forms basis for a number of application in molecular biology. The most important application are :

Evolutionary analysis (also called Molecular phylogenetics analysis/ homology detection/fold detection).

homology modeling (also called comparative modeling).

2.3 Sequence Alignment and Alignment Programs

Alignments can be local or global. In global alignment whole sequences are considered whereas in local alignments only parts of sequences are considered. In both cases the basic goal is to achieve an alignment, which gives rise to maximum number of matches (i.e., high sequence similarity). Such an alignment is known as optimum alignment. Both the type of alignments have advantages as well as disadvantages and are applied based on type of application. For example, in comparative modeling global sequence alignment is essential where as local alignment is sufficient to detect functional domains. Computer software Like CLASTALX, MALIGN does global alignments and Heuristic software like BLAST, FASTA do local alignments. Global alignment is computationally more time consuming than the local alignment. Typically one would use local alignment for data-base searches for detecting sequentially similar sequences and global alignments for doing in-depth analysis on residue conservation pattern, residue mutation and residue deletion and insertions.

2.4 Comparison of Two Sequences Schematic Comparison

Principle of sequence alignment

Let us assume the following two sequences :

```
My1.seq        tgatggtcaagtaaactatgaagagttt
Unknown seq    atggtaatggcacaattgactttcctgaatttctga
```

If we want to align those, we will try to write the two sequences in a way, which allows a pair wise comparison of each sequence symbol. As you might guess, there are lots of possible options to do so, and the longer the sequences are, the more options to align two sequences will exist. In order to find the best alignment, we need to judge the quality of the alignment. To allow computations and comparisons, this judgement shall result in a numerical value, which is called a score. The determination of this score relies on a symbol comparison table, where each symbol pairing gets a value assigned, in order to determine the overall score by adding up the comparison value of each observed pair in our alignment. These tables are very important in the protein field, but also used in DNA comparison. A typical, simple scoring table for nucleotides will give a value of 1 to a match (treating U and T as "match"), and assign a value of 0 to each mismatch :

```
Match value : 1
Mismatch value : 0
```

```
+ - - - - +- - - - -+- - - - -+- - - - -+- - - - -+- - - - -+
|        |  A  |  G  |  C  |  T  |  U  |
+ - - - - +- - - - -+- - - - -+- - - - -+- - - - -+- - - - -+
|  A  |  1  |  0  |  0  |  0  |  0  |
+ - - - - +- - - - -+- - - - -+- - - - -+- - - - -+- - - - -+
|  G  |  0  |  1  |  0  |  0  |  0  |
+ - - - - +- - - - -+- - - - -+- - - - -+- - - - -+- - - - -+
|  C  |  0  |  0  |  1  |  0  |  0  |
+ - - - - +- - - - -+- - - - -+- - - - -+- - - - -+- - - - -+
|  T  |  0  |  0  |  0  |  1  |  1  |
+ - - - - +- - - - -+- - - - -+- - - - -+- - - - -+- - - - -+
|  U  |  0  |  0  |  0  |  1  |  1  |
+ - - - - +- - - - -+- - - - -+- - - - -+- - - - -+- - - - -+
```

Fig. 2.1

This matrix is perfectly symmetric and would be sufficient if printed as half-populated table.

One additional value is missing: If the two sequences have different size, some symbols of one sequence will never have a counterpart. The score of any symbol to "nothing" is therefore assumed to be 0.

To get started, we will write the two sequences amongst each other like in the painting above. However, we can either align the beginning, the end, or arrange the sequences arbitrarily. Figure A below shows our two sequences shifted by various positions. The score is determined according to the table above.

Figure A : Sequence alignments produced by shifting. Scores are calculated using a match value of 1 and a mismatch value of 0. Numbers in parenthesis refer to the calculation with mismatch values of -0.5.

```
tgatggtcaagtaaactatgaagagttt
       | |      |        ||
     atggtaatggcacaattgactttcctgaatttctga

                        shift 4: score 5 (-4.5)

tgatggtcaagtaaactatgaagagttt
    |  ||     || || |    |
     atggtaatggcacaattgactttcctgaatttctga

                        shift 3: score 9 (+1.0)

tgatggtcaagtaaactatgaagagttt
   ||||   |  |    |||       |
     atggtaatggcacaattgactttcctgaatttctga

                        shift 2: score 10 (+2.0)

tgatggtcaagtaaactatgaagagttt
    |    | | | |         |
    atggtaatggcacaattgactttcctgaatttctga

                        shift 1: score 6 (-5.5)

tgatggtcaagtaaactatgaagagttt
            |         |
atggtaatggcacaattgactttcctgaatttctga

                        shift 0: score 2 (-11.0)
```

```
tgatggtcaagtaaactatgaagagttt
||      |     ||      |
atggtaatggcacaattgactttcctgaatttctga
```

shift -1: score 6 (-5.0)

```
tgatggtcaagtaaactatgaagagttt
 |           |      |          |
atggtaatggcacaattgactttcctgaatttctga
```

shift -2: score 4 (-8.0)

```
  tgatggtcaagtaaactatgaagagttt
   | ||                   ||
atggtaatggcacaattgactttcctgaatttctga
```

shift -3: score 5 (-6.5)

```
    tgatggtcaagtaaactatgaagagttt
  | ||||   | |  |||      || |||
atggtaatggcacaattgactttcctgaatttctga
```

shift -4: score 15 (+8.5)

```
   tgatggtcaagtaaactatgaagagttt
  | ||||   | |        |   |   |
atggtaatggcacaattgactttcctgaatttctga
```

shift -5: score 10 (+1.0)

Figure A allows to conclude elementary findings :

- Two sequences can always be aligned, whether they are similar or not.

- It is possible to score sequence alignments and use the obtained numbers as measure to discriminate in between several alignments.

- Alignments will possibly yield more than one possible solution with similar score.

The scoring table, if written as best-score listing of the top four alignments, will read as :

```
Score     Shift    Length
- - - - - - - - - - - - - - - - - - - - - - -
  15        -4        29
  10         2        27
            -5        29
   9         3        26
```

This means that one alignment with shift -4 is calculated to be "best" but the alignments with shift 2, -5 and 3 are of a similar score.

This type of scoring will favour long alignments and will produce higher scores, the longer the alignments are. However, the mismatches are not penalized, which implies that long stretches of different sequences might be in the alignment. The result will be that the score gets better if the alignment gets longer, regardless the amount of mismatches encountered. In order to discriminate better between similar sequences and those, which have accidental similarity on a long range of symbols, such as expected in G/C rich sequences, we need to change scoring to penalize mismatches. As an example, we use the scoring

```
Match value : +1.0
Mismatch value : -0.5
```

and recalculate scores. Figure A shows the values in parenthesis. The scoring table, if written as best score listing of the top four alignments, will now read as :

```
Score    Shift    Length
- - - - - - - - - - - - - - - - - - - - - - -

+8.5      -4        28

+2.0       2        26

+1.0      -5        28

           3        25
```

The main benefit of this scoring schema is quality discrimination: All alignments, which have twice as much, mismatches than matches will score negatively. This implies that we can now introduce a threshold and indicate a "reasonable" alignment to be of a "positive score". However, we have not tried all of the possible shifts, and it is not easily feasible to compare several kb of sequences this way. Therefore, we need an automatism, which allows to judge sequence alignments after visual inspection.

2.5 Dot –Matrix Analysis

This is a graphical method primarily used for finding regions of local matches between two sequences and was first introduced by Gibbs and McIntyre (1970). This is a very simple method. The two sequences to be compared are placed as row and columns of matrix and the matrix is filled with dots as follows :

All residues of the first sequence placed column wise are compared against all residues of the second sequence placed row wise. Whenever a match is found a dot is placed on the corresponding position in the matrix.

A modification of the method has been suggested. Instead of looking for matches at every residue position, some amount of match in every successive overlapping window of residue is sought. Usually for DNA sequences a window of 11 residues is sought with atleast 7 matches and for Protein sequences a window of 3 residues with minimum 2 matches are considered. This kind of smoothening procedure leads to a plot with dots representing only significant matches.

In a Dot Matrix certain pattern of dots may appear to sketch out paths. There are number of programs available for dot matrix analysis. Some of the programs are listed below.

1. DOTTER
2. PALIGN
3. DOTLET

From the Dot Matrix plot it can be seen that a number of alignments are possible for a given pair of sequences. From these alignments how to identify an alignment which best represents true similarity between the sequences giving rise to one to one match for functionally and structurally important residues and therefore enabling one to deduce evolutionary relationship between the two sequences. This question can be asked as how to get an optimum alignment which maximizes sequence similarity between sequences.

(i) *Principle of dot plots*

The dot plot method allows visual inspection of all possible alignments in schematic fashion, and is shown in Figures 2.2 and 2.3.

Figure 2.2 displays the very basic dot plot: Two sequences are plotted as a matrix, and identical symbols get an x (for technical reasons only, in graphic output this is a "dot"). As the two sequences are 28 and 36 base pairs in length, we will have 28 x 36 = 1008 positions to calculate. Our DNA alphabet is a 4-letter alphabet (as we treat T and U as equal), which means that the random chance of an identical symbol at any given position is 1/4 = 0.25. Therefore, if the two sequences are totally unrelated, we expect 0.25 x 1008 = 252 dots, or, as formula,

```
Number of possible dots =
(Probability of pair) * (length of sequence A) *
(length of Sequence B)
```

Counting the x in Figure 2.2 gives 278 dots, which is fairly close to the expected value.

Figure 2.3 : Dot-plot created by painting a dot (x) at each match.

Looking at Figure 2.2, we can draw several conclusions :

- It is possible to display the relationship between two sequences in a graphic fashion.
- The result in the view of numbers is rather discouraging, as the obtained figures seem to be close to the expected statistical value.
- No direct sequence homologies can be derived from this kind of plot.

Obviously, we still need to improve the so-called signal-to-noise ratio. The signal is a line or otherwise visible pattern, which we could use, in the visual inspection. The noise is what we can expect from statistics. If we use a mathematical approximation to count the probability in a four-letter alphabet, we expect 25% of a random hit probability, which is too high if we ask for weak similarities – remember that the best score we had was the one which is given below :

```
    tgatggtcaagtaaactatgaagagttt
    | |||| | | |||      || |||
atggtaatggcacaattgactttcctgaatttctga
```
shift -4: score 15   (+8.5)

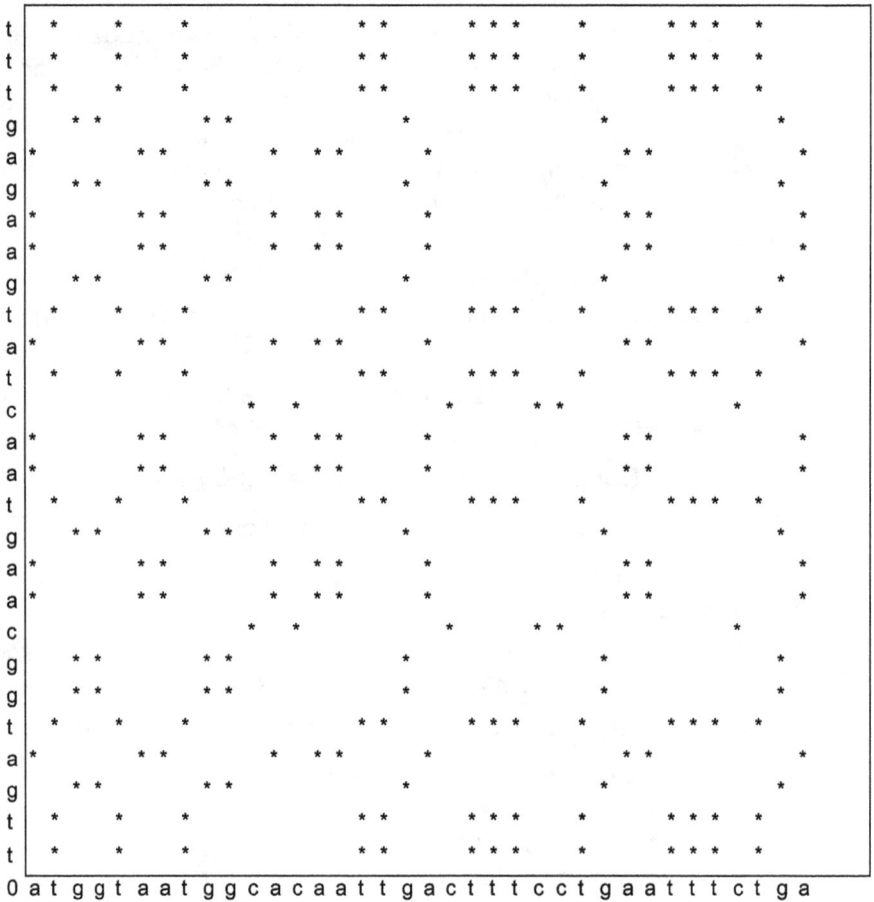

Fig. 2.2 Principle of dot plots

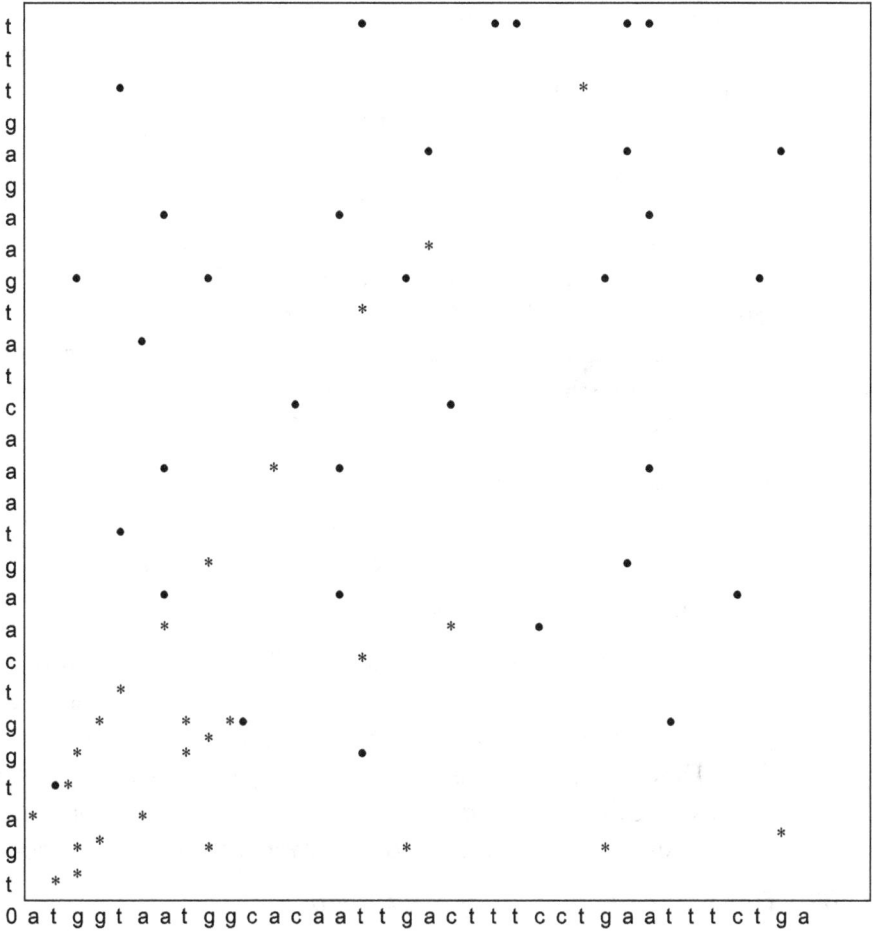

Fig. 2.3 Dot plot principle improved

(ii) *Dot plot Principle - Improved*

We need an improvement for the dot plots with the word method: In our example, on a length of 28 base pairs, we have only 15 matches, which is approximately every second nucleotide. This is a relatively weak signal. Therefore, we use a first approximation: We do no longer point a dot in if each nucleotide matches, but we use oligomers (called words) and paint a dot if these words match. This reduces the chance of a random match. If we use di-nucleotides, accidental matches will be $(1/4)*(1/4) = 1/16 = 6.25\%$ which is already much lower than the 25% obtained earlier. The GCG program suite uses the default word size of 6 - this is $(1/4)$ to the power of 6, which results in a random choice probability of 0.025%. There is, however, an undesired side effect: the larger the word size, the lower is the probability that a given word matches in between two different sequences. Expressed as formula, this will read,

```
Number of possible dots =
(Probability of word) * (length of sequence A) *
(length of Sequence B)
```

See Figure 2.3. Dot plot principle improved.

The result of the application in case of a di-nucleotide match (word size 2) is shown in Figure 2.3. In total, 65 dots (painted as o) are painted in the view of $(1008 \times 0.0625) = 63$ expected. In the figure, dots (.) have been painted in suggestively in order to show the position of the two best hits obtained in the alignments displayed in. The reason for the weak appearance is the low similarity of the two sequences.

(iii) *Dot plot Principle - Improved Again*

The problem with the sensitivity (too few subsequent identities in the case of low similarity) can be overcome with the permission of mismatches in a word. This is the already known windows technique; We select a window and request that a minimal number of matches within this window is obtained. The GCG programs call this stringency. Therefore, using a window/stringency algorithm, we will be able to paint dots at the middle of a window rather than a word, which means that, given the values 9/5 for window/stringency, we obtain the plot as shown in Figure 2.4. Figure 2.4 shows Dot-plot with a dot (0) at each matching window of 9 - with a minimum of 5 matches (stringency) per window.

Three conclusions can be drawn from Figure 2.4:

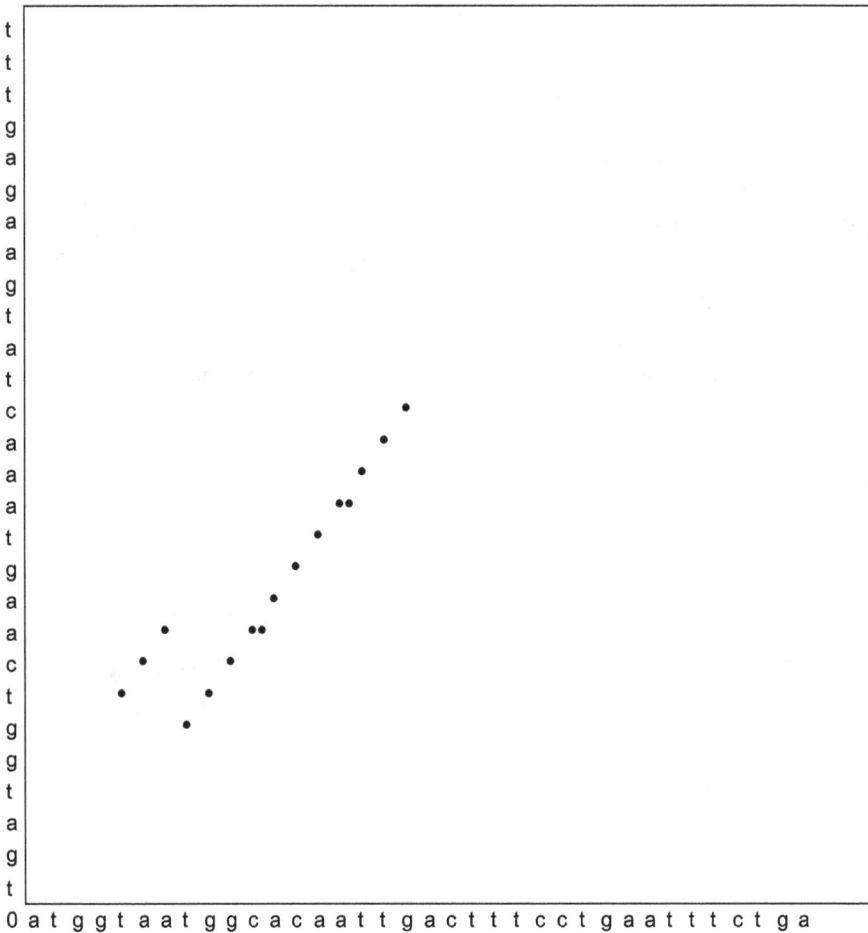

Fig. 2.4   Dot plot principle - Improved again

- The noise is low compared to the signal.
- The top-score alignments are exposed well.
- The definition of start and stop of the similar regions is blurred.

Interpretation of Dot plots

Looking at Figure 2.4, two main diagonals can be identified:

	Vertical Sequence	horizontal sequence
Short diagonal	5-10	4-9
Long diagonal	5-15	9-21

This is an important conclusion, as the vertical sequence has obviously a region in its beginning which is similar to the horizontal sequence in two different areas (4-9 and 9-15 respectively). However, be careful if you use window/stringency as the coordinates plotted, as diagonals will be affected by the size of the window. The actual region of similarity, therefore, will need to be expanded by (window size/2). If we schematically write the sequences in a letter-by-letter format, however, it will become immediately obvious that the window/stringency algorithm averages tremendously:

```
    tgatggtcaagtaaactatgaagagttt    vertical sequence
     ||||| | |   |     ||          (short diagonal)
 atggtaatggcacaattgactttcctgaatttctga horizontal sequence
     | ||||   | |  |||      || |||  (long diagonal)
    tgatggtcaagtaaactatgaagagttt    vertical sequence
```

In this case, experimental evidence will be required to consolidate the computer prediction of whether either the "short" or "long" diagonal are of biological relevance. The protein comparison will be valuable if available or possible.

Tip for the Interpretation of Dotplots : Always try to write down diagonals of interest in the way as depicted above. If you need computerized assistance, use the 'gap' program of the GCG package with very high gap penalty values (e.g., 50).

2.6 Scoring Schemes and Substitution Matrixes

To Work out an optimum alignment computationally which maximizes similarity between sequences we need to use some scoring methods. For example we could use scores based on residues to residue matching, we could see a score of 1 for match and 0 for mismatch. Therefore we could write a scoring matrix as identity matrix. Similarly we can write 20*20 identity matrix for 20 amino acids residues with all the diagonal elements carrying a score of 1 and all non–diagonal elements carrying a score of 0. Identity matrix can be used for sequence alignments. However we need to use more robust scoring schemes. Evolutionarily it has been observed that residues often get substituted or mutated without causing any harm to the native structure and function of the protein. The residues involved in such mutations are considered similar. For example substitutions like isoluecine to valline both hydrophobic and serine to threonine (both polar). Researches have analyzed many homologous protein sequences and have noted down the residue pairs that are similar. They have also found that residues do show mutational preferences (i.e., only certain pairs most often get interchanged). Probably due to evolutionary pressures as well as structural and functional restraint. As a consequence of mutational preferences some pairs of residues become more similar than the other pairs. For computational purposes residues to residue similarity is expressed in terms of similarity scores. A (20*20) matrix of similarity scores is known as similarity matrix (also called as a substitution matrix).

A number of similarity matrices has been derived considering various similarity features of the residues. The most widely used ones are discussed below.

(i) **PAM matrices :** The first substitution matrices, which gain very wide usage and acceptance, were derived by Dayhoff and coworkers (1978). These are based on the Point Accepted Mutation (PAM) model of evolution.

This Model assumes that the evolutionary changes occur as Markov Model i.e., residue mutation occur independent of the previous mutations. One PAM is a unit of evolutionary divergence in which 1% of the amino acids have been changed; this does not imply that after 100 PAMs every amino acid will be different. Some positions may change several times, perhaps reverting to the original amino acid, where as others may not change at all. As mentioned earlier, in homologous proteins residues substitutions are subjected to restrictions due to necessity of retaining the Native 3-Dimentional structure and Function. In fact certain residues remain conserved all along evolution. For example the catalytic residues D, T and G in aspartic Proteases. The mutations that do not cause serious disruption of protein native structure and function are said to be accepted point mutation. Dayhoff and his colleagues calculated frequencies of accepted mutations for 1 PAM by analyzing closely related protein sequences (i.e., those homologues which can be aligned manually without the aid of a substitution matrix). The similarity scores were calculated as natural logarithm of ratio of observed substitution frequencies (referred to as target frequencies). These similarity scores are also referred to as log odds ratio. The method of calculation first adopted by Dayhoff has been used as basis for calculation of all kinds of similarity scores known till today. The data calculated for 1PAM were extrapolated to a distance of 250 PAMs and the resulting matrix was published in 1978. This matrix has popularly reffered to as PAM20.

The data for 1 PAM has been extrapolated to other PAM distances to produce a family of matrices (e.g., PAM200) to suit different alignments situations. For example to derive PAM100 matrix PAM1 matrix is multiplied by itself 100 times. In general PAMN matrix can be obtained by multiplying PAM1 by itself N number of times. As for as the usage of PAM matrices is concerned as a rule of thumb, it has been suggested to use lower distance PAM matrices for closely related proteins and higher PAM matrices for more diverged proteins sequences. For example, PAM30 for closely related proteins whereas PAM250 for highly diverged proteins.

(ii) **BLOSUM Matrics :** BLOSUM is the abbreviated form of BLOCKS amino acid substitution matrices. These matrices have been constructed in a similar fashion as PAM matrices. However the data were derived from local alignments for distantly related proteins deposited in the BLOCKS database. Unlike PAM matrices there is no evolutionary basis in the data used for computing target frequencies. BLOSUM also has several versions. For example, BLOSUM 62 was derived from a set of sequences which are 62% or less similar. It is a good practice to use appropriate versions of BLOSUMS while doing sequence comparisions. For example BLOSUM 30 should be used for comparing highly diverged sequences and BLOSUM 90 for very close sequences.

Other matrices available in addition to the matrices discussed above, a number of matrices have also been derived. Without going in to details of those we simply mention them below.

A similarity Matrix based on the assumption that genetic code is the only influencing factor for amino acid substitution by Benner and co-workers.

Matrices based on chemical similarity of amino acids side chains, molecular volume, and polarity and hydrophobicity of amino acids side chains. (Vogt et al, (1995)).

Matrices derived from structurally aligned proteins by Johnson and Overington.

Matrix by Gonnet (1994), which is a 400*400 dipeptide substitution matrix, derived on that probability that amino acid substitutions at a particular site are influenced by neighboring amino acids and thus the environment of an amino acid plays a role in protein evolution.

Jones at al. (1994) matrix prepard specially for aligning transmembrane Proteins.

So far we discussed about different matrices for assigning scores for residues to residue substitution. As we saw in the example we had to introduce a gap for increasing the number of matches. From the evolutionary point of view a gap represents deletion or insertion of a residue. Introduction of gap is not viewed as favourable and it is penalized. The score associated with the gap is generally called a gap penalty. Two types of scoring schemes are followed when dealing with the gaps in alignments. They are as follows :

Linear Score : This has a form S (g)= –d where –d is called the gap opening penalty. We want to introduce more than one gap the penalty becomes S (g) = –gd, where g = the number of gaps (in other words the length of the gap).

Affine Score : It is often observed in proteins that gaps often occur in Tandem. Application of linear gap score leads to heavy penalty. Therefore a modification has been introduced and this is called Affine Score. The form is as follows.

$$S (g) = -d - (g - 1) e,$$

Where d and e are called the gap opening penalty and the gap extension penalty respectively. The penalty for e is set lower than d so that when gap has to be extended. It is done at lesser penalties.

2.7 Dynamic Programming
Needleman-Wunch and Smith-waterman Algorithm

Dynamic Programming is the computational method used for aligning two protein or nucleotide sequences. The method compares every pair of residues/nucleotides in the two sequences and generates an alignment. In the alignment, matches, mismatches and gaps in the two sequences are positioned in such a way that the number of matches between the identical or similar residues is the maximum possible. Dynamic programming method as used for global alignment is called as Needleman-Wunch algorithm and that as used for local alignment is called as Smith-Waterman algorithm.

Needleman-Wunch algorithm : Let us consider that we have two sequences X and Y with residues x_1, x_2, and x_3 .... and y_1, y_2, y_3 .... respectively. The idea is to build an optimal alignment using previous solutions for optimal alignments of smaller subsequences. In order to achieve this matrix M is constructed such that each element of M i.e., M (i, j) is the score of the best alignment possible between the segment x_1 to x_i and the segments y_1 to y_j.

Each element M (i, j) is set equal to the maximum of the scores obtained by following expressions

$$M (i - 1, j - 1) + s (xi, yj)$$

$$M (i - 1,j) + d$$

$$M (i, j - 1) + d$$

Where s (xi, yj) is the similarity score for the residues xi and yj taken from a given substitution matrix and d is the linear gap penalty.

For example we have two sequences AGCTTA and CCGA. Let us assume that we have a scoring scheme as follows.

Every match has a score of 10, every mismatch has a score of -1 and the gap penalty is -5. By using the above algorithm we can work out a matrix as shown in Fig. 2.5.

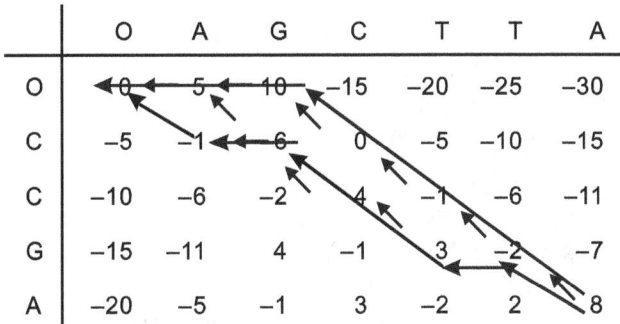

	O	A	G	C	T	T	A
O	0	5	10	-15	-20	-25	-30
C	-5	-1	6	0	-5	-10	-15
C	-10	-6	-2	4	-1	-6	-11
G	-15	-11	4	-1	3	-2	-7
A	-20	-5	-1	3	-2	2	8

Fig. 2.5 Dynamic programming scoring matrix

To derive an optimum alignment using the matrix M following trace back approach is adopted. In this approach the alignment is built in reverse, starting from the final element of the matrix with highest score of 8. This score corresponds to the total alignment score because this is the last element of the matrix. At each step of the trace-back process a move is made from the current element (i, j) to one of the elements(i-1, j-1),(i-1, j) or (i, j-1) from which the value of M (i, j) was derived at the same time a pair of symbols is added to the front of the current alignment, that is , residue pair xi and yi is added if the track back leads to the element (i-1, j-1) or the pair residue xi and gap "-" is added if the elements is (i-1, j) or the pair a gap "-" and residue yj is added if the element is (j, i-1).

Smith-waterman Algorithm : Most often it is sufficient to do alignments of subsequences rather than global alignments from one end to the other end of the sequences. For example when we compare highly diverged sequences it is always better to do local sequence alignments, as there can be conserved domains in them. This is because residue matches are stronger in conserved domains than the other parts. In order to identify the subsequences which give rise to maximum match locally Smith and Waterman introduced two modifications into the dynamic programming as discussed below.

The first modification is in the way the matrix updation is carried out. Unlike Needleman–wunch algorithm the element M (i, j) is set equal to either the maximum of the scores calculated using the three expressions mentioned above or zero. The value zero is selected when all the expressions give rise to scores less than zero. The importance of choosing zero is to stop the best alignment at some point when it gives rise to a negative score at that point and start a new alignment.

The second modification introduced is in the trace back procedure followed. Unlike in Needelman-Wunch algorithm where the trace back begins from the last element of the matrix here the trace back starts from any where in the matrix where the element M (i, j) has the highest score.

So far we assumed linear gap scheme when deriving the elements of the dynamic programming matrix. The other alternative is to use Affine gap score scheme, which is more robust than linear gap score scheme. In the Affine gap score scheme we need to calculate three matrices M, ix and iy instead of one. Here ix and iy matrices explicitly corresponds to scores calculated when a gap is introduced for a residue in the sequence x and y respectively. The three matrices are updated as follows.

M (I,j) is set to the maximum of the following

$$M (i - 1, j - 1) + s (x_i, y_j)$$

$$Lx (i - 1, j - 1) + s (x_i, y_j)$$

$$Ly (i - 1, j - 1) + s (x_i, y_j)$$

Lx (I, j) is set equal to the maximum of the following

$$M (i - 1, j) - d$$

$$Lx (i - 1, j) - e$$

Ly (i, j) is set equal to the maximum of the following

$$Ly\ (i, j-1) -e;$$

M (i, j) is set equal to the maximum of the following

$$M\ (i, j-1) - d$$

It should be noted that the trace back process to deduce optimum alignment now involves three matrices.

2.8 Heuristic Methods BLAST and FASTA

The alignment algorithms discussed above are guaranteed to find the optimal alignment according to the scoring scheme adopted for calculations. In particular the scheme involving Affine gap score is generally regarded as providing the most sensitive sequence matches. However, they are not fastest sequence alignment procedures. For applications like homology searches using large database speed becomes a prime issue. The dynamic algorithm has time complexity of the order of $O\ (n* m\ )$ where n and m are the lengths of the sequences considered for comparisons (i.e., n and m are number of residues/ nucleotides) to make a search in a data base containing 100 million residues we need to evaluate about 10 to the power 11 matrix elements.

This may take several hours of computer time. If we want to make homology searches for many sequences it becomes very tiring job as far as computer time is concerned.

In order to reduce the time consumed for comparison a few heuristic methods have been developed. The word heuristic means an alternative procedure mostly based on probably an educated guess. In heuristic methods there is always trade-off between sensitivity and speed. The most popular methods are BLAST and FASTA.

(i) **BLAST Method** : BLAST is a short form of Basic Local Sequence Alignment Search Tool. This was proposed by Altchul et al. in 1990. BLAST provides software tools for finding high scoring local alignments between two sequences. The basic assumption adopted by BLAST is that within the segments in a high scoring local alignments there exists short stretches of matching segments i.e., very high scoring segments. It is therefore first seed alignments are made between the short matching segments. The lengths of the seed segments are 3 residues in proteins and 11 for nucleic acids in DNA sequences.

Once the seed alignments are made the ungapped alignments are extended on both the direction up to a certain length where the alignment score stops increasing further. In other words BLAST tries to get a high scoring local alignments from the seed alignments.

One of the attractive feature of BLAST is that it tries to report as many high scoring local alignments as possible for a pair of given sequences. Hence it becomes easy for a researcher to analyze the hits. The high scoring pairs constituting the query and the subject (i. e., the sequence from the database) are generally called as HSPs (High scoring pairs).

The most widely used implementation of BLAST finds ungapped alignments only. However, gapped version of BLAST is also available.

There are several variants of BLAST each distinguished by the type of sequences (DNA and protein). BLAST P program compares a protein sequence against a protein sequence database. BLAST N compares a DNA sequences against a database of DNA. BLAST X compares a DNA subsequence after translation against a protein database. TBLASTN program compares a protein sequence against a DNA sequence database (after translation), and TBLAST X compares a DNA sequence (translated) against a DNA sequence database (translated).

The complete set of BLAST programs along with the substitution matrices and non-redundant protein sequence databases and DNA sequence database are freely available from the FTP file ftp.ncbi.nlm.nih.gov.blast.

While doing database searches using BLAST one of the important things done is to Mask the so-called low-complexity regions (LCR). These are the regions of biased composition. These regions can be homopolymeric runs or short period repeats or subtle cases where one or more residues are over represented. LCR pose problems while doing database searches, as they do not fit into the model of residue-to-residue sequence conservation. Further more methods for assessing the statistical significance of alignments are based on certain notion of randomness which LCRs do not obey, consequently many false positives may be observed in the out put of a database search.

BLAST : BLAST (Basic Local Alignment Search Tool) is a popular program for searching biosequences against databases. BLAST was developed and is maintained by a group at the National Center for Biotechnology Information (NCBI). Salient characteristics of BLAST are :

Local alignments : BLAST tries to find patches of regional similarity, rather than trying to find the best alignment between your entire query and an entire database sequence.

Ungapped alignments : Alignments generated with BLAST do not contain gaps. BLAST's speed and statistical model depend on this, but in theory it reduces sensitivity. However, BLAST will report multiple local alignments between your query and a database sequence.

Explicit statistical theory : BLAST is based on an explicit statistical theory developed by Samuel Karlin and Steven Altschul (1990). The original theory was later extended to cover multiple weak matches between query and database entry (1993).

Caution : the repetitive nature of many biological sequences (particularly naive translations of DNA/RNA) violates assumptions made in the Karlin & Altschul theory. While the P values provided by BLAST are a good rule-of-thumb for initial identification of promising matches, care should be taken to ensure that matches are not due simply to biased amino acid composition.

Caution : The databases are contaminated with numerous artifacts. The intelligent use of filters can reduce problems from these sources. Remember that the statistical theory only covers the likelihood of finding a match by chance under particular assumptions; it does not guarantee biological importance.

Rapid : BLAST is extremely fast. You can either run the program locally or send queries to an e-mail server maintained by NCBI

blast@ncbi.nlm.nih.gov

Heuristic : BLAST is not guaranteed to find the best alignment between your query and the database; it may miss matches. This is because it uses a strategy, which is expected to find most matches, but sacrifices complete sensitivity in order to gain speed. However, in practice few biologically significant matches are missed by BLAST, which can be found with other sequence search programs. BLAST searches the database in two phases. First it looks for short subsequences, which are likely to produce significant matches, and then it tries to extend these subsequences.

A substitution matrix is used during all phases of protein searches (BLASTP, BLASTX, TBLASTN)

Both phases of the alignment process (scanning & extension) use a substitution matrix to score matches. This is in contrast to FASTA, which uses a substitution matrix only for the extension phase. Substitution matrices greatly improve sensitivity.

BLAST comes in 4 flavors :

BLASTP : Search a protein sequence against a protein database.

BLASTN : Search a nucleotide sequence against a nucleotide database.

TBLASTN : Search a protein sequence against a nucleotide database, by translating each database nucleotide sequence in all 6 reading frames.

BLASTX *:* Search a nucleotide sequence against a protein database, by first translating the query nucleotide sequence in all 6 reading frames.

BLASTN, BLASTP, TBLASTN were described in the original BLAST paper a later paper describes BLASTX. Analysis of BLAST reports can be aided by a number of tools such as the filters XNU, SEG, and XBLAST.

Detecting New Sequence Similarities :

Currently, the characters most widely used for phylogenetic analysis are DNA and protein sequences. DNA sequences may be compared directly, or for those regions that code for a known protein, translated into protein sequences. Creating phylogenies from nucleotide or amino acid sequences first requires aligning the bases so that the differences between the sequences being studied are easier to spot. The introduction of NCBI's **BLAST**, or the **B**asic **L**ocal **A**lignment **S**earch **T**ool, in 1990 made it easier to rapidly scan huge databases for overt homologies, or sequence similarity, and to statistically evaluate the resulting matches. BLAST works by comparing a user's unknown sequence against the database of all known sequences to determine likely matches. In a matter of seconds, the BLAST server compares the user's sequence with up to a million known sequences and determines the closest matches.

Specialized BLASTs are also available for human, mouse, microbial, and many other genomes. A single BLAST search can compare a sequence of interest to all other sequences stored in GenBank, NCBI's nucleotide sequence database. In this step, a researcher has the option of limiting the search to a specific taxonomic group. If the full scientific name or relationship of species of interest is not known, the user can search for such details using NCBI's Taxonomy Browser, which provides direct links to some of the organisms commonly used in molecular research projects, such as the zebra fish, fruit fly, bakers yeast, nematode, and many more.

BLAST next tallies the differences between sequences and assigns a "score" based on sequence similarity. The scores assigned in a BLAST search have a well-defined statistical interpretation, making real sequence matches easier to distinguish from random background hits. This is because BLAST uses a special algorithm, or mathematical formula, that seeks local as opposed to global alignments and is therefore able to detect relationships among sequences that share only isolated regions of similarity. Taxonomy-related BLAST results are presented in three formats based on the information found in NCBI's Taxonomy database. The Organism Report sorts BLAST comparisons, also called hits, by species such that all hits to a given organism are grouped together. The Lineage Report provides a view of the relationships between the organisms based on NCBI's Taxonomy database. The Taxonomy Report provides in-depth details on the relationship between all the organisms in the BLAST hit list.

(ii) **FASTA Method :** The first widely-used database searches was FASTA and this was developed by Lip man and Pearson in 1985. A comparative assessment on the performances of BLAST and FASTA have shown that FASTA is more sensitive than BLAST. The FASTA package is available by anonymous FTP from ftp.virginia.edu/pub

In the first step FASTA uses a lookup table to locate all identically matching words of length ktup between the two sequences. For Proteins ktup is typically 1 or 2 and for DNA it may be 4 or 6. It then looks for diagonals with mutually supporting word matches. This is a very fast operation, which for example can be done by sorting the matches on the difference of indices (i-j).

The best diagonals are pursued further in step (2), which is analogous to the hit extension step of BLAST algorithm, extending the exact word matches to find maximal scoring ungapped regions. Step (3) then checks to see if any of these ungapped regions can be joined by a gapped region allowing gap costs. In the final step the highest scoring candidate matches in a database search are realigned using the full dynamic programming matrix forming a band around the candidate heuristic match.

Because the last step of FASTA uses the dynamic programming the scores it produces can be handled exactly like those from full dynamic programming. One can tradeoff between the speed and sensitivity by choosing ktup values. High values of Ktup sensitivity increases however the search becomes slow.

(iii) ***Statistical significance of sequence alignment :*** One of the most important recent advances in sequence analysis is the development of methods for assessing the significance of an alignment between DNA and protein sequences. For sequences that are quite similar such as two proteins that are clearly in the same family such an analysis is not necessary. The question or significance arises when comparing two sequences that are not so clearly similar but are shown to align in a promising way. In such a case significant test can be helpful to biologist to decide whether an alignment obtained by a computer program is one that would be expected between related sequences or just as likely to be found if the sequences were not related. This test becomes highly important when one is doing database searches using BLAST or FASTA the test applied to every sequence match (alignment) and the most significant matches are reported.

For global alignment the following method is adopted.

One of the sequences in the pair is shuffled several times and every shuffled sequence is used for producing an alignment which gives rise to a score. The alignment scores are compared with the original alignment score to see any of the randomized alignments are also able to give rise to the original alignment score. If the randomized alignment scores are significantly smaller than the original score then the original alignment produced is considered as significant.

For local alignments such as those produced by BLAST, significance test is carried out on the basis of the statistical framework provided by Karlin and Altschul in 1990. They showed that the random sequence alignments follows a distribution called the extreme value distribution which is somewhat like normal distribution but with a positive skewed tail in the higher score range. By relating an observed alignment score S to the expected distribution it is possible to calculate statistical significance in the form of an E value. The simple interpretation of E value is the number of alignments with scores atleast equal to S that would be expected by chance alone. Therefore lower E values indicate alignments are statistically significant.

2.9 Searching Patterns

Programs to find patterns in DNA sequences were already mentioned in the single sequence analysis section. The programs mentioned their search for patterns using compositional analysis. However, restriction-mapping programs do also use pattern approaches.

(i) Pattern principles

Computers are fast if the comparison of letters or numbers tests whether these are equal or not. In order to apply this principle to biology, we need to define this "matching" in a simple table. E.g., if we compare two protein sequences and find a letter D, this is a symbol for aspartic acid. The test for "equal" or "not equal", therefore, reads as

```
D meeting D        => match
meeting any other  => mismatch
```

This is not very sophisticated, in particular, as certain proteins with specific sites (such as calcium binding) tend to be ambivalent and allow either aspartic or glutamic acid. We could use the comparison matrices as mentioned in the pairwise sequence comparison section. As already explained there, the comparison of sequences on the basis of matrices is computationally expensive. This is not the main reason, however, for using patterns.

The main benefit of patterns is that defined substitutions can occur as the result of a combination of examples – in contrast to a sequence comparison based on a comparison matrix derived from a sequence–independent generalization of alignments.

(ii) *Example of pattern benefit*

This example refers to a calcium-binding site where we have proven examples of sequences containing E or D at a given position. To write our pattern, we will allow either of the two sequence characters to be a 'match' at this position. An example of this in a short alignment stretch is printed below:

```
Sequence fragment 1:     GDRD
Sequence fragment 2:     GERL
```

Our sequence match table, therefore, reads for aspartic acid (for the symbol D in position

```
D    meeting D              => match
     meeting E              => match
     meeting any other      => mismatch
```

A suitable matrix would allow this as well. However, keep in mind that a matrix covers symbol pairings at any position. To make this clearer, look at the fourth position of the sequence fragments above. If we have a leucine residue at a position where we find aspartic acid usually, this were (for the symbol D in position 4)

```
D    meeting D              => match
     meeting L              => match
     meeting any other      => mismatch
```

Again, a suitable matrix would possibly cover this occurrence, but we would have a problem with our first case: As we now allowed L in parallel to D, this were bad for our definition D or E earlier. The solution, therefore, is to define substitutions as a function of the sequence:

```
D     meeting D              => match
      meeting E at pos. 2    => match
      meeting L at pos. 4    => match
      meeting any other      => mismatch
```

(iii) *Definition of a pattern language*

Our example requires that we apply different criteria to different positions of a sequence alignment. In order to have the position-specific comparison done by a computer, a sophisticated program is required which will do this type of calculation for us. Note the difference to the pairwise alignment programs: The comparison of symbols was position-independent there. Now, using patterns, we do **position-dependent comparison** calculations. As we cannot expect to get a specific program for each special pattern, we need to have a pattern-matching program, which will define the rules of patterns in a pattern language.

The creation of such a convention to describe patterns in a flexible fashion is not as difficult as one might assume because patterns are typically short in length (a few amino acids up to some dozen, but rarely more than hundred symbols) if compared to a query sequence which we want to screen for the occurrence of a pattern. By reading pattern definitions, the pattern-matching program will be able to search a given sequence for this pattern defined in a specific language. There are various ways to define such a language, and the "regular expressions" of some essential programs of the

UNIX operating system use such a language. The GCG software package searches with a straightforward definition, the most important features are listed below.

- Alternative Residues

  The residues to be allowed in a given position are listed with a comma (,) as a separator and are embraced by parenthesis (and). To specify our example above, it were sufficient to have

  ```
  sequence fragment 1 :      GDRD
  sequence fragment 2 :      GERL

  Pattern description :      G(D,E)R(D,L)
  ```

- Repetitions

  The number of residues in a pattern might be repeated or vary in any symbol in a certain range. The pattern language allows repetitions in the syntax {minimum, maximum} which consists of two numbers in curled braces. Loops in proteins, for example, might be described as

  ```
  sequence fragment 1 :      GDGTRD
  sequence fragment 2 :      GERL
  sequence fragment 3 :      GDMRD

  Pattern description:      G(D,E)(X){0,2}R(D,L)
  ```

- Alternative Residues, Exclusion

  Occasionally, the number of residues to be allowed in a given position becomes fairly large. Then, it is easier to define which residues are not found at this place. The pattern language uses a tilde (~) in front of a character or a list embraced with parenthesis in order to define these undesired residues. Note that, in the description of the four sequence motifs below, the positions 2 and 3 are identical for the sake of demonstration. Whereas exclusion was used to define position 2, the explicit listing of allowed residues in position 3 seems to be more efficient in this case.

However, real-world examples exist where exclusion can be used beneficially.

```
sequence fragment 1:      GDD
sequence fragment 2:      GEE
sequence fragment 3:      GNN
sequence fragment 4:      GQQ
pattern description :

G~(A,C,F,G,H,I,K,L,M,P,R,S,T,V,W,Y)(D,E,N,Q)
```

2.10 The Statistics of Sequence Similarity Scores

(i) *Introduction*

To assess whether a given alignment constitutes evidence for homology, it helps to know how strong an alignment can be expected from chance alone. In this context, "chance" can mean the comparison of (i) real but non-homologous sequences; (ii) real sequences that are shuffled to preserve compositional properties; or (iii) sequences that are generated randomly based upon a DNA or protein sequence model. Analytic statistical results invariably use the last of these definitions of chance, while empirical results based on simulation and curve fitting may use any of the definitions.

(ii) *The statistics of global sequence comparison*

Unfortunately, under even the simplest random models and scoring systems, very little is known about the random distribution of optimal global alignment scores. Monte Carlo experiments can provide rough distributional results for some specific scoring systems and sequence compositions, but these can not be generalized easily. Therefore, one of the few methods available for assessing the statistical significance of a particular global alignment is to generate many random sequence pairs of the appropriate length and composition, and calculate the optimal alignment score for each. While it is then possible to express the score of interest in terms of standard deviations from the mean, it is a mistake to assume that the relevant distribution is normal and convert this Z-value into a P-value; the tail behavior of global alignment scores is unknown. The most one can say reliably is that if 100 random alignments have score inferior to the alignment of interest, the P-value in question is likely less than 0.01. One further pitfall to avoid is exaggerating the significance of a result found among multiple tests.

When many alignments have been generated, e.g. in a database search, the significance of the best must be discounted accordingly. An alignment with P-value 0.0001 in the context of a single trial may be assigned a P-value of only 0.1 if it was selected as the best among 1000 independent trials.

(iii) *The statistics of local sequence comparison*

Fortunately statistics for the scores of local alignments, unlike those of global alignments, are well understood. This is particularly true for local alignments lacking gaps, which we will consider first. Such alignments were precisely those sought by the original BLAST database search programs. A local alignment without gaps consists simply of a pair of equal length segments, one from each of the two sequences being compared. A modification of the Smith-Waterman or Sellers algorithms will find all segment pairs whose scores can not be improved by extension or trimming. These are called high-scoring segment pairs or HSPs.

To analyze how high a score is likely to arise by chance, a model of random sequences is needed. For proteins, the simplest model chooses the amino acid residues in a sequence independently, with specific background probabilities for the various residues. Additionally, the expected score for aligning a random pair of amino acid is required to be negative. Long alignments would tend to have high score independently of whether the segments aligned were related, and the statistical theory would break down.

Just as the sum of a large number of independent identically distributed (i.i.d) random variables tends to a normal distribution, the maximum of a large number of i.i.d. random variables tend to an extreme value distribution. (We will elide the many technical points required to make this statement rigorous.) In studying optimal local sequence alignments, we are essentially dealing with the latter case. In the limit of sufficiently large sequence lengths m and n, the statistics of HSP scores are characterized by two parameters, K and *lambda*. Most simply, the expected number of HSPs with score at least S is given by the formula

$$E = Kmn\ e^{-\lambda s} \qquad\qquad .....(2.1)$$

we call this the E-value for the score S.

This formula makes eminently intuitive sense. Doubling the length of either sequence should double the number of HSPs attaining a given score. Also, for an HSP to attain the score $2x$ it must attain the score x twice in a row, so one expects E to decrease exponentially with score. The parameters K and *lambda* can be thought of simply as natural scales for the search space size and the scoring system respectively.

(iv) *Bit scores*

Raw scores have little meaning without detailed knowledge of the scoring system used, or more simply its statistical parameters K and *lambda*. Unless the scoring system is understood, citing a raw score alone is like citing a distance without specifying feet, meters, or light years. By normalizing a raw score using the formula

$$S' = \frac{\lambda S - \ln K}{\ln 2} \qquad \qquad .....(2.2)$$

one attains a "bit score" S', which has a standard set of units. The E-value corresponding to a given bit score is simply

$$E = mn\, 2^{-S'} \qquad \qquad .....(2.3)$$

Bit scores subsume the statistical essence of the scoring system employed, so that to calculate significance one needs to know in addition only the size of the search space.

(v) *P-values*

The number of random HSPs with score $>= S$ is described by a poisson distribution. This means that the probability of finding exactly a HSPs with score $>=S$ is given by

$$e^{-E}\frac{E^a}{a!} \qquad \qquad .....(2.4)$$

where E is the E-value of S given by equation (2.1) above. Specifically the chance of finding zero HSPs with score $>=S$ is e^{-E}, so the probability of finding at least one such HSP is

$$P = 1 - e^{-E} \qquad \qquad .....(2.5)$$

This is the *P*-value associated with the score *S*. For example, if one expects to find three HSPs with score $>= S$, the probability of finding at least one is 0.95. The BLAST programs report *E*-value rather than *P*-values because it is easier to understand the difference between, for example, *E*-value of 5 and 10 than *P*-values of 0.993 and 0.99995. However, when $E < 0.01$, *P*-values and *E*-value are nearly identical.

(vi) *Database searches*

The *E*-value of equation (2.1) applies to the comparison of two proteins of lengths *m* and *n*. How does one assess the significance of an alignment that arises from the comparison of a protein of length *m* to a database containing many different proteins, of varying lengths? One view is that all proteins in the database are equally likely to be related to the query. This implies that a low *E*-value for an alignment involving a short database sequence should carry the same weight as a low *E*-value for an alignment involving a long database sequence. To calculate a "database search" *E*-value, one simply multiplies the pairwise-comparison *E*-value by the number of sequences in the database. Recent versions of the FASTA protein comparison programs take this approach.

An alternative view is that a query is more likely to be related to a long than to a short sequence, because long sequences are often composed of multiple distinct domains. If we assume the chance of relatedness is proportional to sequence length, then the pair wise *E*-value involving a database sequence of length *n* should be multiplied by *N/n*, where *N* is the total length of the database in residues. Examining equation (2.1), this can be accomplished simply by treating the database as a single long sequence of length *N*. The BLAST programs take this approach to calculating database *E*-value. Notice that for DNA sequence comparisons, the length of database records is largely arbitrary, and therefore this is the only really tenable method for estimating statistical significance.

(vii) *The statistics of gapped alignments*

The statistics developed above have a solid theoretical foundation only for local alignments that are not permitted to have gaps. However, many computational experiments and some analytic results strongly suggest that the same theory applies as well to gapped alignments.

For ungapped alignments, the statistical parameters can be calculated, using analytic formulas, from the substitution scores and the background residue frequencies of the sequences being compared. For gapped alignments, these parameters must be estimated from a large-scale comparison of "random" sequences.

Some database search programs, such as FASTA or various implementation of the Smith-Waterman algorithm, produce optimal local alignment scores for the comparison of the query sequence to every sequence in the database. Most of these scores involve unrelated sequences, and therefore can be used to estimate *lambda* and *K*. This approach avoids the artificiality of a random sequence model by employing real sequences, with their attendant internal structure and correlations, but it must face the problem of excluding from the estimation scores from pairs of related sequences. The BLAST programs achieve much of their speed by avoiding the calculation of optimal alignment scores for all but a handful of unrelated sequences. They must therefore rely upon a pre-estimation of the parameters *lambda* and *K*, for a selected set of substitution matrices and gap costs. This estimation could be done using real sequences, but has instead relied upon a random sequence model, which appears to yield fairly accurate results.

(viii) *Edge effects*

The statistics described above tend to be somewhat conservative for short sequences. The theory supporting these statistics is an asymptotic one, which assumes an optimal local alignment, can begin with any aligned pair of residues. However, a high-scoring alignment must have some length, and therefore cannot begin near to the end of either of two sequences being compared. This "edge effect" may be corrected for by calculating an "effective length" for sequences; the BLAST programs implement such a correction. For sequences longer than about 200 residues the edge effect correction is usually negligible.

(ix) *The choice of substitution scores*

The results of a local alignment program produces depend strongly upon the scores it uses. No single scoring scheme is best for all purposes, and an understanding of the basic theory of local alignment scores can improve the sensitivity of one's sequence analyses.

As before, the theory is fully developed only for scores used to find ungapped local alignments, so we start with that case.

A large number of different amino acid substitution scores, based upon a variety of rationales, have been described. However the scores of any substitution matrix with negative expected score can be written uniquely in the form

$$S_{ij} = \frac{\left(\ln \frac{q_{ij}}{p_i\, p_j}\right)}{\lambda} \qquad .....(2.6)$$

where the q_{ij}, called target frequencies, are positive numbers that sum to 1, the $p_i\, p_j$ are background frequencies for the various residues, and *lambda* is a positive constant. The *lambda* here is identical to the *lambda* of equation (2.1).

Multiplying all the scores in a substitution matrix by a positive constant does not change their essence: an alignment that was optimal using the original scores remains optimal. Such multiplication alters the parameter *lambda* but not the target frequencies q_{ij}. Thus, up to a constant scaling factor, every substitution matrix is uniquely determined by its target frequencies. These frequencies have a special significance:

A given class of alignments is best distinguished from chance by the substitution matrix whose target frequencies characterize the class.

To elaborate, one may characterize a set of alignments representing homologous protein regions by the frequency with which each possible pair of residues is aligned. If valine in the first sequence and leucine in the second appear in 1% of all alignment positions, the target frequency for (valine, leucine) is 0.01. The most direct way to construct appropriate substitution matrices for local sequence comparison is to estimate target and background frequencies, and calculate the corresponding log-odds scores of formula (2.6). These frequencies in general cannot be derived from first principles, and their estimation requires empirical input.

(x) *The PAM and BLOSUM amino acid substitution matrices*

While all substitution matrices are implicitly of log-odds form, the first explicit construction using formula (2.6) was by Dayhoff and coworkers. From a study of observed residue replacements in closely related proteins, they constructed the PAM (for "point accepted mutation") model of molecular evolution. One "PAM" corresponds to an average change in 1% of all amino acid positions. After 100 PAMs of evolution, not every residue will have changed: some will have mutated several times, perhaps returning to their original state, and others not at all. Thus it is possible to recognize as homologous proteins separated by much more than 100 PAMs. Note that there is no general correspondence between PAM distance and evolutionary time, as different protein families evolve at different rates.

Using the PAM model, the target frequencies and the corresponding substitution matrix may be calculated for any given evolutionary distance. When two sequences are compared, it is not generally known a priori what evolutionary distance will best characterize any similarity they may share. Closely related sequences, however, are relatively easy to find even with non-optimal matrices, so the tendency has been to use matrices tailored for fairly distant similarities. For many years, the most widely used matrix was PAM-250, because it was the only one originally published by Dayhoff.

Dayhoff's formalism for calculating target frequencies has been criticized, and there have been several efforts to update her numbers using the vast quantities of derived protein sequence data generated since her work. These newer PAM matrices do not differ greatly from the original ones.

An alternative approach to estimating target frequencies, and the corresponding log-odds matrices, has been advanced by Henikoff & Henikoff. They examine multiple alignments of distantly related protein regions directly, rather than extrapolate from closely related sequences. An advantage of this approach is that it cleaves closer to observation; a disadvantage is that it yields no evolutionary model. A number of tests suggest that the "BLOSUM" matrices produced by this method generally are superior to the PAM matrices for detecting biological relationships.

(xi) *DNA substitution matrices*

While we have discussed substitution matrices only in the context of protein sequence comparison, all the main issues carry over to DNA sequence comparison. One warning is that when the sequences of interest code for protein, it is almost always better to compare the protein translations than to compare the DNA sequences directly. The reason is that after only a small amount of evolutionary change, the DNA sequences, when compared using simple nucleotide substitution scores, contain less information with which to deduce homology than do the encoded protein sequences.

Sometimes, however, one may wish to compare non-coding DNA sequences, at which point the same log-odds approach as before applies. An evolutionary model in which all nucleotides are equally common and all substitution mutations are equally likely yields different scores only for matches and mismatches. A more complex model, in which transitions are more likely than transversions, yields different "mismatch" scores for transitions and transversions. The best scores to use will depend upon whether one is seeking relatively diverged or closely related sequences.

(xii) *Gap scores*

Our theoretical development concerning the optimality of matrices constructed using equation (2.6) unfortunately is invalid as soon as gaps and associated gap scores are introduced, and no more general theory is available to take its place. However, if the gap scores employed are sufficiently large, one can expect that the optimal substitution scores for a given application will not change substantially. In practice, the same substitution scores have been applied fruitfully to local alignments both with and without gaps. Appropriate gap scores have been selected over the years by trial and error, and most alignment programs will have a default set of gap scores to go with a default set of substitution scores. If the user wishes to employ a different set of substitution scores, there is no guarantee that the same gap scores will remain appropriate. No clear theoretical guidance can be given, but "Affine gap scores", with a large penalty for opening a gap and a much smaller one for extending it, have generally proved among the most effective.

(xiii) *Low complexity sequence regions*

There is one frequent case where the random models and therefore the statistics discussed here break down. As many as one fourth of all residues in protein sequences occur within regions with highly biased amino acid composition. Alignments of two regions with similarly biased composition may achieve very high scores that owe virtually nothing to residue order but are due instead to segment composition. Alignments of such "low complexity" regions have little meaning in any case: since these regions most likely arise by gene slippage, the one-to-one residue correspondence imposed by alignment is not valid. While it is worth noting that two proteins contain similar low complexity regions, they are best excluded when constructing alignments. The BLAST programs employ the SEG algorithm to filter low complexity regions from proteins before executing a database search.

3

Calculation of Sequence Alignments for Evolutionary Inferences and to Aid in Structural and Functional Analysis

---

Although it is not possible to *completely* predict the function or shape (structure) of a protein from its sequence *de novo*, some **useful inferences about structure and function can be drawn**, especially by comparing the sequence of a protein of unknown structure and function to sequences of proteins with known structure and function. Second, if the goal of structure/function prediction is to be reached in the future, it will be because of **partial analyses done in the present.** Third, by comparing the sequence of equivalent proteins from different species of animals (such equivalent proteins are called "homologues"), one can draw inferences about the **evolution of these species from their common ancestors.**

One of the most useful things people do with sequences is to compare them to other sequences. However, such comparisons are not as easy to make as one might first think. One factor that complicates analysis is that the sequences biologists need to compare are usually not identical, but only similar. In addition to having a small number of substitutions (e.g. a Guanine for an Adenine at one position in a DNA sequence) there will be insertions and deletions in one sequence relative to the other. Also, depending on what you are comparing and what you want to learn from the comparison, how you do the comparison will be different. For these reasons, there have been many different kinds of programs written to compare sequences

3.1 Principle of Multiple Sequence Alignment

Once a sequence search is completed, the question arises whether the found similarities do share similarity amongst each other. This can be achieved either automatic or manual fashion by using programs which will align the sequences of interest.

If you painted a map from the result of your sequence search as described earlier, it might be obvious that sequences do usually share similarity only in parts. This will leave the ends or over hang parts of two sequences badly aligned due to low similarity, therefore before alignments are attempted, it is a good practice to create sequence fragments of approximately the same length which will allow programs to operate more easily.

If sequences are not specifically tailored for multiple sequence alignment programs, they might fail to report alignments unreliably.

(i)   **Finding the Best :** The approach used for automatic sequence alignment can be described as "clustering," of the most similar sequences .In a first step, the program will need to find the sequence pair (s) which share (s) the most obvious similarity .To achieve this, each sequence is compared to each, which results in (n*n)/2 comparison if we have n sequences to compare. As in rigorous sequences searching, a comparison is made using sequence comparison tables to compute the best possible alignment and score this appropriately. Note that the score will be not as desired if the sequences have not been tailored as mentioned above.

(ii)   **Grouping :** Once the comparison for each possible sequence pair has been completed, the best candidates serve as nuclei, and additional sequences are aligned to the already existing alignment. This will work well with similar proteins but too many gaps, in particular on DNA level, will most probably not yield the desired result. The largest errors will occur if regions with low similarity are used as "closest" set, as this will cause trouble for additional sequences to be matched.

         If problems are encountered because similarity can, not be determined well enough automatically, either manual alignment is required or the selection of sequences must be improved by tailoring or Omission of very remotely related fragments.

(iii)   **Result Evaluation :** The result of a multiple sequence alignment will be a block of sequences, which are nicely painted on top of each other. Programs exist which will plot the degree of similarity along the sequence coordinate. Other programs allow to print or paint the output nicely. The GCG programs also produce a figure which schematically displays the level of similarity as a dendrogram.

(iv)   **Limitation :** Multiple sequence alignment is not the tool for you if you are working on fragment assembly or shortgun sequencing. In order to align multiple sequences reliably, the similarity amongst the members of the alignment should be extensive along the entire length rather than only overlapping fragments.

3.2 Global Alignments

The Needleman and Wunsch algorithm for finding the best global alignment of two sequences can readily be extended to multiple sequences. The problem is that the time the computer needs for such a job is roughly proportional to the product of the sequence lengths. So, if aligning two sequences of 300 positions takes 1 second, aligning 3 sequences takes 300 seconds and aligning 10 sequences would take $300 \wedge 8$ seconds, which is longer than the lifetime of the universe!

Since searching for a best global alignment using a rigorous algorithm is not realistic for more than three sequences, a number of strategies have been developed to carry out a multiple global alignment in a reasonable amount of time with a reasonable chance of finding the best alignment. The GCG program pileup first aligns all possible pairs of sequences according to Needleman and Wunsch (for n sequences, this makes $n*(n-1)/2$ alignments). Then it uses the pairwise similarity scores to construct a tree using the UPGMA method. Finally, this tree serves as a guide for a progressive multiple alignments starting from the tips. Once two sequences have been aligned, their relative alignment is no longer changed. Clusters of previously aligned sequences are treated as a linearly weighted profile when they are subsequently aligned with another sequence or another cluster.

3.3 Local Alignments

There are cases where sequences share a similar region but are otherwise completely different. Take, for example, the amino acids in the active site of an enzyme or transcription factor binding sites in a DNA sequence. To handle these cases local multiple alignment algorithms have been developed. Usually they only look for ungapped alignments thereby avoiding the problem of choosing the optimal gap penalty. Two such programs have been developed at the NCBI :

MACAW by Schuler, Altschul and Lipman first tries to find high scoring segment pairs (HSPs) for each possible pair of sequences using the BLAST algorithm (with the sensitivity set high). It then assembles overlapping HSPs into blocks. An interesting feature of MACAW is that it does not try to align all sequences, but can pick out only those that share similar regions. There are versions of MACAW for the PC under Windows and for the Mac.

The MACAW distribution also contains Gibbs (see below) and a pattern searcher.

The Gibbs sampler algorithm involves iteratively making a profile with stretches of n bases or amino acids, selected from the sequences, and then searches this profile against one of the sequences. The result of the search is used to weight the selection of the stretches at the next run. A drawback is that the user must choose the width n and the number of elements in each sequence and thus must have a certain idea of the outcome, or run the program several times. An interesting feature is that the Gibbs sampler algorithm avoids the choice of an externally added scoring scheme since it derives the highest scoring profile, in a self-consistent manner, from the data. Gibbs is available for UNIX.

3.4 What is a Multiple Alignment?

The purpose of multiple sequence alignment is to bring the large no of similar features into register in the same column of the alignment, optimally.

If the sequences in the MSA (Multiple sequence alignment) align well, they are likely to be derived from a common ancestor sequence presence of several similar domain in several sequences suggests a biochemical function, this may become the basis of further experimental investigation.

Based on similarities obtained by MSA. Similar proteins have been organised into databases of protein families – multiple sequence alignment of a set of sequences can provide information as to the most alike regions in the set. In proteins such regions may represent conserved functional or structural domains.

A good alignment is that which includes a series of columns where majority of sequences have same aminoacid or an aminoacid that is a conservative substitution for that aminoacid. In the same column very few examples of other substitutions or gaps may be present. These columns should be present throughput the alignment, often clustered into domains.

In case of Nuclei acids, multiple sequence alignment can reveal structural and functional relationships. In case when promoter regions of a set of similar sequences aligned well, they may represent consensus binding sites for regulatory proteins.

Classes of multiple sequence alignment :

(a) **Global alignment** *:* Global sequence alignment is the entire length sequence alignment. It is an extension of dynamic programming global alignment algorithm.

(b) **Sequence block** *:* Sequence block is a common pattern of alignment in a group of sequence where matches, mismatches but no gaps are included. Sequence block can be found by pattern matching / pattern finding algorithms.

(c) **Profile** *:* A profile is a type of scoring matrix which is produced from an alignment of common patterns in protein sequences that includes matches, mismatches, insertions and deletions.

Scoring multiple sequence Alignments

S.P. Model for Scoring MSA :

S.P stands for sum of pairs.

M.S.A - Multiple sequence alignment.

With S.P. model we can score the MSA by adding all the possible combination of pairs scores of aminoacids in a column of a MSA.

This model assumes that any sequence could be ancestor of the other sequence.

When the number of mismatched residues pairs increases, scores in the MSA column decreases rapidly. This decrease should be greater for a large number of sequences say more than five sequnces with all R, or with one or two S substitutions, because there will be more R–R matched pairs relative to mismatched R – S pairs However, the opposite is true with the SP method of scoring. We can understand it more clearly from the below mentioned illiustrations in Fig. 3.1.

Sequence	Column P	Column Q	Column R
1	– – R – – – – – – – –	R – – – – – – – – R	R – – – – – – – – R
2	– – R – – – – – – – –	R – – – – – – – – R	R – – – – – – – – R
3	– – R – – – – – – – –	R – – – – – – – – R	R – – – – – – – – R
4	– – R – – – – – – – –	R – – – – – – – – R	R – – – – – – – – S
5	– – R – – – – – – – –	S – – – – – – – – S	R – – – – – – – – S

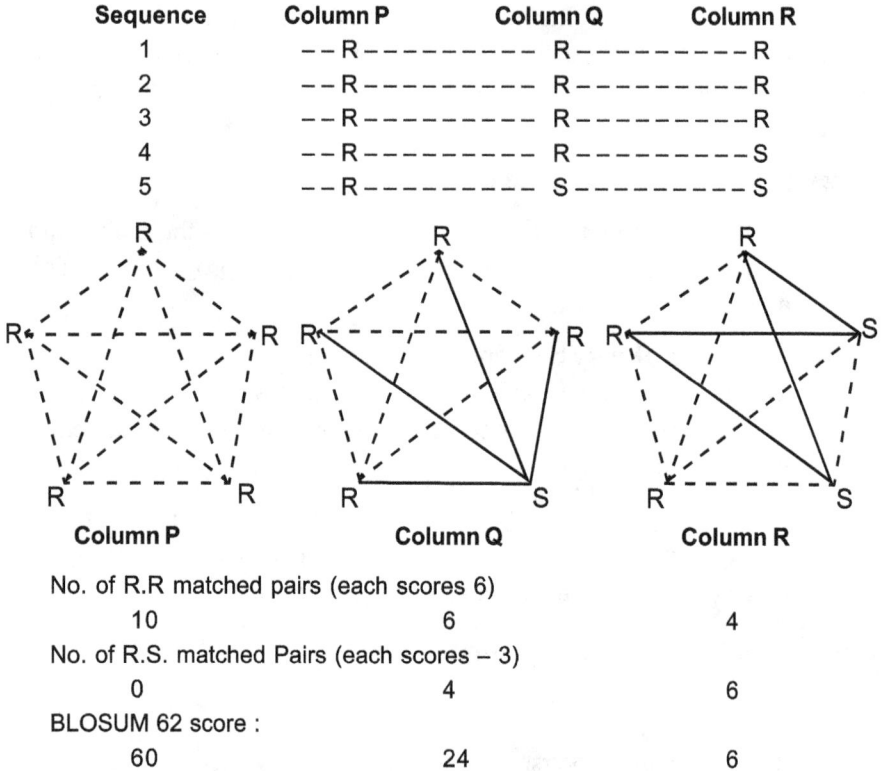

No. of R.R matched pairs (each scores 6)

10	6	4

No. of R.S. matched Pairs (each scores – 3)

0	4	6

BLOSUM 62 score :

60	24	6

Fig. 3.1 The SP model for soring a msa.

SP method is an optimization method where maximization of number of matched pairs score is performed by minimising the cost or number of mismatched pairs) in all columns in the msa.

See Fig. 3.1 there are three columns of a five sequence msa. In column P all residues i.e R are matched, in column Q four R are matched and one S is mismatched, where as in column R three R are matched and two S mismatched.

With SP method cumulative scores for columns of a msa can be calculated. SP method can be illustrated by means of graph with five sequnces as vertices and representing the ten possible sequnce pair wise sequence comparisions as shown Fig. 3.1.

Solid lines represnts a matched pair and dotted liner a mismatched pairs.

BLOSUM 62 scores are calculated as shown in last row.

→ Solution for calcuting Blosum 62 scores.

1. for column P

The number of R – R matched pairs for column P is 10. For each match pair the score is 6.

The no. 6 is by our convention we can put any score the first column P has no R – S matched pair therefore score is zero. Therefore the effective score of the column is 10×6 = 60. (Blosum score 62)

Similarly the Blossum score for column Q is calculated as below.

The number of matched pairs of R–R in column Q is 6 each pair has score 6 i.e 6×6 = 36

However, the no of R – S matched pairs in same column is 4 each with a score of – 3. i.e

$$4 \times -3 = -12.$$

The effective score or the Blosum 62 score for the same column is 36 – 12 = 24.

In the same manner as above the Blossum 62 score for the R column is 6.

The number of combinations of pairs in a column for n sequnces is n (n – 1)/2.

In Fig. 3.1 there are five sequnces therefore n = 5.

$$5(5 -1) /2$$

$$5 \times \frac{4}{2} = 5 \times 2 = 10$$

Therefore 10 possible combinations of pairs is possible for each column.

Note : For a larger number of sequences than five with all R, or with one or two S substitutions, the scores in the msa column should decrease rapidly as the no. of mismatched residue pairs increases. (because there will be more R – R matched pairs relative to mismatch R – S pairs. However, the reverse is true with SP method of scoring).

In column P, as all are amino acid R, then the BLOSUM 62 score for the column is $6 \times n(n-1)/2$.

It comes out to be 60. We have already calculated this above. Now there is one S in column Q. Then $(n-1)$ matched R – R pairs will be replaced by $n-1$ mismatched R – S pairs, giving a score $9(n-1)$ less.

Now we consider the relative difference for column where there is mismatched combinations of pair for calculating the relative difference, the score for one S in the column is divided by that for zero S in column i.e.

$$\frac{9(n-1)}{\dfrac{6n(n-1)}{2}} = 3/n.$$

for column Q it is 3/n.

Where n = no. of sequnces

For 3 sequnces relative difference is 1 where as for six sequnces the relative difference is 2.

As more sequences are present in the column the relative difference increases, not in agreement with expectation (See: note). Henc, the SP method is not providing a reasonable result when this type of scoring matrix is used.

3.5 Pair Wise Sequence Alignment Verses Multiple Sequence Alignment

One of the important contributions of molecular biology to evolutionary analysis is the discovery that the DNA sequences of different organisms are often related. Similar genes are conserved across widely diverged species, often performing a similar or even identical function, and at other times, mutating or rearranging to perform an altered function through the forces of natural selection. Thus many genes are represented in highly conserved forms in organisms. Through simultaneous alignment of the sequences of these genes sequence patterns that have been subject to alteration may be analyzed.

Because the potential for learning about the structure and function of molecules by multiple sequence alignment (msa) is so great, computational methods have received a great deal of attention. In msa sequences are aligned optimally by bringing the greatest number similar characters into register in the same column of the alignment of more than two sequences that includes matches, mismatches and gaps and that takes into account the degree of variation in all of the sequences at the same time poses a very difficult challenge. The dynamics programming algorithm used for optimal sequence alignment of pairs of sequences can be extended to three sequences, but for more than three sequences, only small number of relatively short sequences may be characterized. Thus approximate methods are used, including

Progressive global alignment of the sequences starting with an alignment of the most alike sequences and then building an alignment by adding more sequences.

Iterative methods that make an initial alignment of group of sequences and then revise the alignment to achieve a more reasonable result.

Alignment based on locally conserved patterns found in the same order in the sequences. Use of statistical methods and probabilistic models of the sequences.

Just now we discussed about statistical method. A second computational challenge is identifying a reasonable method of obtaining a cumulative score for the substitution in the column of a MSA. Finally, the placement and scoring of gaps in the various sequences of an MSA presents an additional challenge.

The MSA of a set of sequences may also be viewed as an evolutionary history of the sequences. If these sequences in the MSA align very well, they are likely to be recently derived from a common ancestor sequence. Conversely a group of poorly aligned sequences share a more common complex and distant evolutionary relationship. The task of aligning a set of sequences, some more closely and other less closely related is identical to that of discovering the evolutionary relationship among the sequences.

As with aligning a pair of sequence the difficulty in aligning a group of sequences varies considerably with sequence similarity. On the one hand, if the amount of sequence variation is minimal, it is quite straightforward to align the sequences, even without the assistance of a computer program. On the other hand, if the amount of sequence variation is great, it may be difficult to find an optimal alignment of the sequences because so many combinations of substitutions, insertions and deletions, each predicting a different alignment, are possible.

The availability of a subset of the Many MSA Programs are shown below

CLUSTAL W or CLUSTALX; MSA; PRALINE; DIALIGN; MULTALIN

PRRP; SAGA; HMMER; MACAW; SAM;

Websites :   clustal W   www.ebi.ac.vk/clustalw or clustalx
              clustal X   available at Ebi or Expary websites

When dealing with a sequence of unknown function the presence of similar domains in several similar sequences implies a similar biochemical function or structural fold that may become the bias of further experimental investigation. A group of similar sequences may define a protein family that may share a common biochemical function or evolutionary origin. Similar proteins have been organized into databases of proteins families, which will be discussed later.

One application MSA is in genome sequencing Projects. Instead of cloning and arranging a very large number of fragments of a Large DNA molecule and then moving along the molecule and sequencing the fragments in order, random fragments of the large molecules are sequenced and those that overlap are found by the MSA program. This approach enables automated assembly of large sequences. Bacterial genome has been quite readily sequenced by this method.

Just as the alignment of a pair of nucleic acid or protein sequences can reveal whether or not there is an evolutionary relationship between the sequences, so can the alignment of three or more sequences reveal relationship among multiple sequences. MSA of a set of sequences can provide information as to the most alike regions in the set. In Proteins, such regions may represent conserved functional or structural domains. If the structure of one or more members of the alignment is known it may be possible to predict which amino acids occupy the same spatial relationship in other proteins in the alignment. In nucleic acids, such alignments also reveal structural and functional relationships. For example, aligned promoters or set of similarity-regulated genes may reveal consensus-binding sites for regulatory Proteins.

Another use of consensus information retrieved from a MSA is for the prediction of specific probes for other members of the same group or family of similar sequences in the same or other organisms. There are both computer and molecular biology applications. Once a consensus pattern has been found database-searching programs may be used to find other sequences with a similar pattern. In the laboratory a reasonable consensus of such patterns may be used to define polymerase chain reaction (PCR) primers for amplification of related sequences.

Once MSA has been found, the number or types of changes in the aligned sequence residues may be used for a phylogenetic analysis. The alignment provides a prediction as to which sequence character corresponds. Each column in the alignment predicts the mutations that occurred at one site during evolution of the sequence family.

The close relationship between MSA and evolutionary tree construction shown is a short section of one MSA of four Protein sequences including conserved and substituted positions, an insertion (of K) and a deletion of L below MSA shown an hypothetical evolutionary tree that could have generated these sequence changes. Each outer branch in the tree represents one of the sequences. The outer branches are also referred to as leaves. The deepest, oldest branch is that of the sequence D, followed by A, then by B and C . The optimal alignment of several sequences can thereby be thought of as minimizing the number of mutational steps in an evolutionary tree for which the sequences are the outer branches or leaves. The mathematical solution to this problem was first outlined by Sankoff (1975).

Fast MSA programs that are tree based have since been developed. However, such an approach depends on knowing the evolutionary tree to perform an alignment. Often this is not the case. Usually, pair wise alignments are generated first and then used to predict the tree. In this example, the alignment could be explained by several different trees including the one shown. (Fig. 3.2).

Seq A	N	•	F	L	S
Seq B	N	•	F	•	S
Seq C	N	K	Y	L	S
Seq D	N	•	Y	L	S

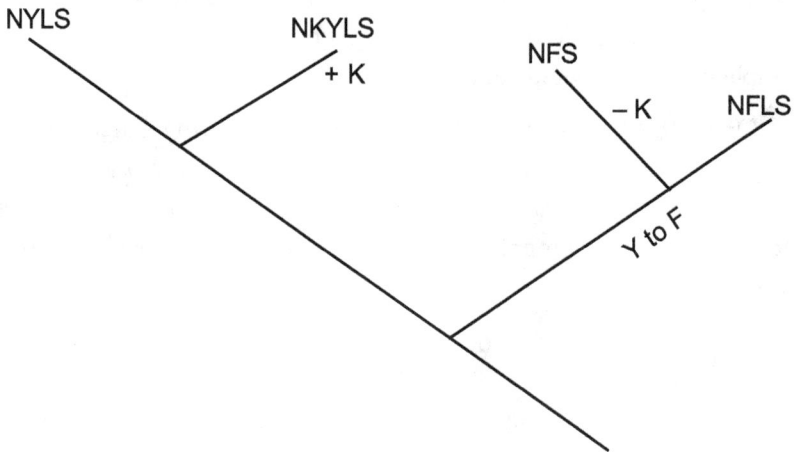

Fig. 3.2 Tree diagram

Within the column are original characters that are present early, as well as other derived characters that appeared later in evolutionary time. In some cases the position is so important for function that mutational changes are not observed. In other cases the position is less important and substitutions are observed. Deletions and insertions may also be present in some regions of the alignment. Thus, starting with the alignment one can hope to dissect the order of appearance of the sequences during evolution.

3.6 Phylogenetic Trees

Ideally a researcher would like to have a black box in which to throw sequences and get out a fully annotated phylogenetic tree. This is, however, not possible for two reasons. First, an algorithm that considers all possible multiple sequence alignments and then, for each alignment, all possible phylogenetic trees and picks out the best one, would take too much time. That is why most phylogenetic programs work on previously aligned sequences. Second, the result is always strongly influenced by the criteria that are used to define the best tree. Phylogenetic analysis will be the subject of a separate chapter. However, a few remarks seem appropriate here. There are three main kinds of tree building methods : Distance matrix, Maximum likelihood and Parsimony.

Distance matrix methods first estimate the pairwise distances between the sequences (which means that the information in the alignment of two sequences is reduced to one number) while the other methods construct many trees from all the information in the multiple alignments and decide which is best.

The simplest distance based method is UPGMA (unweighted pair-group method using arithmetic averages) which involves iteratively taking together the two sequences that have the shortest distance from each other, placing them at the end of branches on a node of the tree, and replacing their distances from the other sequences by an average value.

The guide tree used by pileup and CLUSTAL should never be used to infer phylogeny! It has been derived from the distances between pairwise aligned sequences and these distances are not necessarily the same as the distances between sequence pairs taken from the multiple sequence alignment.

3.7 Tools Used Such as Clustal X

CLUSTAL X provides graphical interface to the program CLUSTAL X. Clustal was developed by Higgins and sharp in 1988 and much improved versions were developed later. CLUSTAL W is the more recent version of CLUSTAL with W standing for weighing to represent the ability of the program to provide weights to the sequence and program parameters.

CLUSTAL performs a global-multiple sequence alignment by a stepwise process. In step I it performs pair wise alignments of all the sequences provided by the user. In step II the scores obtained for the pairwise alignment are used to produce a phylogenetic tree and in step III the phylogenetic tree is used as a guide to align sequences sequentially thus the most closely related sequences are aligned first, and then additional sequences are added one by one to a profile of an existing MSA. The scoring of gaps is done in a manner different from that followed for a pairwise alignment. CLUSTAL W calculates gaps in a novel way. The graphical version of CLUSTALX provides a versatile environment for doing MSA of sequences. Alignments can also be produced in profile mode. Profile mode is typically used when MSA is already known for a set of sequences and one wants to align a sequence of another MSA to that MSA. This is very useful feature for finding conserved domains.

Family specific sequence profiles, sequence signatures, their importance in sequence alignments and homology searches, psi-blast; MSA obtained for a family of sequences typically contains columns of conserved residues and the columns of similar residues. Such residues taken together may specify a pattern or signature or groups of functionally related sequences sharing similar patterns. From the columns of the residues in the MSA one can work out a consensus sequence (variously known as a pattern, motif, signature, or finger print) characterizing that family. Using that appropriate computational tools, PROSITE is a database where many consensus sequence patterns of many protein families have been deposited.

3.8 Multiple Sequence Alignments Using ClustalX (PRACTICAL)

Clustal X can be obtained from the following website :

www.ebi.ac.uk/clustal x

ClustalX is a graphical version of the Clustal program that not only aligns sequences but also draws pretty pictures of the alignments.

1. Convert your sequences, which are probably in Fasta format, into "PIR" format, which is only slightly different. If fasta format is...

2. >SequenceName1

3. GSAVVALTNDRDTSYFGEIGIGTPPQKFTV

4. IFDTGSSVLWVPSSKCINSKACRAHSMYES

5. >SequenceName2

6. GNTTSSVILTNYMDTQYYGEIGIGTPPQTF

7. KVVFDTGSSNVWVPSSKCSRLYTACVYHKL

...Then PIR format is...

>SequenceName1

GSAVVALTNDRDTSYFGEIGIGTPPQKFTV

IFDTGSSVLWVPSSKCINSKACRAHSMYES

*

>SequenceName2

GNTTSSVILTNYMDTQYYGEIGIGTPPQTF

KVVFDTGSSNVWVPSSKCSRLYTACVYHKL

*

8. To keep Clustal happy, make sure the first word of the header line is unique for each sequence. If

9. >1hrn A

10.

11. GSAVVALTNDRDTSYFGEIGIGTPPQKFTV

12. IFDTGSSVLWVPSSKCINSKACRAHSMYES

13. *

14. >1hrn B

15.

16. GNTTSSVILTNYMDTQYYGEIGIGTPPQTF

17. KVVFDTGSSNVWVPSSKCSRLYTACVYHKL

18. *

...Change to...

>1hrnA

GSAVVALTNDRDTSYFGEIGIGTPPQKFTV

IFDTGSSVLWVPSSKCINSKACRAHSMYES

*

>1hrnB

GNTTSSVILTNYMDTQYYGEIGIGTPPQTF

KVVFDTGSSNVWVPSSKCSRLYTACVYHKL

*

...else Clustal will think there are two sequences for 1hrn.

19. Load your sequences into ClustalX by typing:

    /usr/local/apps/clustalx/clustalx my_alignment.pir &

20. Align the sequences by clicking the "Alignment" menu and selecting "Do complete alignment".

21. Save the alignment in PIR format by selecting "File"/"Save sequences as" and checking the appropriate format on the dialog box.

22. Save a picture of the alignment by choosing "File"/"Write Alignment as Postscript" and checking the options in the "write postscript" dialog box. Dismiss any printing-related error or warning messages (these are unimportant) then close the dialog box once ClustalX has saved the .ps file. Postscript (abbrev. "ps") is a printer language and postscript files can be viewed or printed under unix. View the postscript file by typing:

```
gs my_alignment_pic.ps &
```

Ask a demonstrator to print this picture out in colour.

23. Multiple sequence alignments can indicate which positions or regions are important for the structure and/or function of a protein, and which regions may vary with little consequence.

Look at your alignment. Are there any positions that are completely conserved? Are there any positions that show only conservative substitutions, i.e., like substituting for like? Are there any regions of one sequence unmatched by the other sequences? If the proteins in your alignment have identical functions, what does this suggest about the relative importance of these unmatched regions? Which regions of sequence might correspond to loops in the structure?

24. When all the sequences in an alignment are highly similar it can be difficult to distinguish important from unimportant positions; the sequences may be so closely related that less important regions have not had time to diverge and so appear conserved.

Look at the BLAST outputs for the sequences in your alignment. How similar are your sequences to each other? If you have time, add some of the lower scoring BLAST hits to your alignment, i.e., sequences in the 30-40% identity range (no lower, else they may not be genuine relatives). Make another alignment with this larger set. How does this alignment differ from your original ?

Note : Blast can be found at www.ncbi.n/m.nih.gov/blast

3.9 What is the Use of Sequence Patterns

It is often observed that a new protein is too distantly related to any protein of known structure to detect its resemblance by overall sequence alignment. But it can be identified by the occurrence in its sequence of a particular motif. These motifs arise because of particular requirement on the structure of specific regions of a protein, which may be important for example for the binding properties or for their enzymatic activity. These requirements impose very tight constraints on the evolution of those limited in size but important portion of a protein sequence. The use of protein sequence patterns (or motifs) to determine the function of proteins is becoming very rapidly one of the essential tools of sequence analysis.

As it is clear now from the above discussion that MSA of Proteins can be used to develop sequence pattern. The first and the most important criterion is that a good signature pattern must be as short as possible, should detect all or most of the sequences it is designed to describe and should not give too many false positive results. In other words it must exhibits both high sensitivity and high specificity. Therefore while deriving a motif particular attention is paid to the residues and regions thought or proved to be important to the biological function of the group of Proteins. These biologically significant regions or residues are generally :

Enzyme catalytic sites; prosthetic group attachment sites (heme, pyridoxal-phosphate, biotin etc)

Amino acids involved in binding a metal ion.

Cysteine involved in disulphide bonds.

Regions involved in binding a molecule (ADP/ATP, GDP/GTP, CALCIUM, DNA)

Or another Protein.

For example from the following MSA one can derive a sequence pattern a [R, T or D]-[D, A or Q]-[F, E or A]-A-T-H-[D or E]. Please note the shorter motif viz., the conserved A-T-H could have been sufficient. However, in order to increase the specificity the sequence pattern in the flanking regions have also been have been taken.

ALRDFATHDDF
SMTAEATHDSI
ECDQAATHEAS

There are a number of protein families as well as functional or structural domains that cannot be detected using patterns due to their extreme sequence divergence. But by using family specific sequence profiles it is possible to detect such proteins or domains.

A profile (also called, as weight matrix) is a table of position specific amino acid weights and gap costs. These numbers (also referred to as scores) are used to calculate a similarity score for any alignment between a profile and a sequence, or parts of a sequence and a profile. An alignment with a similarity score higher than or equal to a given cut off value constitutes a motif occurrence. As with patterns, there may be several matches to a profile in one sequence, but multiple occurrences in the same sequences must be disjoint (non-overlapping) according to a specific definition included in the profile.

Profile can be constructed by a large variety of different techniques. The classical method developed by Gribskov and coworkers requires a multiple sequence alignment as input and uses a symbol comparison table to convert residue frequency distribution into weights.

Unlike patterns, profiles are usually not confined to small regions with high sequence similarity. Rather they attempted to characterize a protein family or domain over its entire length. This can lead to specific problems not arising with PROSITE patterns. With a profile covering conserved as well as diverged sequence regions, there is a chance to obtain a significant similarity score even with a partially incorrect alignment. This possibility is taken into account by our quality evaluation procedures. In order to be acceptable, a profile must not only assign high similarity scores to true motif occurrences and low scores to false matches. In addition it should correctly align those residues having analogues functions or structural properties according to experimental data.

Profiles are supposed to be more sensitive and more robust than patterns because they provide discriminatory weights not only for the residues already found at a given position of a motif but also for those not yet found. The weights for those not yet found are extrapolated from the observed amino acid compositions using empiric knowledge about amino acid substitutability.

3.10 PSI –BLAST

As mentioned earlier it is quite advantageous to use a sequence profile that represents a sequence pattern in a protein family instead of a single query sequence to search a database. The search of database thereby will be expanded to identify additional related sequences that might other wise be missed. A new version of blast called Position specific iterated blast has been designed to build profiles iteratively and then to do blast search. As name itself indicate the methods of Psi- Blast involves a series of repeated steps or iterations. First a database search of protein sequence database is performed using query sequence. Second the results of the search are checked to include only the convincing hits in other words only the high scoring sequence matches. These sequences are aligned and a weigh matrix is produced from the alignment. The database is again searched with this scoring matrix. Again the hits are aligned and the weight matrix is updated. This type of database search and updating of weight matrix are repeatedly carried out until no new hits are found (converged).

PSI-BLAST is highly sensitive as well as specific due to the use of family specific profile which gets updated iteratively and that is used as the scoring matrix for next database search. An analysis on the performance of PSI-BLAST has demonstrated that BLAST can detect weak similarities that exist between distant homologues.

PSI-BLAST can be accessed from the following website:
             www.ncbi.nlm.nih.gov/BLAST

3.11 Structure Based Sequence Alignment-COMPARER

So far we discussed about alignment of sequences using some scoring matrices. It is also possible to align sequences of proteins based on their structures. Such alignments are called as structure based sequence alignments. In fact structure based sequence alignments more accurately represents the similarities between the Proteins than the alignments purely based on sequence scoring matrices. The basic underlying fact is that even the proteins, which have diverged very much with respect to their amino acid sequences, still retain their overall 3D structure. The fact has led to the development of many computational algorithms.

The basic prerequisite to carry out structure-based alignments is that the 3D structures of the proteins in the form of PDB (Brookhaven Protein Data Bank) files are known. A PDB file contains Cartesian coordinates of all the amino acids residue of a protein. Using the atomic coordinate the protein 3D structures are superimposed on to each other. After the best superposition the residues that are within a distance usually 3 Angstroms are listed. Such residues are called as topologically equivalent residues. The topologically equivalent residues have similar structural environments. From topologically equivalent residues an unequivocal sequence alignment is worked out.

COMPARER is a computational tool developed by Sali and Bundall (1990) to carry out structural based sequence alignments of Proteins. The underlying idea in this method is that the protein is not only viewed as a string of amino acids which makes its primary structure but also additionally as string of structural features such as secondary structures, the degree of residue solvent accessibilities, and hydrogen bonds. All these structural features along with the residues are used and an alignment is produced using dynamic programming algorithms.

Other approaches include :

- The very popular CLUSTAL program differs only from pileup in that it performs the initial pairwise alignments using the fast algorithm of Wilbur and Lipman.

  CABIOS 8:189 (1992). You can obtain versions of CLUSTAL for UNIX.

- Starting with a search for words of n bases or amino acids that are common between the sequences. An example is Martin Vingron's program MALI.

  CABIOS 5:115 (1989). MALI is not distributed freely but may be obtained from its author Martin Vingron (vingron@embl-heidelberg.de)

- PIMA uses pattern matching, rather than profile matching, while making the progressive alignment. PNAS 87:118 (1990).

  PIMA can be obtained for UNIX.

- Building a phylogenetic tree, using a more elaborate algorithm, as the sequences are progressively aligned. An example is Jotun Hein's program Tree Align.

  Meth.Enzymol. 18:626(1990)

  TreeAlign can be obtained for UNIX from the same address as given for Clustalw (see above)

- Making the best multiple alignments in a limited area of alignment space. This can only realistically be performed with eight to ten sequences.

3.12 Blast3

It is also worth mentioning the program blast3. This searches a protein against a protein databank using the BLAST algorithm (with the sensitivity set high) and then makes threefold alignments between the query sequence and each possible pair of databank sequences that have been found. Only the statistically significant threefold alignments which are made from three nonsignificant pairwise alignments are retained. Blast3 is useful in finding proteins that share a region of only weak similarity. Occasionally it can show that a query sequence makes the bridge between two databank sequences whose relationship had not yet been suspected.

It is possible to access a BLAST (including blast3) server at the NCBI, either through WWW or with a specific blast Internet client that you can install on your computer.

Note : www.ncbi.nlm.nih.gov/BLAST

3.13 Multiple Sequence Alignments and Patterns

Multiple sequence alignment is the process of aligning several related sequences, showing the conserved and unconserved residues across all of the sequences simultaneously. These conserved/unconserved residues form a pattern that can often be used to retrieve sequences that are distantly related to the original group of sequences. These distant relatives are extreemly helpful in understanding the role that the groups of sequences play in the process of life.

3.14 Global Multiple Sequence Alignments

Global multiple sequence alignments are sequence alignments that require the participation of all sequence residues. A multiple sequence alignment shows the residue juxtaposition across the entire set of sequences; thus showing the conserved and unconserved residues across all of the sequences simultaneously.

3.15 Dynamic Programming Approach

In order to understand the multiple sequence alignment algorithms, we first, need to review aligning two sequences using the dynamic programming approach. In a straightforward implementation, this problem would require memory proportional to the lengths of the sequences. Thus if *sequence A* had *length L* and *sequence B* had *length M* this problem could be solved using $N \times M$ cells of memory. For example if sequence A was 8 residues long and sequence B were 5 residues long, 40 memory cells would be needed : (Fig. 3.3).

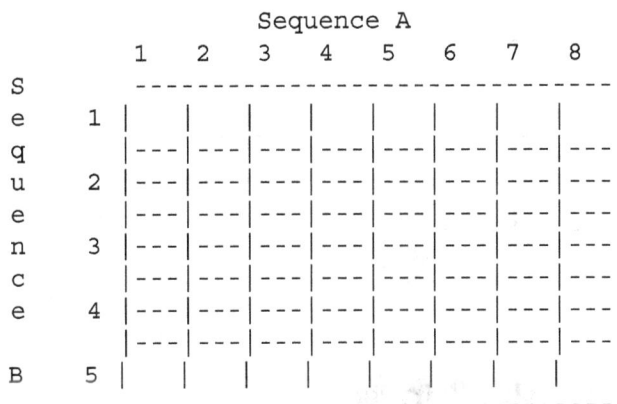

```
                        Sequence A
                1    2    3    4    5    6    7    8
   S         ----------------------------------------
   e     1  |    |    |    |    |    |    |    |    |
   q        |---|---|---|---|---|---|---|---|
   u     2  |---|---|---|---|---|---|---|---|
   e        |---|---|---|---|---|---|---|---|
   n     3  |---|---|---|---|---|---|---|---|
   c        |---|---|---|---|---|---|---|---|
   e     4  |---|---|---|---|---|---|---|---|
            |---|---|---|---|---|---|---|---|
   B     5  |    |    |    |    |    |    |    |    |
         ----------------------------------------
```

Fig. 3.3

If we were to align *3* residue third sequence, *sequence C*, with the original two sequences we would need 8x5x3=120 memory cells : shown in Fig. 3.4.

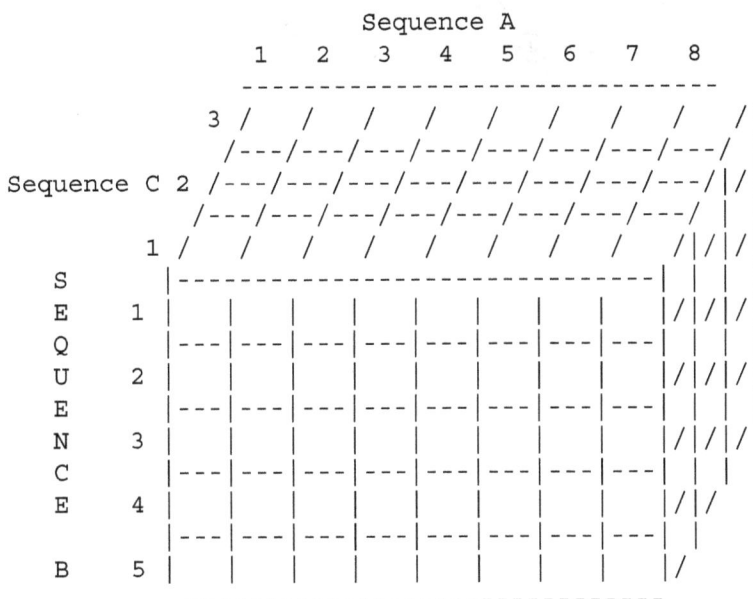

Fig. 3.4 Memory cells representation.

This approach is not practical for more than three average sized protein sequences. Lets look at the memory required to align average sized (300 residue) protein sequences :

Sequences	Cells	Memory (4 bytes/cells)
2	300^2 = 90000	351Kb
3	300^3 = 27000000	105Mb
4	300^4 = 8.1 × 10^9	31640Mb

3.16 Progressive Pairwise Approach

The progressive pairwise approach relies on exhaustive pairwise alignments between all of the sequences to produce a measure of sequence relatedness. From this measure, an algorithm (UPGMA in **Pileup**, Neighbor Joining in **Clustalw**) is used to develop a joining order. This joining order corresponds to a tree that is used to produce the multiple sequence alignment. It should be noted that this tree is **not an evolutionary tree** - Do not make the mistake of using it as one. The tree is shown in Fig. 3.5.

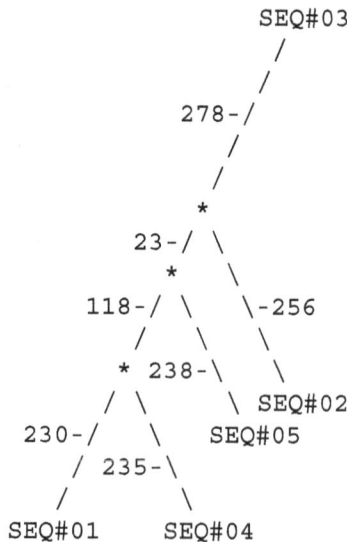

```
                              SEQ#03
                               /
                              /
                       278-/
                           /
                          /
                         *
                  23-/ \
                    *    \
              118-/ \     \-256
                  / \      \
                 * 238-\    \
                / \     \ SEQ#02
            230-/   \    SEQ#05
            / 235-\
           /       \
        SEQ#01     SEQ#04
```

Fig. 3.5 Tree of multiple sequence alignment (Progressive pairwise approach)

After the joining order has been determined, sequences close to each other are aligned first. In the example above, *SEQ#01* and *SEQ#04* are the first two sequences to be aligned. The third sequence, *SEQ#05*, is then aligned with the two previously aligned sequences, *SEQ#01* and *SEQ#04*. *SEQ#02* is then aligned, followed by *SEQ#03*.

Note :For understanding it better see UPGMA method in phylogentics chapter.

While this approach produces adequate results for many sets of sequences, the alignment produced by the procedure will vary depending on the joining order. Thus, joining the sequences in this order :

[[[[SEQ#03 + SEQ#02] + SEQ#05] + SEQ#04] + SEQ#01]

may not produce the same alignment as joining the sequences in the original order :

[[[[SEQ#01 + SEQ#04] + SEQ#05] + SEQ#02] + SEQ#03]

The advantages to this approach are that it requires only modest computer resources and that it is capable of aligning hundreds of sequences.

3.17 Modified Dynamic Programming Approach

If we had a good global alignment between two related sequences, the memory cells that contain this alignment would be near the center diagonal of the two dimensional grid. Likewise if we had a good global alignment between three related sequences we would expect its alignment path to make use of the memory cells near the center of the cube.

The MSA program uses a clever approach to restrict the amount of memory by computing bounds that approximate the center of a multi-dimensional hypercube. The first bound is produced by computing pairwise alignments between the set of sequences. Weights are usually applied to this value to produce the lower bound used by the program. Next a heuristic alignment is produced for the sequences. This heuristic alignment is produced by a procedure similar to progressive pairwise approach outlined above.

Weights are usually applied to this value to produce the upper bound used by the program. A *delta* value is then computed to be the difference between these two values. The *epsilon* values shown by the program is the computed delta value broke down per pairwise alignment. To produce good optimal alignments, *epsilon* and *delta* are the two most important parameters that you need to pay attention to. The delta and epsilon values are preliminary measures of the divergence between the set of sequences. Thus, closely related sequences will have low epsilons and deltas while distantly related sequences will have high epsilons and deltas.

Even though MSA reduces the space required to produce a multiple alignment dramatically, it is still uses much more memory than the progressive pairwise technique. Generally speaking, MSA will produce better alignments than most multiple sequence alignment programs such as Clustal or Pileup. The drawback with using MSA is that it requires an enormous amount of both computer time and memory to align more than a few distantly related sequences. However, we have been able to use MSA to optimally align 20 Phospholipase A2 sequences (approximately 130 residues), 14 Cytochrome C sequences (approximately 110 residues), 6 Aspartal proteases (approximately 350 residues), and 8 Lipid binding proteins (approximately 480 residues) on our computers. All of these problems approached the limits of the problems that can be solved optimally by the MSA program. The size of the problems solved by MSA are directly related to the sequence lengths, the number of sequences, and the amount of sequence diversity.

An example for best results running the program, first produce only a heuristic alignment with your set of sequences. Examine the alignment and the epsilons. If you are only using a few short sequences and the computed epsilons are relatively low *(epsilons < 50)* then the sequences are closely related. Continue on to produce an optimal alignment. If you are using a more complicated set of sequences, a *ramping* strategy is suggested. First, align three of your sequences optimally, than four, then five ... etc., until you exceed 32Mb of memory. Then double, triple, or quadruple the memory requirements and add one last sequence. You may or may not be able to get this last sequence to align. If you are dealing with long sequences, you may want to divide your sequences into two or three sub regions, and align the sub regions separately. The chart below illustrates using this strategy.

#	Sequences	Elapsed	CPU Time	Memory
1	humcetp	na	na	na
2	hupltp	00:00:00	00:00:00	608,056
3	rrrya3	00:00:24	00:00:24	632,863
4	bovbpi	00:01:53	00:01:53	20,432,143
5	ratlbp	00:20:52	00:20:51	75,296,490
6	rry2g5	16:48:04	16:04:10	10,129,449,583

3.18 Patterns

Patterns derived from aligned families

Early patterns were first reported as **consensus sequences**. These patterns were essentially composite sequences consisting of the most common residue occurring at a position in an alignment. Today, these patterns are of little use unless if the sequences are highly conserved. A later approach stored the pattern as a **regular expression**. A regular expression is much more flexible than a consensus sequence because more than one residue can be stored at each position. There are many patterns that can be described as regular expressions. Many of these excellent patterns can be found in the PROSITE dictionary of sites and patterns. The GCG program **motifs** make use of this data. The **findpatterns** program can be used to search a database for an ambiguous pattern. A more recent approach is to use a **weight matrix** to represent the pattern. This approach is much more sensitive to patterns that are not strongly conserved. The profile analysis method can be used to create a weight matrix patterns from a sequence alignment. These patterns, (called profiles) can then be used to search the sequence databases for additional sequences that contain the pattern. The **profilemake** program can be used to create a profile, with the **profile search** or **PROFILE-SS** programs can be used to scan a database for a profile. The **profilescan** program can be used to see if a sequence contains a pattern placed in the profile library.

3.19 Patterns Derived from Unaligned Sequences

Deriving patterns from unaligned sequences is a new area of research. One successful method uses an information content measure to discover patterns. This approach is incorporated into the **MEME** program. MEME essentially finds a position-dependent letter frequency matrix that is similar to a gapless profile. This gapless profile can then be used to search a database for copies of the profile. An experimental approach being used today is that of a hidden markov model. At the current time software using this technique is still very experimental. We anticipate that in a few years this approach may become useful technique.

3.20 Optimal and Sub Optimal Alignments

We discussed about optimal alignment between two sequences and how to achieve it using dynamic programming method. In several instances especially when the two sequences are highly diverged, there can be alternative alignments with nearly same probability or more generally the same score as the optimal alignment. Such alternative alignments that are worthy of examination are known as sub-optimal alignments.

There are two classes of sub optimal alignments. One class where the scores are closer to that of optimal alignment but differ in a few positions from the optimum alignment. The second class of sub-optimal alignments

4

Computational Biology (Biological Database Management System)

4.1 Introduction to Databases

Database : A collection of information organized in such a way that a computer program can quickly select desired pieces of data. You can think of database as an electronic filing system.

Traditional database are organized by fields, records and files. A field is a single piece of information; a record is a complete set of fields; and file is a collection of records. For example, telephone book is analogous to a file. It contains a list of records, each of which consists of three fields: name, address, and telephone number.

An alternate concept in database design is known as hypertext. In a hypertext database, any object, whether it be a piece of text, a picture, or a film, can be linked to any other object. Hypertext databases are particularly useful for organizing large amounts of desperate information, but they are not designed for numerical analysis.

To access information from a database, you need a database management system (DBMS). This is a collection of programs that enables you to enter, organize, and select data in a database.

Increasingly the term database is used as shorthand for a database management system.

(i) **Representation of data :** Database is used to abstract very specific sorts of information about a reality and organize it in a way that will prove useful. The database should be viewed as a representation or model of the world developed for a very specific application.

One of the reasons that there are so many softwares and hardware systems employed for databases is because each system allows users to represent and model certain types of phenomena.

(ii) **Organizing data :** It is important to realize that data can be filed away in several different forms depending on how it needs to be used and accessed. Perhaps the simplest method is the flat file or spreadsheet. Where each field is matched to one row of data.

(iii) **Flat files and spread sheaths :** Flat file or spread sheath is a simple method for storing data. All records in this database have the same number of fields. Individual records have different data in each field with one field serving as a key to locate a particular record. When the number of fields becomes lengthy a flat file is cumbersome to search. Also the key field is usually determined by the programmer and searching by other determinants may be difficult for the user. Although this type of database is simple in its structure, expanding the number of fields usually entails reprogramming. Additionally, adding new records is time consuming, particularly when there are numerous fields. Other methods offer more flexibility and responsiveness.

(iv) **Hierarchial files :** Hierarchial files store data in more than one type of record. This method is usually described as a "parent child, one to many", relationship. One field is key to all records, but data in one record does not have to be repeated in another. This system will allow records with similar attributes to be associated together. The records are linked to each other by a key field in a hierarchy of files. Each record except for the master record has a higher-level record file linked by a key field pointer. In other words, one record may lead to another and so on in a relatively descending pattern. An advantage is that when the relationship is clearly defined, and queries follow a standard routine, a very efficient data structure results. The database is arranged according to its use and needs. Acess to different records is easily available, or easy to deny to a user by not furnishing that particular file of the database. One of the disadvantages is one must access the master record, with the key field determinant, in order to link downward to other records.

(v) **Relational files :** Relational files connect different files or tables without using internal pointers or keys. Instead a common link of data is used to join or associate records. The link is not hierarchial. A " matrices of tables" is used to store the information. As long as the tables have a common link they may be combined by the user to form new inquires and data out put. This is the most flexible system and is particularly suited to SQL (structured query language). Queries are not limited by a hierarchy of files, but instead are based on relationship from one type of record to another that the user establishes. Because of its flexibility this system is the most popular database model.

(vi) **Object Oriented Databases :** The methods of the file organization discussed above depends upon the careful description of real-world phenomenon in terms of their attributes, such as height, weight, or age. It is these attributes that are stored in the database and together they provide a sort of abstracted depiction of the real world feature. Much recent attention has focused on how to organize this information in ways that are more readily represent the way users gather and use information about the world around them. That is, humans recognize objects immediately in terms of their totality or wholesomeness. Houses and skyscrapers are recognized immediately by form and function. The differences can be described in terms of the underlying attributes, but the people recognize these from experience.

The idea of object oriented database is to recognize information into the sort of wholes that people recognize, instead of decomposing each feature a distinctive list of attributes, emphases is placed on grouping the attributes of a given object into a unit or template that can be stored or retrieved by its natural name.

Object Oriented database has the advantage of organizing information in ways that scores often find easier to use the database, it has an intuitive feel because it employs that categories which users uses naturally in day-to-day life. For this reason object oriented databases are gaining increased attention.

(vii) Importance of Biological Databases : Bioinformatics which is basically convergence of two technology revolutions the explosive growth in biotechnology, paralled by the explosive growth in information technology. In last 10 years both the size of sequence databases (gene bank) and the power of computers have been doubling at about the same rate 18-24 months. Internet has radically affected the way data are provided, handled and analysed. This powerful combination of data and tools, which allow easy access and analysis has changed and will continue to change our approach to the design and practice of biological research.

One of the major challenges for the academicians and researchers working in the field of Bioinformatics is to manage the growing biological resources on Internet. Because it is important for the bench scientists working in biology to have easy and efficient ways of wading through the data and finding what is important to his or her research.

Hence biological data is becoming increasingly important to the modern research community. The task of managing this data is important, yet the task of presenting this data to the researchers is of even greater importance. Within the last two decades, new technologies have enabled the automated generation of data on a large scale that was never anticipated. The best example of this is automated DNA sequencing developed by Gilbert and Sanger. This technology has spawned many large scale-sequencing projects including the systematic sequencing of the human genome project. The human genome project is the single large multinational effort spearheaded by the United State Department of Energy with an estimated cost of 5 million dollars. The human genome is some three billion bases in length and promised to unlock the secrets of nearly every human genetic disease. Scientists are eager to access this data and as a result they are getting better at generating sequence data. In fact advancements in this technology have resulted in a doubling of sequencing rates every four years.

4.2 Introduction to Molecular Biology Databases

Recent years have seen an explosive growth in biological data, which is often not published anymore in a conventional sense, but deposited in a database. Sequence data from mega-sequencing projects may not even be linked to a conventional publication. This trend and the need for computational analysis of the data made databse essential tool for biological research. The goal of this material is to describe the different molecular biology database available to the researchers. There are so many specialized databases that is not reasonable to list the URLS of all of them, especially since this category of database is quite changeable and any list provided here would be outdated.

(i) **Bibliographic databases :** Services that abstract the scientific literature began to make their data available in machine-readable form in the early 1960. You should be aware that none of the abstracting services has a complete coverage. The best known is MEDLINE and now PUBMED abstracting mainly the medicinal literature.

MEDLINE and PUBMED are best accessible through NCBI, sENTREZ. EMBASE is a commercial product for the medical literature. BIOSS the inheritor of the old biological abstracts covers a broad biological field; the zoological record indexes the zoological literature. CAB international maintains abstracts database in the field of agricultural and parasitic diseases. AGRICOLA is for the agricultural field, what MEDLINE is for the medical field.

(ii) **Taxonomy databases :** Taxanomy databases are rather controversial since the soundness of the taxonomist classification done by the one taxonomist will be directly questioned by the next. Various efforts are going on to create a taxanomy resource. International Organization for Plant Information. Integrated Taxonomic Information System. The most generally used taxanomy databases are that maintained by the NCBI. This heirarchial taxanomy is used by the nucleotide sequence databases, SWISS-prot, and TREMBL, and is curated by an informal group of experts.

(iii) **Nucleotide sequence databases :** The International Nucleotide Sequence Database Collaboration (often though inaccurately referred to as Gen Bank) is a joint production of the nucleotide sequence database by the DDBJ (DNA Data Bank of Japan), EBI (European Bioinformatics Institute) and NCBI (National Centre for Biotechnology Information). In Europe the vast majority of the nucleotide sequence data produced is collected, organized and distributed by the EMBL Nucleotide Sequence database, located at the European Bioinformatic Institute, an outstation of the European Molecular Biology Laboratory. (EMBL) in Heidelberg, Germany. The Nucleotide Sequence databases are Data Repositories, accepting nucleic acid data from the community and making it freely available. The database strives for completeness, with the aim of recording every publicly known nucleic acid sequence. These data are heterogeneous, they vary with respect to the source of the material (e.g., genomic, viruses and cDNA), the intend quality (e.g. Finished verses single pass sequence), the extent of sequence annotation and the intended completeness of the sequence relative to its biological target (e.g. complete verses partial coverage of a gene or a genome). EMBL, NCBI and DDBJ automatically update each of their entry after every 24 hours with the new sequence they have collected or updated. The result is that they contain exactly the same information, except for sequences that have been added in the last 24 hours.

Each entry in a database must have a unique identifier that is a string of letters and or numbers that only that record has. This unique identifier, which is known as the accession number can be quoted in the scientific literature, as it will never change. As the accession number must always remain the same, another code is used to indicate the different versions due to sequence corrections. You should therefore always take care to quote both the unique identifier and the version number when referring to records in a nucleotide sequence database.

The accession number line in a nucleotide sequence record lists the accession numbers associated with the entry. The accession numbers consists of one letter followed by the five digits (X12345) or (more recently) two letters followed by six digits (XY 123456).

An example of an accession number line is shown here: AC YOO321; JO5348;

An accession number is dropped from the database only when the data to which it was assigned have been completely removed from the database.

The SV (Sequence version) line contains the nucleotide sequence identifier, which allows you to recognize the sequence version of this record. An example of a sequence version line is shown here: SV AJ000012.1; The Nucleotide sequence identifier is of the form of accession Version (eg, AJ000012.1). The first part is the never changing accession number, followed by a period and a version number. The accession number part will be stable but the version part will be incremented when the sequence changes.

Although the nucleotide sequence data are checked for integrity and obvious errors by the data library staff, the quality of the data is the responsibility of the submitter. As a consequence, there are many errors in the database; many sequence entries are either mislabeled, contaminated incompletely or erroneously annotated, or contain sequencing errors. In addition to this the databases is very redundant, in the sense that the same sequence from the same organism may be included many times, simply reflecting the redundancy of the original scientific reports. Sequence cluster databases such as unigene and stack (sequence tag alignment and consensus knowledge base) address the redundancy problem by coalescing sequences that are sufficiently similar that one may reasonably infer that they are derived from the same gene. Several specialized sequence databases are also available. Some of these deal with particular classes of sequence e.g., the ribosomal database project (RDP), the HIV sequence database and IMGT, the immunogenetics database. Others are focusing on particular features, such as TRANSFAC for transcription factor and transcription factor binding sites and EPD (Eukaryotic Protein Database) for promoters and REBASE (for restriction enzymes and restriction enzyme sites. GOBASE is a specialized database of organelle genome. A database for Mitochondria genome is Mit base from the EBI.

(iv) Genetics Databases : For organism of major interest to geneticists, there is a long history of conventionally published catalogues of genes or mutations, in the past few years most of these have been made available in an electronic form and a variety of new databases have been developed. These various databases vary greatly in form and content varying in the classes of data captured and how these data are stored.

There are several databases for Escherichia coli, CGSC, the *E.Coli* genetic stock center, maintains a database of E coli genetic information including genotypes and reference information for the strains in the CGSC collection, gene names, properties and linkage map, gene product information, and information on specific mutations. The E.coli database collection (ECDC) the Encyclopedia of E.coli Genes and Metabolism is a database of E. coli genes and metabolic pathways.

The MIPS yeast database is an important for information on the yeast genome and its products. The saccharomysis genome database is another major yeast database.

ACeDB is the database for genetic and molecular data concerning Caenorhabditis elegens. The database management system written for ACeDB by Durbin and j *Thierry-Mieg* has proved very popular and has been used in many other species-specific databases. ACeDB is now the name of this database management system, resulting in some confusion relative to the C.Elegens Database. The entire database can be downloaded from the Sanger Centre. Two of the best curated genetic databases are Fly base, the database for Drosiphila Melanogaster and the Mouse Genome (MGD). ZFIN a database for another important model organism, the zebra fish, Brachydanio rerio, has been implemented recently. Two major database for human genes and genomics are in existence McKusicks Mendelian inheritance in Man (MIM) is a catalogue of Human genes and genetic disorders and is available in an online form (OMIM) from the NCBI. The Genome Database (GDB) is the major human database including both molecular and mapping data. Both OMIM and GDB include information on genetic variation in humans but there is also the human mutation server at the EBI; and to the SRS interface to many human mutation databases.

(v) Protein sequence databases : The protein sequence databases are the most comprehensive source of information on proteins. It is necessary to distinguish between universal database covering proteins from all species and specialized data collections storing information about specific families or group of proteins, or about the protein of a specific organism. Two categories of universal protein sequence database can be discend; simple archives of sequence data; and annotated database where additional information has been added to the sequence record. In the following sections you will find a short description of the Protein Information Resource (PIR) the oldest protein sequence database, and a more detailed description of SWISS-PROT, annotated universal sequence database, and of TrEMBLE, the supplement of SWISS-PROT, which can be classified as computer-annotated sequence repository.

(vi) Structure database : The number of known Protein structures is increasing very rapidly through the Protein Data Bank (PDB). The Nucleic Acid Database (NDB) is the database of structures of small molecules of interest to biologist concerned with protein-ligand interactions.

(vii) Integration of databases : The increase use of databases in recent years has lead to the situation where semantically related information is stored in separate database at different sites. Researchers today face a Herculean task if they seek answers to questions that cross the boundaries of existing database on the characteristics of microorganisms. At present there are many databases, each covering some aspect of microbial life nomenclature, phylogeny and taxonomy, biochemistry, physiology, phenotypic information, ecology, genetics, alignment and sequence data (including the important recent availability of completely sequenced genomes).

Several database are there with protein and nucleic acid at various places worldwide web (for example at EBI and EMBL). These databank consists of readable flat files of data. Each databank contains a different kind of data and each has its own format for its entry. This growing mass of information is geographically scattered and are organized in almost as many ways as there are databases. To achieve easy access to all information gathered in a subject, it is desirable to have a global view of the data distributed in the different systems.

One way to examine entries in these databanks is to browse interactively. This can be done by using browsing tools like Netscape. In doing this databank entries are presented as HTML documents, with links to enable the user to jump to related entries in other databanks. However the user has to control the navigational search, which is awkward when sets of results satisfying various criteria are wanted. Instead, it is better to use a database query language.

(viii) **Intelligent data organization :** Comparison is the most commonly used methodology in computational molecular biology. Many biological objects come in families that share structural or functional features. Specifically for proteins the concept of super families was elaborated by Dayhoff (1976) And Zuckerkandi (1975) following the early observation that many protein share sequence similarity, suggesting their common evolutionary origin. While in the early days of Bioinformatics protein sequence and structure comparison were made on a case-by-case basis. More recently many systematic efforts to organize protein related information in the form of added value data collections have been undertaken. A very successful attempt to cluster protein sequences in the P FAM database of protein domain family. That contains mutually curated automatic components. Automatic approaches allow the delineation of the most conserved segments in related amino acid sequences that serve as characteristic signatures of protein families. Through aligning protein sequences with sequence of known three-dimensional coordinates, it is possible to augment the amount of available structural information about proteins by an order of magnitude.

(ix) **Data quality and control by databanks :** Databanks at two extremes function as passive data repositories (Archives) or as active reference compendia, issuing modification of data and information content. Data in biological databanks contains facts, e.g. representations of biological macromolecules as strings or coordinates, and associated information, which might be fuzzy, incomplete of subject to individual interpretation or conflicting nomenclature. Data quality has several elements, correctness, completeness, timeliness of capture, applied both to the newly measured properties and the annotation.

Quality control should not be restricted to the semantic checking of individual entries, but also include relationships to the other pats of the databases; the growth in rates of data generation has implication for data quality. On the one hand, most new data entries are related to previously described objects and can inherit some part of their annotation. However, many, newly determined data entries have no associated experimentally confirmed facts, and their annotations are based on their prediction.

(x) **The need for a common language :** Public database distribute their contents as flat files in some cases including indices for Rapid data retrieval. In principle, all flat file formats are based on the organizational hierarchy of databases entry, record. Entries are fundamental entities of molecular databases, but in contrast to the situation in the living cell that they purport to describe, database entries at one object in the form of atomic, isolated, nonheirarchial structures. Different databases may describe different aspects of the biological unit, e.g the nucleic acid and amino acid sequence of a gene and the relationship between them must be established by links that not intrinsically part of the data archives themselves.

The development of individual databases has generated a large variety of formats in their implementations. There is consensus that a common language, or at least that mutual intelligibility, would be a good thing, but this goal has proved difficult to achieve. Attempts to unify data formats have included application of Backusnaur based syntax; the development of an object oriented database definition language. None of these approaches has achieved the degree of acceptance. Underlying the question of mechanisms of inter communications between the databases of different structure and formats there is a need for common semantic standards and controlled vocabulary in annotations. This problem is especially acute in comparative genomics. From the technological point of view, intergenome comparisons are interdatabase comparisons, which means that the database to be compared have to speak the same language: keywords, information, fields, weight factors, object catalogues etc. General biological data resources are databases rather than knowledge bases: they describe miscellaneous objects according to the database schema, but no representation of general concepts and their relationship is given.

(xi) Integrated data retrieval system : An early attempt to provide a comprehensive interface to a variety of molecular biology databases was made by George and Orcutt in their Atlas system. ATLAS generated data indices by parsing the heterogeneous formats into common fields allowing for cross-database multi term queries. Avoiding the need for reformatting the database sources.

Several highly sophisticated retrieval systems have emerged, over the recent years. Entrez is gateway to the data collections maintained by the NCBI, those include nucleic acid and protein sequence data, 3D structures, genomes, taxonomic information and the only freely available general literature database, PUBMED. Perhaps the most powerful and unique feature of the Entrez system is that in addition to the static cross-reference inherent to the underlying database, extraction of related documents is also possible through the mechanism of neighbors. For example, it is possible to retrieve bibliographic references related to the article you are currently looking at. This is done through lexicographical analysis of the abstract text and keywords. Sequence neighbors can be extracted by performing a BLAST similarity search. Entrez also has excellent graphical capabilities and is directly bundled with a protein structure viewer and an extensive genome browser.

(xii) Data retrieval: Sequence retrieval system: Browsing across databases facilitated by the SRS system. The sequence retrieval system called the paragon of connectivity allows the user to explore virtually all existing molecular biology databanks installed at different locations, making full use of the inter database links.

SRS maintains indexes relating entries in one databank to entries in others. Thus, SRS maintains a large network of related databank entries. SRS provides search tools that enables users to retrieve particular entries or to find the accession code of entries that satisfy specific criteria e.g., entries with fields that match a given pattern strings, or fields with numeric values in a given range. SRS also provides link operators that enables the user to follow a chain of cross references where there is no direct link between the two.

The system includes a specifically designed language, ICARUS, for describing the structure of databanks and the syntax of the data fields. The SRS user interface, which started as a system of pulldown menus on a VT 100 terminal achieved in its WEB incarnation an unprecedented degree of sophistication. Various web query forms are adopted for interrogation by the users of different levels of expertise. Logical operators can be applied to field subsets. For instance it is logical to ask for all sequences larger than 200 residues from Escherichia coli, containing the word kinase but the glucokinase in the description line and published before 1995. Query forms can be adapt themselves to the particular sets of databanks selected by the user. Out put formats may also be customized, ranging from simple ID list to complicated property views. SRS creates indices of all possible cross-links between all databases.

SRS is relatively easier to install and maintain, which makes it suitable for running in-house bioinformatics Websites. Second it has a powerful command line language allowing complex queries to perform from programs and scripts.

Alternatively, the C language API is available for creating calls to all SRS functions from C programs. Finally anyone who creates a new databank can easily add it to the system by creating the appropriate description and indexing. DBGET at KYOTO University and the Human Genome Centre of Tokyo University, another integrated retrieval system for molecular biology data banks provides access to a variety of general data collection as well as to the Kyoto Encyclopedia of Genes and Genomes.

QGB based on another intelligent database query system, which is essentially a parser for the feature table field of the databases conforming to the DDBJ/ ENBL/ GENBANK format. The system includes three components the flat file parser, the SQL like query language and the sequence entry parser itself, which analyses the logical strucuture of the feature table records and their relationships.

4.3 Biological System Databases

(i) **The emergence of databases :** Around 1970 a researcher called
Ted Codd had developed the relational data model which was to
become the foundation stone of modern database technology in the
mid 70s. However computer databases particularly in the hands of
end users were not a common thing.

It wasn't until the beginning of the 80s with the development of dBaseII
(There was no dBase I) that microcomputer based databases started
coming into their own. Although riddled with bugs, dBase put
enormous power into the hands of microcomputer developers and it
remained the prominent database programs until the advent of
Windows 3,x with Windows 3 came a new breed of PC database,
designed to be much easier to use than their DOS based predecessors.

What is a Database? Lets take a step back and define exactly what is
a database is. If spread sheets are the number crunchers of the digital
world, databases are the real information crunchers database excel
at managing and manipulating structured information.

What does the term structured information mean consider that most
ubiquitous of databases–the phone book? The phone book contains
several items of information–that Name, address and phone numbers–
about each phone book is a table, which contain a record for each
subscriber. Each subscriber contains three fields: name, address and
phone number. The records are sorted alphabetically by the name
field, which is called the key field.

Other examples of the databases are the club membership lists,
customer list, library catalogues, business cards files and parts of
inventories. The list is, in fact, infinite. Using a database program you
can design a database to do anything from tracking the breeding
program on a horse stud to collecting information from the Mars
Rover. And increasingly, databases are being used to build websites.

(ii) **Database programs :** To create and maintain a database, you need a computer database; you need a database program, often called a database management system, or DBMS. Just as database range from simple, single line table lists to complex multiple systems, database systems too range in complexity. Some such as the database component of Microsoft works, are designed purely to manage single file databases. With such a product you cannot built a multi-table database, You can certainly create numerous tables for sorting different types of information, but there's no way to link information from one table to another. Such programs are sometimes called flat file database, or list managers.

Other database programs, called relational database programs or RDBMS, are designed to handle multi-file databases. File maker Pro is a relational database that's easy to use and fairly inexpensive.

The most popular relational databases are the offering from the big three software companies. Lotus, Corel and Microsoft each produces a full-featured relational database application available both as a standalone Program and as apart of its integrated suite. Lotus as Approach, Coral has Paradox and Microsoft has Access.

(iii) **Database programs tools :** A database program gives you the tools to:

To design the structure of your Database

Create the data entry forms so you can get information into the databases.

Validate the data entered and check for inconsistencies

Sort and manipulate the data in the database.

Query the database (that is, ask questions about the data).

Producer flexible reports, both on screen and on paper, that make it easy to comprehend the information stored in the database.

Most of the more advanced database programs has built in programming or macro languages, which let you automate many of their functions.

(iv) Using a Database : if the mention of programming languages makes you feel, you are getting out of your depth, don't worry. Most of the databases programs you're likely to encounter can be used at a variety of levels.

If you are a beginner, you will find builtin templates, Sample databases, Wizards and Experts that will do the much of the hard work for you. If you find the builtin database don't quite work for you, it is easier to modify an existing database so it fits your needs, and it is not at all difficult to learn to create your own simple database structure from scratch.

For more advanced users the more powerful database programs enable you to create complete, custom-built, application specific systems which can be used by others in your organization or business.

4.4 DNA Databanks

There are two main types of databases DNA nucleotide database and protein databases. The growth rate of DNA databases is much higher because most of the DNA is not coding for proteins and because DNA sequencing is the most prominent source of these data.

The DNA databanks are, genbank at NCBI, DNA databank of JAPAN (DDBJ) AND EMBL nucleotide sequence database (EMBL) which are part of the International Nucleotide Sequence Database Collaboration, Exchange Data on a daily basis.

What is a Gene Bank? Gen Bank is the NIH Genetic sequence Database, an annotated collection of all publicly available DNA sequences. There are approximately 12,419000000 Bases in 11,546000 Sequence Records as on April 2001.

Access to gen bank : Gen bank is available for searching at NCBI via several Methods :

1. *Text and Similarity Searching :* Entrez Browser
2. *Blast Sequence Similarity Searching :* Nucleotides or the protein sequences against the specified databases using the BLAST suite.

4.5 The EMBL Nucleotide Sequence Database

The EMBL nucleotide sequence database constitutes Europe's primary nucleotide sequence resource. Main sources for DNA and RNA sequence are direct submission from individual researchers, genome sequencing projects and patent applications. The current database release is 67 (June 2001)

Over view of EMBL databases : Established in 1980 the database was historically tightly coupled top the publication of sequences in the scientific literature. Electronic submission via the WWW is now usual practice. Today, the vast majority of data submitted by direct transfer of data comes from the major sequencing centers, such as the Sanger Centre. The EMBL database has nearly tripled in size within the last months and on September 1, 2000 contained more than 9.6 Gigabytes in 8.3 Million records.

Data management and representation : Data is managed in a robust database management system (ORACLE) using a scheme, which facilitates integration and interoperability with other databases, especially protein sequences. Quarterly releases and daily updates for distribution and installation at remote sites are generated from this system.

4.6 Data Bank of Japan

DDBJ The DNA data Bank of Japan in 1986 at the National Institute of Genetics (NIG) with the endorsement of Ministry of Education, Science, Sports and Culture. From the begining, DDBJ has been functioning as one of the international DNA database, including EMBL in Europe and NCBI in the USA as the two major centers for Biotechnology information responsible for GEN BANK. Consequently this has been collaborating with the two databanks through exchanging data and information on Internet as the international databanks collaboration.

The Center for information Biology At NIG was reorganized as the Centre for Information Biology and DNA Data Bank of Japan in 2001. The new Center is to play a major role in carrying out research in biology. Today requires both computer and experimental equipments equally well. In particular, this relies on computers to analyze DNA sequences data accumulating at a remarkable rapid rate. Actually, this triggers the birth and the development of Information Biology.

DDBJ is the sole DNA data bank in Japan which is officially certified to collect DNA Sequences from researchers and to issue the internationally recognized number to data submitters. We collect data mainly from the Japanese researchers, but of course accept data and issue the Accession Number to researchers in any other countries. Also many tools for retrieval and analysis worldwide are provided which are developed at DDBJ and others.

4.7 SWISS–PROT

SWISS–PROT is a curated protein sequence database which strives to provide a high level of annotations such as the function of proteins, its domains structure, post-translational modifications, variants etc., with a minimum level of redundancy and a high level of integration with other databases.

SWISS–PROT is an annotated protein sequence database established in 1986 and maintained collaboratively, since 1987, by the department of Medical Biochemistry of the University of Geneva and the EMBL data entry library (Now the EMBL – Out station –the EBI. The swiss-port consists of sequence entries.

The SWISS-PROT protein sequence database differs with other databases by three distinct criteria:

Annotation : In SWISS–PROT, as in most other sequence databases two classes of data can be distinguished: the core data and the annotation. For each sequence entry the core data consists of the sequence data; the citation information and the taxonomic data while the annotation consists of the description of the following terms.

Functions of the proteins

Post-translational modifications

Domains and sites

Secondary structures

Quarternarary structure

Similarities to other proteins

Disease associated with deficiencies in the proteins

Minimum redundancy : Many sequence databases contain, for a given protein sequence separate entries, which corresponds to different literature reports. IN Swiss-prots, as much as possible all these data will be merged so as to minimize the redundancy of the databases. If conflicts exists between various sequencing reports, they are indicated in the feature table of the corresponding entry.

Integration with other databases : It is important to provide the user of molecular databases with a degree of integration between the three types of databases as well as with specialized data collection. SWISS-PROT is currently cross-referenced with 30 different databases. Cross-references are provided in the form of pointers to the information related to SWISS-PROT entries and found in data collections other than SWISS-PORT.

4.8 Protien Information Resource

The protein information resource (PIR) in collaboration with Munich Information Center for Protein Sequences (MIPS) and Japan Information Database (JIPID), produces the PIR International Protein Sequence Database (PIR-PSD); a comprehensive, non redundant, expertly annotated, fully classified and extensively cross referenced protein sequence database in the Public Domain. The primary objective for its continuing development and enhancement is to achieve the properties of comprehensiveness, timeliness, non-redundancy, quality annotation, and full classification.

The Protein Information Resource (PIR) for over three decades has been a community resource that provides protein database and analysis tools to support research on molecular evolution, functional genomics and computational biology.

To further support genomic and poteomic research they have greatly improved in the Bioinformatics infrastructure in the last 2 years.

To continue to provide quality protein sequence data and annotation, while keeping pace with the large influx of data being generated by genome sequencing Projects.

To develop an integrated system of protein databases and analytical tools for expert annotation and knowledge discovery, and

To improve accessibility of resource and interoperability of their databases.

The primary sources of PSD data are naturally occurring wild-type sequences from gene bank/EMBL/DDBJ translations, published reports, and direct subimission to PIR International.

4.9 PFAM

PFAM is a collection of Protein Families and Domains. PFAM contains multiple protein alignments and profiles–HMM of these families. PFAM is a semiautomatic protein family database, which aims to be comprehensive as well as accurate.

PFAM is a database of multiple alignments of protein domains or conserved protein regions. The alignments represents some evolutionary conserved structure, which has implications for the protein's function. Profile Hidden Markov Models (ProfileHMM) built from the Pfam alignments can be very useful for automatically recognized that a new protein belongs to an existing protein family, even if the homology is weak. Unlike standard pair wise alignment methods. (e.g. BLAST, FASTA), PFAM HMMS deal sensibly with multidomain proteins.

PFAM is composed of two parts; the first part, PFAM-A, contains curated families each with an associated Profile Hidden Markov Model (ProfileHMM) that can be used for alignment and database searching. The second part of PFAM is PFAM-B, in which sequence segments that are not included in P-FAM-A are clustered automatically, allowing PFAM to be comprehensive.

Each P-Fam–A Family consists of four elements :

1. Annotations
2. A seed alignments
3. A profile HMM
4. A full alignment

Using PFAM : The PFAM web sites allow the database to be queried in one of three ways: First, a user may have a new sequence for which they know nothing. In such a case, this sequence can be searched against the current collection of PFam Profile HMMs to locate regions of the sequence that belongs to known domain families. Protein matches to PFAM–A Profile HMMs are now displayed using a graphical representation.

Second, if the user already has a SISS-PROT or SP- TrEMBL identifier for the sequence they can access pre–calculated matches using the SWISSPFAM resource. In such cases the regions of the target sequence belonging to PFAM-A and PFAM-B are displaced. Finally, users can browse the information in PFAM by family or use a text search of PFAM and related PROSITE annotation to find families of interest.

Changes to PFAM-B : PFAM–B is an automatically generated supplement to Pfam–A, that provides completeness in terms of coverage. It has also provided a useful resource for new PFAM-A families. PFAM-B in principle is made from the parts of PRODOM not covered by PFAM-A.

Searching PFAM : The US and UK PFAM servers provide users the ability to search query protein sequences against one, all or a few PFAM HMMs. Results are returned in tabular forms, and both GIF and JAVA based graphical representation are available optionally.

Users can also use HMM profiles to search protein sequences locally using the freely available HMMER software package.

For comparing Genomic Data and EST Data to PFAM HMM profiles, the Programs Gene wise, and EstWise are available.

4.10 INTERPRO

INTERPRO is an integrated documentation resource for protein families : Domains and sites, developed initially as a means of rationalizing the complementary efforts of the PROSITE,PRINTS,PFAM and PRODOM and links are made back to the relevant member database, allowing the user to see at a glance whether a particular family or domain has associated patterns, profiles, fingerprints, etc. merged and individual entries are assigned unique accession numbers. Each InterPro entry lists contains all the matches against SWISS-PROT and TREMBL.

InterPro aims to reduce duplication of efforts in the labour-intensive, rate-limiting process of annotation, and will facilitate communication between the disparate resources. By uniting these databases, their individual strengths are capitalized, producing a single entity that is as far greater than the sum of its parts. As it evolves, InterPro will streamline the analysis of newly determined sequences for the individual user, and will make a significant contribution in the demanding task of automatic annotation of predicted proteins from genome sequencing projects.

What is InterPro ? Protein signature database have become vital tools for identifying distant relationships in novel sequences and hence for inferring protein function. Currently, the most commonly used protein signature database include :

PROSITE home of Regular expressions and Profiles;

PFAM, keeper of Hidden Markov Model

PRINTS, and Providers of Fingerprints (Group of aligned, un-weighted motifs) and Blocks, the source of aligned, weighted motifs or Blocks.

Diagnostically, these resources have different areas of optimum application owing to different strengths and weaknesses of their underlying methods. In terms of Family coverage, the protein signature databases are similar in size but differ in content. While all of the resources share a common interest in protein sequences classification, some focus on divergent domains (e.g., PFAM), some focus on functional sites (e.g., PROSITE) and others focus on families, specializing in hierarchical definitions from super-family down to subfamily levels in order to pin-point specific functions. (e.g. PRINTS).

A number of sequence cluster databases are also commonly used in sequence analysis. For example to facilitate domain identification (e.g., PRODROM). Protein signature database, the clustered resources are derived automatically from sequence database, using different clustering algorithms. This allows them to be relatively comprehensive, because they do not depend on manual crafting and validation of family discriminators. Given these complexities, analysis strategies should endeavor to combine a range of databases, as none alone is sufficient. In the task of sequence characterization, we need reliable, concerned methods for identifying protein family traits and for inheriting functional annotation. This is especially important given our dependence on automatic methods for assigning functions to the raw sequences data issuing from genome projects. InterPro provides an integrated view of a number of commonly used proteins signature databases, and provides an intuitive interface for text and sequence-based searches.

How it will be useful? A primary application of InterPro's Family, Domain and functional site definitions will be in the computational functional classification of newly determined sequences That lack biochemical Characterization. For instance the EBI will use Inter-pro for enhancing the automated annotation of TrEMBL.This process should be more efficient and reliable than using each of the pattern database separately, because InterPro will Provide internal consistency checks and deeper coverage.

Application of InterPro : InterPro is an international initiative that was conceived in an attempt to streamline the efforts of the signature database. A primary application of InterPro's family, domain and functional site definition will be in annotation and functional classification of uncharacterized sequences. The EBI is Using InterPro for enhancing the automated annotation of TREMBL. This is more efficient and reliable than using each of the signature databases separately, because interpro provides internal consistency checks and deeper coverage. InterPro also has proven its usefulness for whole Proteome analysis in the comparative genome analysis of Drosophila Melanogaster. Ceanorhabditis elegans and saccharomyces cerevisieae.

Another major use of InterPRo will be in identifying those families and domains for which the existing discriminations are not optimal and could hence be usually supplemented with an alternative patten. Where a regular expression identifies lrge numbers of false matches, it could be useful to develop an HMM.

4.11   PROSITE DATABASE : Database of Protein Families and Domains

PROSITE is a method of determining what is the function of uncharacterized proteins translated from genomic or cDNA sequence. It consists of a database of biologically significant sites and patterns, formulated in such a way that with appropriate computational tools, it can rapidly and reliably identify to which family of proteins the new sequence belongs.

In some cases the sequences of an unknown protein is too distantly related to any protein of known structure to detect its resemblance by overall sequences alignment, but it can be identified by the occurrence in its sequence of a particular cluster of residue types, which is variously known as pattern, motif, signature, or fingerprint. These motifs arise because of particular requirement on the structure of specific regions of a protein, which may be important, for example, for their binding properties or for their enzymatic activity. These requirements impose very tight constrains on the evolution of those limited but important portions of a protein sequence (to paraphrase or well in animals).

PROSITE contains a few patterns, which have been published in the literature, but the majority has been developed in the last ten years by the author (Amos Bairoch Swiss institute of Bioinformatics).

There are a number of protein families as well as functional or structural domains that cannot be detected using patterns due to their extreme sequence divergence; the use of techniques based on weight matrices (also known as profiles) allows the detection of such proteins or domains. Such Profiles are added to PROSITE through a collaborative project with P.Butcher of The Swiss institute of Cancer research in Lausanne.

The design of PROSITE follows the leading concepts :

Completeness : for such a compilation to be useful in the determination of protein structure it is important that it contains as many biologically meaningful patterns and profiles as possible.

High specificity : In the majority of cases if patterns or profiles that are specific enough that they do no detect too many unrelated sequences were chosen yet they will detect most, if not all, sequences that clearly belong to the set in consideration.

Documentation : Each of the entries in the PROSITE is fully documented. The documentation includes a concise description of the protein family or Domain that it is designed to detect; as well as a summary of the reasons leading to the development of the pattern or profile.

Periodic reviving : It is important that each entry in be periodically reviewed to ensure that it is still valid.

A very tight relationship with the SWISS-PROT Protein sequence Data bank.

How make use of profile : Interactive access to PROSITE using the WORLD WIDE WEB :

It is available at EXPASY .CH

To make use of the PROSITE patterns and profiles, you can make use of the following software tools :

Scan PROSITE : Allows the user to either scan a protein database sequence from the SWISSPROT or provided by the user for the occurrence of patterns stored in PROSITE or to scan the SWISSPROT or TrEMBL data-including weekly release for the occurrence of a pattern that can originate from the PROSITE or to be provided by the user.

Profile scan : Allows the user to scan a protein sequence from the SWISSPROT or provided by the user for the occurrence of profiles stored in PROSITE.

4.12 Protein Data Bank

The protein data bank is the single international repository for public data on the 3-dimentional structures of biological micro molecules. The contents are primarily experimental data, derived from the X- ray crystallography and NMR experiments. The primary goals of the resource are:

To enable you to locate structures of interest.

To perform simple analysis on one or more structures.

To act as a portal to additional information available on a structure notably the Cartesian atomic coordinates for further analysis

The database is constantly updated as new structures are deposited by the international scientific community.

The Protein Data Bank (PDB) was established at the Brookhaven National Laboratories (BNL) in 1971 as an archive for biological macromolecular crystal's structures. In the beginning the archive held seven structures and with each year a hand full of more were deposited. In the 1980 the number of deposited structure began to increase dramatically. This was due to the improved technology for all aspects of the crystallographic process. The addition of structures determined by the magnetic resonance (NMR) methods and changes in the community view about data sharing.

The mode of access to the PDB database has changed over the years as a result of improved technology, notably the availability of the WWW replacing distribution solely via the media. Further the need to analyze diverse data sets required the development of modern data management systems.

Search methods : The search Tools can be accessed from the PDB Home Page. The Types of possible searches are :

By Providing a PDB identification code (PDB) ID.

By searching the text found in PDB Files

By searching against specific fields of information - for example, deposition data or author.

By searching on the status of an entry, onHold or Released (Status).

By iterating on a previous search.

PDB ID : Each structure in the PDB is represented by a 4 character alphanumeric identifier, assigned upon its deposition. For example, 4hhb and 9 in are the identification codes for PDB entries for Haemoglobin and insulin, respectively. Many of the PDB WEB site pages, including the PDB Home Page, allow you to enter a PDB ID and retrieve information for the corresponding structure.

4.13 Structural SCOP : Classification of Proteins

Nearly all proteins have structural similarities with other proteins and, in some of these cases, share a common evolutionary origin. A knowledge of these relationships is crucial to our understanding of the evolution of proteins and of development. It will also play an important role in the analysis of the sequence data that is being produced by worldwide genome projects.

The SCOP database aims to provide a detailed and comprehensive description of the structural and evolutionary relationship between all proteins whose structure is known, including all entries in the Protein Data Bank (PDB). Its available as a set of tightly linked hypertext documents which makes the large database comprehensive and accessible.

Classification : Proteins are classified to reflect both structural and evolutionary relatedness. Many levels exist in the hierarchy, but the principal levels are family, super family and fold, described below. The exact positions of boundaries between these levels are to some degree subjective. Our evolutionary classification is generally conservative : where any doubt about relatedness exists, we made new divisions at the family and super family levels. Thus, some researchers may prefer to focus on the higher levels of the classification trees, where proteins with structural similarity are clustered.

The different levels in the hierarchy are :

Family : These proteins are clearly evolutionarily related. Generally, this means that pair wise residue identities between the proteins are 30% and greater. However, in some cases similar functions and structures provide definitive evidence of common descent in the absence of high sequence identity; for example, many globins form aa family though some members have sequence identities of only 15%.

Super Family : Probably common evolutionary origin.

Proteins that have low sequence identities, but whose structural and functional features suggest that a common evolutionary origin is probable are placed together in super families. For example, actin, the ATPASE Domain of the Heat Shock Protein, and Hexakinase together form a Super family.

Fold: Major Structural Similarity : Proteins are defined as having a common fold if they have the same major secondary structures in the same arrangement and with the same topological connections. Different proteins with the same fold often have peripheral elements of secondary structure and turn regions that differ in size and conformation. In some cases, these differing peripheral regions may not have a common evolutionary origin: the structural similarities could arise just from the physics and chemistry of proteins favouring certain packing arrangements and chains topologies.

Class : The different folds have been grouped into classes. Most of the folds are assigned to one of the five structural classes.

1. All-Alpha, Those whose structure is essentially formed by (alpha)-Helices;
2. All- beta, Those whose structure is essentially formed by (beta)-sheaths;
3. Alpha/beta, those with (alpha)-helices and (beta)- sheaths;
4. Alpha+ Beta, those in which Alpha-helices and Beta sheaths are largely segregated, and
5. Multidomain. Those with domains of different class and for which no homologues are known at present.

    Other classes have been assigned for peptides, small proteins, theoretical models, nucleic acids and carbohydrates.

4.14   Class, Architecture, Topology and Homologous Superfamily

CATH – Protein Structure Classification : Cath is a novel hierarchical classification of Proteins domain structures, which clusters proteins at four major levels, Class(c), Architecture (A), Topology (T) and Homologous super family (H).

Class, derived from secondary structure content is assigned for more than 90% of protein structures automatically. Architecture, which describes the gross orientation of secondary structures, independent of connectivities, is currently assigned manually. The topology level clusters structures according to their topological connections and numbers of secondary structures. The homologous super families clusters proteins with highly similar structures and functions, the assignments of structures to topology families and homologous superfamlies are made by sequence and structure comparisons.

The CATH Hierarchy

Class, C-level : Class is determined accordingly to the secondary structure composition and packing within the structure. It can be assigned automatically for over 90% of the known structures using the method of Michie et al. For the remainder, manual inspection is used and where necessary information from the literature taken into account. Three major classes are recognized; mainly alpha, mainly- beta and alpha-beta. This last class alpha-beta includes both alternating alpha/ beta structures and alpha+beta structures, as originally defined by Levitt and Chothia. (1976).

Architecture, A-level

This describes the overall shape of the domain structures as determined by the orientations of the secondary structures but ignores the connectivity between the secondary structures. It is currently assigned manually using a simple description of the secondary structure arrangement e.g. Barrel or 3-layer sandwich. Reference is made to the literature for well-known architectures.

Topologies (fold Family) T- level

Structures are grouped into fold families at this level depending on both the overall shape and connectivity of the secondary structures. This is done using the structures comparison algorithms SAP Structures which have a SSAP score of 70% and where at least 60% of the larger proteins matches the smaller proteins are assigned to the same T LEVEL or fold family.

Homologous super family : *s-level:* Structures within each H-level are further clustered on sequence identity. Domains clustered in the same sequence families have sequence identities > 35% (with At least 60% of the larger domain equivalent to the smaller), indicating highly similar structures and functions.

Organization of the Cath Database : CATH data base can be searched using the keywords or by the PDB identifier itself.

The CATH-PSI BLAST Server has been developed to allow access to the CATH database by the Sequence Searching. Sequences may be submitted in FASTA format.

What is Redundancy ?

A key concept in comparing databases is the issue of redundancy. Many databases try to be "non-redundant". Unfortunately, biological data is too complex to fit a simple definition of redundancy. Are two alleles of the same locus redundant? Two isozymes in the same organism? The same locus in two closely related organisms? Hence, each "non-redundant" database has its own definition of redundancy. Some use automated measures, while others use manual cutting; the former are amenable to large projects, the latter give higher quality. Other databases don't attempt to be non-redundant, but rather sacrifice this goal in favor of ensuring completeness.

5

Computational Biology : Information Retrieval From Databases

The collection and maintenance of data is performed at centers like the EBI (European Bioinformatics Institute, an outstation of EMBL) or the NCBI (National Center for Biotechnology Information). Other centers are similarly active; these two shall only serve as examples.

The end user is not expected to employ the sophisticated software, which these institutions use to collect, maintain, and curate data. After an export procedure to a so-called flat file, the data are distributed to the end users' sites in various formats. The main paradigm is that each biological sequence is described in an entry, which has a title, the sequence data and associated reference information. In a "real" database system, these data are accessible in a smooth and interlinked fashion. To benefit from the databases in their original form, however, the customers would need to install the very expensive and staff-intensive database software (so-called relational database systems). During the export to flat files, a considerable part of structuring information is lost and, therefore, auxiliary information must be printed into each entry.

The application software at the end user's site must use various conventions (called a format) to bring you the information as close to the original comprehensive set as possible.

5.1 Contents of an Entry

Each entry has,

Name (database specific, one per entry)

Accession number (Universally valid, one or more per entry)

Title (Usually similar in between databases, one line of description)

Reference (The literature reference or location of the lab that produced the sequence).

Sequence (Always starting with Position1 in DNA).

Some data, which serve administrative purposes, such as section information or dates of creation or updating, are not listed. Optionally, one or more of the following data are attached to an entry if known.

5.2 Organization Classification

Features of the sequence (reading frame coordinates, protein functional motiffs, etc)

Cross-references to the other databases (DNA refers to protein entry, and vice versa).

If you want to retrieve an entry from a database, it is important to decide what type of query will be most effective.

Query by reference, author, sequence name etc; this is a search in the annotation. The programs described in this chapter perform this type of search after having obtained the keywords to be searched. The results will be a list of entries, which match the key words exactly.

Query by sequence similarity : This is a search in the sequence data. No keywords but similar strings are searched. This will produce a list of entries, which match closely, but not necessarily exactly the query sequence.

5.3 Search Concepts

Boolean search : an advanced query technique used when searching with two or more terms. Terms are combined using the Boolean Operators AND, OR and NOT. The default Boolean Operator is And.

Broadening the search : If the results of a search produce no useful entries, change or remove terms that have been entered.

Narrowing the search : If the results of a search produce too many entries, change or add terms that have been entered.

Proximity search : To search with multiword terms or phrases, place quotes around the terms.

WILD cards : The character can be prepended or appended to a search term to make a search less specific. For example, to look for all authors whose last name begins with Khan, search using Khan.

5.4 Database Searching Basic Considerations

Think about every step. Search a large current database. Compare as protein rather than DNA. Filter query for low complexity regions. Interpret scores with E-values. Recognise that most homologues are not found by pair wise sequence comparision. Consider slower and more powerful methods, but use iterative programs with great caution.

Today's sequence databases have a significant number of cross-references to other databases. A protein sequence, for example, will have one or more references to the DNA sequence(s) coding for the protein, and possibly also hints to databases describing protein motifs (such as the PROSITE database) or organism-specific databases. Recently, the interest of researchers focused on genome projects. Therefore, information on the genetic locus might be contained in the database and also pointers to other databases, which deal with genomics specifically. All these entries will refer to publications, which are described in the literature databases. Your computer does not necessarily have all these databases available within the application software used for sequence analysis (such as the GCG package), but browser programs, like the SRS database browser, are capable of handling these complex networks of databases.

To make the best use of the widely available databases, you first need to find out which databases are storing the information you are looking for in most comprehensive fashion. If you only search for a given accession number, you will be able to search all the sequence databases simultaneously. However, searching a genetic locus of a disease or a protein motif for a specific protein function will succeed more efficiently if you use one of the databases specifically made for this purpose. In the two examples mentioned, the databases of choice are OMIM and PROSITE, respectively. Once you encounter hits in one database, you should use this information to expand to other databases as well-once you have found one description of a sequence, your search is not finished.

5.5 HOW to Perform Database Searching

The access to databases is no longer necessarily performed on the same computer where you usually do sequence analysis. Some programs operate via networks exclusively, such as the famous SRSWWW browser. The sections below reflect this fact. It is, however, important to note that the retrieved sequences will be in specific formats. The data will be ordered in a way that the software you want to use for further analysis can or cannot interpret them correctly. Therefore, you must determine the formats of the entries you get via computer networks and apply appropriate procedures for reformatting if the data shall be used in the GCG program package.

Security notice : Once you use wide area computer networks, you will most probably access databases and computers, which are not under local control. Information quality, therefore, might not apply in the usual way. This consideration is particularly important for environments beyond firewalls (commercial companies.

The two main ways of searching are: Text based search, querying the annotation and sequence based search.

Text based searching : There are three data retrieval systems of particular relevance to molecular biologist: Sequence Retrieval System (SRS), ENTREZ, and DBGET. These three systems allow searching in a multitude of molecular biology database and provide links to relevant information, for entries that match the search criteria. The three systems differ in the databases they search and the links they have to other information.

(i) **SRS** : The sequence retrieval system is a homogeneous interface to over 80 biological databases that had been developed at the European Bioinformatics Institute (EBI). It includes databases of sequences, metabolic pathways, (BLAST, SSEARCH, FASTA), transcription factors, application results like protein 3d structures, genomes, mappings, mutations and locus specific mutations. The webpagelisting of all the database contains a link to a description page about each database including the data on which it was last updated. You select one or more of the databases to search before entering your query. After getting you choose an alignment algorithm (like CLUSTALW, PPHYLIP) enter parameters and run it. The SRS is highly recommended for use.

(ii) **ENTREZ** : This is a molecular biology database and retrieval system, developed by the National Center for Biotechnology Information (NCBI).

It is entry point for exploring distinct but integrated databases. Of the three texts-based databases systems, Entrez is the easiest to use but also offers limited information to search.

Entrez is a combined bibliographic, protein sequence, and nucleotide sequence database maintained by the National Center for Biotechnology Information (NCBI). A major advantage of Entrez is interconnections between the various databases; you can move quickly from a sequence to its reference to another sequence. Another central concept in Entrez is neighboring, the grouping together of sequences and references by computed similarity scores. Entrez has sprouted several variants. First, the Entrez database can be accessed by either CD ROM or over the Internet. Second, Entrez can be used with either a custom Graphical Interface client, using a World Wide Web browser, with a command line browser (CLEVER), or via NCBI's toolkit written in C.

World Wide Web / Gopher

Many biosequence databases are available as hypertext on the World Wide Web, or as flat files from gophers.

(iii) **DBGET** : This is an integrated database retrieval system developed by the institute for Chemical Research, Kyoto University and the Human Genome Center of the University of Tokyo, provides access to 20 databases one at a time having more limited options. The DBGET is less recommended than the two others.

5.6 Tools for Searching

There are three Main tools : FASTA (better for nucleotides than for proteins), BLAST (better for proteins than for nucleotides) and SW-Search (more sensitive than FASTA or BLAST.

(i) **FASTA** : FASTA is a sequence comparison software that uses the method of Pearson and Lipman.The basic Fasta algorithm assumes a query sequence and a database over the same alphabet. It searches a DNA sequence in a DNA database or a protein sequences in a protein database. Practically FASTA is a family of programs, allowing also queries of DNA vs. a protein database or vice versa. In these variants there is further distinction which regards the location of gaps: One may assume that gaps occur only in the codon frames corresponding to amino acid insertion; alternatively, one can assume gap location to be arbitrary, accounting for insertion/deletion of nucleotides.

Under different circumstances it is favorable to use different programs: to identify an unknown protein sequence use either; Fasta3 ortFASTX3.

To identify structural DNA sequence use FASTA3, first with ktup = 6 and then with ktup = 3.

To identify an EST use FASTX3; Use ktup = 1 for oligonucleotides (length <20).

Search speed and selectivity are controlled with the ktup (word size) parameter. Searches with ktup=1 are slower, but more sensitive, while ktup=2 is faster but less sensitive.

For Proteins the default is ktup=2.

For DNA, the default is ktup = 6. Use ktup = 3 or ktup = 4 more sensitivity.

FASTA Steps

Hashing : FASTA locates regions of the query sequence and matching regions in the database sequences that have high density of exact word matches (without gaps). The length of the matched word is called the ktup parameter.

Scoring : The ten highest scoring regions are rescored using a scoring matrix. The score for such a pair region is saved as the intial score.

Introduction of gaps : FASTA determines if any of the initial regions from different diagonals may be joined together to form an approximate alignment with gaps. Only non-overlapping regions may be joined. The score for the joined regions is the sum of the scores of the initial regions minus a joining penalty for each gap. The score of the highest scoring region, at the end of this step is saved as the intial score.

Alignment : After computing the initial scores, fasta determines the best segment of similarity between the query sequence and the search set sequence, using a variation of the Smith Waterman algorithm. The score for this alignment is the opt score.

Random sequence simulation : In order to evaluate the significance of such alignments empirically estimats the score distribution from the alignment of many random pairs of sequences. More precisely the characters of the query sequence are reshuffled to maintain bias due to length and character composition and searched against a random subset of the database. This empirical distribution is extrapolated, assuming it as an extreme value distribution, and each alighnment to the real query is assigned a z-score and an e-score.

(ii) ***Blast-basic local allignment search tool :*** Blast programs use a heuristic search algorithm. The programs use the statistical methods of Karlin and Altschul. BLAST programs were designed for fast database searching, with minimum sacrifice of sensitivity for distantly related sequences. The programs search databases in a special compressed format. To use your own private database with Blast you need to convert it to the BLAST format.

The BLAST at NCBI also can be run through one of the retrieval systems. For example, Gene web mirror site at Weizman institute. BLAST is a family of programs. The BLAST program compares the query to each sequence in the database using heuristic rules to speed up the pair wise comparison. It first creates sequence abstraction by listing exact and similar words between the query and each database sequence. It then extends such words to obtain high scoring sequence pairs. It also calculates statistically like Fasta does. BLAST 2 is a new version with new capabilities (also called Advance BLAST). It can perform gapped alignments such as gapped BLAST and PSI-BLAST. The gapped BLAST algorithm allows gaps to be introduced into the alignments. That means that similar regions are not broken into several segments (as in the older versions). This Method reflect biological relationship much better than ordinary BLAST.

PSI-BLAST : PSI-BLAST (Position Specific Iterated BLAST) provides a new automatic profile like search the program first performs a gapped BLAST search of the database. The significant segments are then used by the program to construct a Position Specific Score Matrix (PSSM). This Matrix may be iterated until no new significant alignments are found.

The Smith-Waterman tool : Smith-Waterman (SW) searching method compares the query sequence to each sequence in database using the full Smith-Waterman algorithm for pair wise comparisions. It also uses search results to generate statistics. Since SW searching is exhaustive it is the slowest method. We use special software and hardware to accelerate the application. A bioaccelerator can be found in the TAV bioinformatics department, Direct Pointer. It can also be run through Weizmann institute site.

Tips for database search : Use latest database version. Run BLAST first then depending on your results run a finer tool like (FASTA, Search, SW.BLOCKS, etc.,). When ever possible use the Translated Sequence.

5.7 Homology Searches

Homology searches means you search with your own sequence to find out if there are other sequences in the sequence database that are related to your sequence-similarity search.

Homology searching profiles consists of user supplied sequence data, a designation of preferred search algorithm (BLAST or FASTA) and a selection of database to be searched.

Profiles of this type should be search for new DNA or protein sequences, which are similar to the query sequence. Once established profiles are compared on a regular basis (weekly) to the updated versions of the available databases.

> **Input sequence :** This user supplied data should be entered by cutting/pasting or direct typing into the supplied text Box, or by using the Upload form to upload data directly from your local computer. Data should be in FASTA FORMAT or one of the standard recognized data formats. PEPTIDE mixtures must be entered as a variation of the FASTA format.

> **Database to search :** The Database available for Searching

> GEnBank, SwissProt, GenPept, PDB (SWISS-PROT + GENPEPT + PDB) all three combined.

COMPARISION PROGRAMS

> **BLAST :** Based on the input sequence (Protein / Nucleic acid) and the database chosen the appropriate BLAST Program will be run.

> **Type of output :** Top Scores Only.

> **FASTA :** Based on the input sequence (Protein/ or Nucleic acid / Peptide Mix) and the database chosen the appropriate FASTA program will be run.

> **Type of output :** Top Scores and Alignments.

5.8 Finding Domain and Functional Site Homologies with Database Search

This is a simple exercise: find functional predictions by database search. Here you find a number of protein sequence examples in one-letter form. Copy one of them and submit it to the following e-mail server :

SBASE
DOMAIN

Sample sequences for domain and function identification

1.

```
ELHKGIMVNG VDEATILDLL TKKYNAQRHH
LKAVYIQETG EPLDETLKKA LTGHIQELLL
AM
```

2.

```
APARSCAEEP CGAGTCKETE GHVICLCPPA
YTGEHCNI
```

3.

```
APTEQRPGVQ ECYHGNGQSY RGTYSTTVTG
RTCQAWSSMT PHSHSRTPEY YPNAGLIMNY
CRNPDAVAAP YCYTRDPGVR WEYCNLTQCS
DAEGTAVAPP TVTPVPSLEA PSEQ
```

4.

```
LRVFVERQAA PLQLAPNVSA LLRWDVPEEH
AGSQSLQYRI SCWRGSELHS ELLLNQSTLE
ARVEHLQPEE TYRFQVQAHV AATGLAAGAT
SHAL
```

5.

```
YHCAGNGSWV NEVLGPELPK CVPVCGVPRE
PFEEKQRIIG GSDADIKNFP WQVFFDNPWA
GGALINEYWV LTAAHVVEGN REPTMYVGST
SVQTSRLAKS KMLTPEHVFI HPGWKLLEVP
EGRTNFDNDI ALVRLKDPVK MGPTVSPICL
PGTSSDYNLM DGDLGLISGW GRTEKRDRAV
RLKAARLPVA PLRKCKEVKV EKPTADAEAY
VFTPNMICAG GEKGMDSCKG DSGGAFAVQD
PNDKTKFYAA GLVSW
```

5.9 Programme & Website for Database Searches

BLOCKS : http://.ww.blocks.fhere.org/blocksmkr/make_blocks.html

Profiles : http://www.psc.edu/general/software/packages/profiles/profile ss.html

PROBE : *Provides a new and powerful approach towards finding a sequence family* : ncbi.nlm.nih.gor/pub/newwald

BCM Search Launcher : http:// dot.imgen.bcm.tmc.edu.9331/ seq.search/ protein.search.html

SEARCH : www. ddbj.nig.ac.jp/E-mail/hamology.html

Blast e-mail server : Blast@ncbi.nlm.nih.gor

FASTA : http://jasta.bioch.virginia.edu/fasta

Anomynous ftp : ftp,virginia.edu/pub/fasta

TIGR gene includes search : http://www.tigr.org

PROSITE : http:www.expasy.ch/prosite

INTERPRO : www.ebi.ac.uk/interpro

PEAM : http: www.Sanger.al.uk/pfam.

PSI-BLAST : http:www.ncbi-nm.nib.gar\blast

   Note :   Prosite :- www. Expasy.ch / prosite is the most important of all websites
                  explore it fully. (You will learn many techniques in bioinformatics from
                  this site).

   Here you will get sites for clusted, Prints, SRS, zEntrez, DBGET & much more.

ENTREZ : http://www.ncbi.nlm.nih.gor/Entrez.

ENTREZ : htts://www3. ncbi.nlm.nih.gor/Taxonomy/taxonomy http

RDP : (Ribosomel :- http://www..(me msu .edu/RDP/Database project)

Tree of Life : http://Phylogeny. arizena. edu/tree/phylogency.htm

PDB : http://www.resb.org/pdb.

SCOP : http://scop mre-lmb.cam.ac.uk/SCOP
            Programme for viewing Protein Molecules.

Chine : http://www.u mass.edu/microbiol/chine

   - A webbrowser plug in that can be used to display and manipulate dieven
   controls. Excellent for lecture presentations.

Cn3d : http//www.ncbi.nlm.nih.gore/structural /CN3D

   Provides viewing of three dimensional structures from Entrez. CN3D runs
   on windows, Macos, and Unix Simulaneously displays structual &
   Sequence alignment can show multiple superimposed images from NMR
   studies.

Rasmo : http:// www.umass.edu/microbiol/rasimol

   Most commonly used viewer for windows, macos, Unix & VMS operating
   systems. Performs many functions.

Swiss 3D : http//www.expasy.cb/spclbr/mainpage html.\ viewer Spdbr

   Proein molecules can be built by structutal alignment. calculates atmic
   angles & distances, thereading, energy minimizations, & Interacts withswiss
   model seever.

6

Phylogenetic Analysis

6.1 Introduction

When comparing sequence homologues from different source species, there is recognition that they are related. The questions often asked are "how are they related" ? and "when did they diverge"? These are not new questions. Before people started making comparisons at the molecular level, they were using other types of data such as morphology and developmental processes to try to answer these questions. Phylogenetics attempts to reconstruct evolutionary history. In a phylogenetic analysis, one compares the results of evolutionary processes, be its shape and size of specific bones or patterns of DNA or protein sequences, in an attempt to determine how different groups or species may have been derived during evolution. Looking at the molecular sequences can give insight into the nature of the processes, which lead to divergence, in addition to analyzing the relative degree of relatedness.

The mechanisms of change include 1. random mutation, which can be seen as genetic drift in the absence of selective pressure, 2. sequence duplication, which may be duplication of small segments, genes, or even whole genomes, and 3. recombination, which includes transposons, translocations, and viral activity, to mix up sequences within an organism, to remove sequences, or to introduce sequences from another organism.

There is considerable debate regarding the best approach to take when analyzing sequence alignments for phylogenetic relationships. Accepted approaches include distance calculations, parsimony, and maximum likelihood. New on the scene is Bayesian analysis, which is expected to gain popularity as people become familiar with it. It is good to become familiar with the different methods of analysis. It helps in understanding the arguments being made, both in terms of how things should be done and of the resulting analyses. When examining the results of molecular phylogenetic analysis, care should be taken to compare the results to other independent means of analysis and/or to other data sets.

The associated concepts, you need to know in phylogenetic analysis :

- Phylogenetics vs. taxonomy
- Cladistic vs. phenetic
- Clustering
- Parsimony vs. maximum likelihood

Charles Darwin was the first to recognize that the systematic hierarchy represented a rough approximation of evolutionary history. However, it was not until the 1950s that the German entomologist Willi Hennig proposed that systematics should reflect the known evolutionary history of lineages as closely as possible, an approach he called **phylogenetic systematics**. The followers of Hennig were referred to as "cladists" by his opponents, because of the emphasis on recognizing only **monophyletic groups**, a group plus all of its descendents, or clades. However, the cladists quickly adopted that term as a helpful label, and nowadays, cladistic approaches to systematics are used routinely.

6.2 What is Phylogenetic Systematics ?

Carolus Linnaeus was also credited with pioneering **systematics, the field of science dealing with the diversity of life and the relationship between life's components.** Systematics reaches beyond taxonomy to elucidate new methods and theories that can be used to classify species based on similarity of traits and possible mechanisms of **evolution**, a change in the gene pool of a population over time.

   Phylogenetic systematics *is that field of biology that does deal with identifying and understanding the evolutionary relationships among the many different kinds of life on earth, both living (extant) and dead (extinct)*. Evolutionary theory states that similarity among individuals or species is attributable to common descent, or inheritance from a common ancestor. Thus, the relationships established by phylogenetic systematics often describe a species' evolutionary history and, hence, it is **phylogeny**, the historical relationships among lineages or organisms or their parts, such as their genes.

6.3 Understanding the Evolutionary Process

(i) *Genetic variation : changes in a gene pool*

Evolution is not always discrete with clearly defined boundaries that pinpoint the origin of a new species, nor is it a steady continuum. ***Evolution requires genetic variation, which results from changes within a gene pool,*** the genetic make-up of a specific population. A gene pool is the combination of all the **alleles;** *alternative forms of a genetic locus;* for all traits that population may exhibit. Changes in a gene pool can result from **mutation**–variation within a particular gene; or from changes in **gene frequency;** the proportion of an allele in a given population.

(ii) *How does genetic variation occur ?*

Every organism possesses a **genome** that contains all of the biological information needed to construct and maintain a living example of that organism. The biological information contained in a genome is encoded in the nucleotide sequence of its DNA or RNA molecules and is divided into discrete units called **genes**. The information stored in a gene is read by proteins, which attach to the genome and initiate a series of reactions called **gene expression**.

Every time a cell divides, it must make a complete copy of its genome, a process called **DNA replication**. DNA replication must be extremely accurate to avoid introducing **mutations**, or changes in the nucleotide sequence of a short region of the genome. Inevitably, some mutations do occur, usually in one of two ways; *either from errors in DNA replication or from damaging effects of chemical agents or radiation that react with DNA and change the structure of individual nucleotides*. Many of these mutations result in a change that has no effect on the functioning of the genome, referred to as **silent mutations**. Silent mutations include virtually all changes that happen in the non-coding components of genes and gene-related sequences.

Mutations in the coding regions of genes are much more important. Here we must consider the importance of the same mutation in a **somatic cell** compared with a **germ line cell**. *A somatic cell is any cell of an organism other than a reproductive cell, such as a sperm or egg cell. (A germ cell line is any line of cells that gives rise to gametes and is continuous through the generations).* Because a somatic cell does not pass on copies of its genome to the next generation, a somatic cell mutation is important only for the organism in which it occurs and has no potential evolutionary impact. In fact, most somatic mutations have no significant effect because there are many other identical cells in the same tissue.

On the other hand, mutations in germ cells can be transmitted to the next generation and will then be present in all of the cells of an individual who inherits that mutation. Even still, mutations within germ line cells may not change the phenotype of the organism in any significant way. Those mutations that do have an evolutionary effect can be divided into two categories, **loss-of-function mutations** and **gain-of-function mutations**. A loss-of-function mutation results in reduced or abolished protein function. Gain-of-function mutations, which are much less common, confer an abnormal activity on a protein

The randomness with which mutations can occur is an important concept in biology and is a requirement of the Darwinian view of evolution, which holds that changes in the characteristics of an organism occur by chance and are not influenced by the environment in which the organism lives. Beneficial changes within an organism are then positively selected for, whereas harmful changes are negatively selected.

(iii) *The drivers of evolution: selection, drift, and founder effects*

We just discussed that new alleles appear in a population because of mutations that occur in the reproductive cells of an organism. This means that many genes are **polymorphic**, that is, two or more alleles for that gene are present in a population. Each of these alleles has its own **allele** or **gene frequency**, a measure of how common an allele is in a population. Allele frequencies vary over time because of two conditions, natural selection and random drift.

Natural selection : is the process whereby one **genotype**, the hereditary constitution of an individual, leaves more offspring than another genotype because of superior life attributes, termed **fitness**. Natural selection acts on genetic variation by conferring a survival advantage to those individuals harboring a particular mutation that tends to favor a changing environmental condition. These individuals then reproduce and pass on this "new" gene, altering their gene pool. Natural selection, therefore, decreases the frequencies of alleles that reduce the fitness of an organism and increases the frequency of alleles that improve fitness.

"Natural selection" is the principle by which each slight variation, if useful, is preserved.   *Charles Darwin*

It is important to point out that natural selection does not always represent progress, only adaptation to a changing surrounding, that is, evolution attributable to natural selection is devoid of intent something does not evolve to better itself, only to adapt. Because environments are always changing, what was once an advantageous mutation can often become a liability further down the evolutionary line.

Random Drift : The term **random drift** actually encompasses a number of distinct processes, sometimes referred to as outcomes. They include **indiscriminate parent sampling**, the **founder effect**, and fluctuations in the rate of evolutionary processes such as selection, migration, and mutation. **Parent sampling** is the process of determining which organisms of one generation will be the parents of the next generation. Parent sampling may be **discriminate**, that is, with regard to fitness differences, or **indiscriminate**, without regard to fitness differences. Discriminate parent sampling is generally considered natural selection, whereas indiscriminate parent sampling is considered random drift.

6.4 What is Sampling

Suppose a population of red and brown squirrels share a habitat with a color blind predator. Although the predator is color blind, the brown squirrels seem to die in greater numbers than the red squirrels, suggesting that the brown squirrels just seem to be unlucky enough to come into contact with the predator more often. As a result, the frequency of brown squirrels in the next generation is reduced.

More red squirrels survive to reproduce, or are sampled, but it is without regard to any differences in fitness between the two groups. The physical differences of the groups do not play a causal role in the differences in reproductive success. Now, lets say that the predator is not color blind and can now see the red squirrels better than the brown squirrels, resulting in a better survival rate for the brown squirrels. This would be a case of discriminate parent sampling, or natural selection.

6.5 Founder Effect

Another important cause of genetic drift is the **founder effect**, *the difference between the gene pool of a population as a whole and that of a newly isolated population of the same species.* The founder effect occurs when populations are started from a small number of pioneer individuals of one original population. Because of small sample size, the new population could have a much different genetic ratio than the original population. An example of the founder effect would be when a plant population results from a single seed.

Thus far, we have discussed natural selection and random drift as events that occur in isolation from one another. However, in most populations, the two processes will be occurring at the same time. Furthermore, there is great debate over whether, in particular instances and in general, natural selection is more prevalent than random drift.

6.6 Phylogenetic Trees : Presenting Evolutionary Relationships

Systematics describes the pattern of relationships among taxa and is intended to help us understand the history of all life. But history is not something we can see it has happened once and leaves only clues as to the actual events. Scientists use these clues to build hypotheses, or models, of life's history. *In phylogenetic studies, the most convenient way of visually presenting evolutionary relationships among a group of organisms is through illustrations called phylogenetic trees.*

Node : represents a taxonomic unit. This can be either an existing species or an ancestor.

- *Branch :* defines the relationship between the taxa in terms of descent and ancestry.

- *Branch length :* represents the number of changes that have occurred in the branch.

  Topology : the branching patterns of the tree.

- *Root :* the common ancestor of all taxa.

- *Distance scale* : scale that represents the number of differences between organisms or sequences.

- *Clade* : a group of two or more taxa or DNA sequences that includes both their common ancestor and all of their descendents.

- *Operational Taxonomic Unit (OTU)* : taxonomic level of sampling selected by the user to be used in a study, such as individuals, populations, species, genera, or bacterial strains.

A phylogenetic tree is composed of **nodes**, each representing a taxonomic unit (species, populations, individuals), and **branches**, which define the relationship between the taxonomic units in terms of descent and ancestry. Only one branch can connect any two adjacent nodes. The branching pattern of the tree is called the **topology**, and the branch length usually represents the number of changes that have occurred in the branch. This is called a **scaled branch**. Scaled trees are often calibrated to represent the passage of time. Such trees have a theoretical basis in the particular gene or genes under analysis. Branches can also be **unscaled**, which means that the branch length is not proportional to the number of changes that has occurred, although the actual number may be indicated numerically somewhere on the branch. Phylogenetic trees may also be either **rooted** or **unrooted**. In rooted trees, there is a particular node, called the **root**, representing a common ancestor, from which a unique path leads to any other node. An unrooted tree only specifies the relationship among species, without identifying a common ancestor, or evolutionary path.

Phylogenetic trees, a convenient way of representing evolutionary relationships among a group of organisms can be drawn in various ways. Branches on phylogenetic trees may be scaled representing the amount of evolutionary change, time, or both, when there is a molecular clock, or they may be unscaled and have no direct correspondence with either time or amount of evolutionary change. Phylogenetic trees may be rooted or unrooted. In the case of unrooted trees, branching relationships between taxa are specified by the way they are connected to each other, but the position of the common ancestor is not. For example, on an unrooted tree with five species, there are five branches (four external, one internal) on which the tree can be rooted. Rooting on each of the five branches has different implications for evolutionary relationships.

6.7 Methods of Phylogenetic Analysis

Two major groups of analyses exist to examine phylogenetic relationships : **phenetic methods** and **cladistic methods**. It is important to note that Phenetics and cladistics have had an uneasy relationship over the last 40 years or so. Most of today's evolutionary biologists favor cladistics, although a strictly cladistic approach may result in counterintuitive results.

(i) *Phenetic method of analysis :* Phenetics, also known as numerical taxonomy, involves the use of various measures of overall similarity for the ranking of species. There is no restriction on the number or type of characters (data) that can be used, although all data must be first converted to a numerical value, without any character "weighting". Each organism is then compared with every other for all characters measured, and the number of similarities (or differences) is calculated. The organisms are then clustered in such a way that the most similar are grouped close together and the more different ones are linked more distantly. The taxonomic clusters, called phenograms, that result from such an analysis do not necessarily reflect genetic similarity or evolutionary relatedness. The lack of evolutionary significance in phenetics has meant that this system has had little impact on animal classification, and as a consequence, interest in and use of phenetics has been declining in recent years.

(ii) *Cladistic method of analysis :* An alternative approach to diagramming relationships between taxa is called cladistics. The basic assumption behind cladistics is that members of a group share a common evolutionary history. Thus, they are more closely related to one another than they are to other groups of organisms. Related groups of organisms are recognized because they share a set of unique features (apomorphies) that were not present in distant ancestors but which are shared by most or all of the organisms within the group. These shared derived characteristics are called *synapomorphies*. Therefore, in contrast to phenetics, cladistics groupings do not depend on whether organisms share physical traits but depend on their evolutionary relationships. Indeed, in cladistic analysis two organisms may share numerous characteristics but still be considered members of different groups.

Cladistic analysis entails a number of assumptions. For example, *species are assumed to arise primarily by bifurcation, or separation, of the ancestral lineage;* species are often considered to become extinct upon hybridization (crossbreeding); and hybridization is assumed to be rare or absent. In addition, cladistic groupings must possess the following characteristics: all species in a grouping must share a common ancestor and all species derived from a common ancestor must be included in the taxon. The application of these requirements results in the following terms being used to describe the different ways in which groupings can be made:

A *monophyletic grouping* is one in which all species share a common ancestor, and all species derived from that common ancestor are included. This is the only form of grouping accepted as valid by cladists.

A *paraphyletic grouping* is one in which all species share a common ancestor, but not all species derived from that common ancestor are included. A polyphyletic grouping is one in which species that do not share an immediate common ancestor are lumped together, while excluding other members that would link them.

6.8 The Origins of Molecular Phylogenetics

Macromolecular data, meaning gene (DNA) and protein sequences, are accumulating at an increasing rate because of recent advances in molecular biology. For the evolutionary biologist, the rapid accumulation of sequence data from whole genomes has been a major advance, because the very nature of DNA allows it to be used as a "document" of evolutionary history. Comparisons of the DNA sequences of various genes between different organisms can tell a scientist a lot about the relationships of organisms that cannot otherwise be inferred from morphology, or an organism's outer form and inner structure. Because genomes evolve by the gradual accumulation of mutations, the amount of nucleotide sequence difference between a pair of genomes from different organisms should indicate how recently those two genomes shared a common ancestor. Two genomes that diverged in the recent past should have fewer differences than two genomes whose common ancestor is more ancient. Therefore, by comparing different genomes with each other, it should be possible to derive evolutionary relationships between them, the major objective of molecular phylogenetics. Molecular phylogenetics attempts to determine the rates and patterns of change occurring in DNA and proteins and to reconstruct the evolutionary history of genes and organisms. Two general approaches may be taken to obtain this information. In the first approach, scientists use DNA to study the evolution of an organism. In the second approach, different organisms are used to study the evolution of DNA. Whatever the approach, the general goal is to infer process from pattern: the processes of organismal evolution deduced from patterns of DNA variation and processes of molecular evolution inferred from the patterns of variations in the DNA itself.

(i) *Molecular phylogenetic analysis :* Fundamental elements as we just discussed, macromolecules, especially gene and protein sequences, have surpassed morphological and other organismal characters as the most popular forms of data for phylogenetic analysis. Therefore, this next section will concentrate only on molecular data. It is important to point out that a single, all-purpose recipe does not exist for phylogenetic analysis of molecular data. Although numerous algorithms, procedures, and computer programs have been developed, their reliability and practicality are, in all cases, dependent upon the size and structure of the dataset under analysis. The merits and shortfalls of these various methods are subject to much scientific debate, because the danger of generating incorrect results is greater in computational molecular phylogenetics than many other fields of science. Occasionally, the limiting factor in such analyses is not so much the computational method used, but the users' understanding in of what the method is actually doing with the data. Therefore, the goal of this section is to demonstrate to the reader that practical analysis should be thought of both as a search for a correct model (analysis) as well as a search for the correct tree (outcome). Phylogenetic tree-building models presume particular evolutionary models. For any given set of data, these models may be violated because of various occurrences, such as the transfer of genetic material between organisms. Therefore, when interpreting a given analysis, a person should always consider the model used and entertain possible explanations for the results obtained. For example, models used in molecular phylogenetic analysis.

Methods make "default" assumptions, including :

The sequence is correct and originates from the specified source

- The sequences are homologous – all descended in some way from a shared ancestral sequence.
- Each position in a sequence alignment is homologous with every other in that alignment.
- Each of the multiple sequences included in a common analysis has a common phylogenetic history with the other sequences.
- The sampling of taxa is adequate to resolve the problem under study.
- Sequence variation among the samples is representative of the broader group.
- The sequence variability in the sample contains phylogenetic signal adequate to resolve the problem under study.

(ii) **The four steps of Phylogenetic analysis:** A straightforward phylogenetic analysis consists of four steps:

1. Alignment–building the data model and extracting a dataset.
2. Determining the substitution model–consider sequence variation.
3. Tree building.
4. Tree evaluation.

Tree Building :

Key features of DNA-based Phylogenetic trees : Studies of gene and protein evolution often involve the comparison of **homologs**, sequences that have common origins but may or may not have common activity. Sequences that share an arbitrary level of similarity determined by alignment of matching bases are **homologous**. These sequences are inherited from a common ancestor that possessed similar structure, although the ancestor may be difficult to determine because it has been modified through descent.

Homologs are most commonly defined as orthologs, paralogs, or xenologs. **Orthologs** are homologs produced by speciation. They represent genes derived from a common ancestor that diverged because of divergence of the organism. Orthologs tend to have similar function.

Paralogs are homologs produced by gene duplication and represent genes derived from a common ancestral gene that duplicated within an organism and then diverged. Paralogs tend to have different functions.

Xenologs are homologs resulting from the horizontal transfer of a gene between two organisms. The function of xenologs can be variable, depending on how significant the change in context was for the horizontally moving gene. In general, though, the function tends to be similar.

A typical gene-based phylogenetic tree is depicted below. This tree shows the relationship between four homologous genes: A, B, C, and D. The topology of this tree consists of four external nodes (**A, B, C,** and **D**), each one representing one of the four genes, and two internal nodes (**e** and **f**) representing ancestral genes. The branch lengths indicate the degree of evolutionary differences between the genes. This particular tree is unrooted it is only an illustration of the relationships between genes A, B, C, and D and does not signify anything about the series of evolutionary events that led to these genes. A rooted tree is often referred to as an inferred tree. This is to emphasize that this type of illustration depicts only the series of evolutionary events that are inferred from the data under study and may not be the same as the true tree or the tree that depicts the actual series of evolutionary events that occurred.

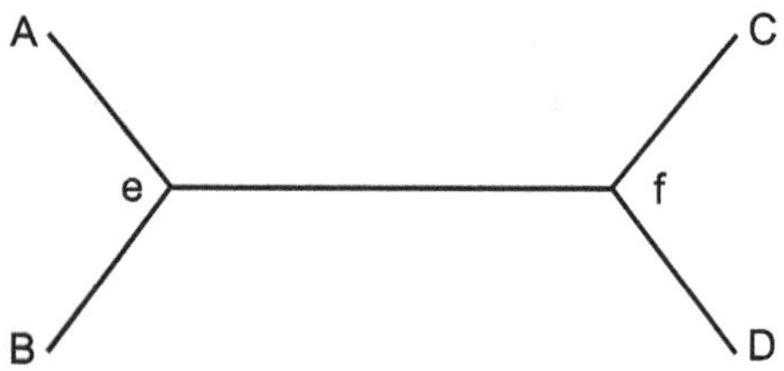

Fig. 6.1 Gene based phylogenetic tree.

To distinguish between the pathways, the phylogenetic analysis must include at least one **outgroup**, a gene that is less closely related to A, B, C, and D than these genes are to each other (panel below). Outgroups enable the root of the tree to be located and the correct evolutionary pathway to be identified. Let's say that the four case, an outgroup could be a gene from another primate, such as baboon, which is known to have branched away from the four species above before the common ancestor of the species. Homologous genes used in the previous tree examples come from human, chimpanzee, gorilla, and orangutan. In this case, an outgroup could be a gene from another primate, such as baboon, which is known to have branched away from the four species above before the common ancestor of the species.

6.9 Gene Trees versus Species Trees – Why are They Different ?

It is assumed that a gene tree, because it is based on molecular data, will be a more accurate and less ambiguous representation of the species tree that is obtainable by morphological comparisons. This may indeed be the case, but it does not mean that the gene tree is the same as the species tree. For this to be true, the internal nodes in both trees would have to be precisely equivalent, and they are not. An internal node in a gene tree indicates the divergence of an ancestral gene into two genes with different DNA sequences, usually resulting from a mutation of one sort or another. An internal node in a species tree represents what is called a speciation event, whereby the population of the ancestral species splits into two groups that are no longer able to interbreed. These two events, mutation and speciation, do not always occur at the same time.

6.10 Molecular Phylogenetics Terminology

Monophyletic : two or more DNA sequences that are derived from a single common ancestral DNA sequence

Clade : a group of monophyletic DNA sequences that make up all of the sequences included in the analysis that are descended from a particular common ancestral sequence.

Parsimony : an approach that decides between different tree topologies by identifying the one that involves the shortest evolutionary pathway. This is the pathway that requires the smallest number of nucleotide changes to go from the ancestral sequence, at the root of the tree, to all of the present-day sequences that have been compared.

6.11 Molecular Clock Hypothesis

States that nucleotide substitutions, or amino acid substitutions in proteins are being compared, occur at a constant rate, that is, the degree of difference between two sequences can be used to assign a date to the time at which their ancestral sequence diverged. The rate of molecular change differs among groups of organisms, among genes, and even among different parts of the same gene. Furthermore, molecular clocks require calibration with fossils to determine timing of origin of clades, and thus their accuracy is crucially dependent on the fossil record, or lack thereof, for the groups under study. Fossil DNA older than about 25,000–50,000 years is virtually empty of phylogenetic signal except in rare instances, and therefore traditional morphological studies of extinct and extant organisms remain a crucial component of phylogenetic analysis.

6.12 The Importance of Molecular Phylogenetics

The field of molecular phylogenetics has grown, both in size and in importance, since its inception in the early 1990s, attributable mostly to advances in molecular biology and more rigorous methods for phylogenetic tree building. The importance of phylogenetics has also been greatly enhanced by the successful application of tree reconstruction, as well as other phylogenetic techniques. Today, a survey of the scientific literature will show that molecular biology, genetics, evolution, development, behavior, epidemiology, ecology, systematics, conservation biology, and forensics are but a few examples of perplexing issues in the many disparate fields conceptually united by the methods and theories of molecular phylogenetics. Phylogenies are used essentially the same way in all of these fields, either by drawing inferences from the structure of the tree or from the way the character states map onto the tree. Biologists can then use these clues to build hypotheses and models of important events in history. Broadly speaking, the relationships established by phylogenetic trees often describe a species' evolutionary history and, hence, its phylogeny; the historical relationships among lineages or organisms or their parts, such as their genes. Phylogenies may be thought of as a natural and meaningful way to order data, with an enormous amount of evolutionary information contained within their branches. Scientists working in these different areas can then use these phylogenies to study and elucidate the biological processes occurring at many levels of life's hierarchy.

6.13 A Brief Review of the Common Tree-building Methods Used in Phylogenetic Inference.

Phylogenetic inference can be defined as the process of determining the estimated evolutionary history by analysis of a given data set (Swofford 1996).

Increasingly, molecular data sets, such as DNA and protein sequences, are used to develop these phylogenies. The reasons for building a phylogenetic tree are as diverse as the methods used to produce the trees. The process of phylogenetic analysis can be summarized in five steps.

The first two steps are preparatory for the subsequent steps that involve tree building and evaluation of the resultant tree.

The first step is the alignment of either the nucleotide or the amino acid sequences for the taxa of interest. It is generally agreed upon that amino acid sequences produce a tree closest to the true tree (Felsenstein 1996, Hershkovitz 1998, Russo, 1996). This is due to the higher rate of conservation of amino acid sequences and protein structure (Felsenstein 1996). Manual alignment editing is recommended over fully computational multiple alignments as the algorithms and programs are not yet optimal for phylogenetic alignment (Hershkovitz 1998). Regardless of the method for alignment, the final alignment should be carefully scrutinized with any independent phylogenetic evidence and other assumptions of structure and function. Once one proceeds to tree building, the computer-generated alignment will be blind to any errors in alignment.

The second step will be to determine the presence of a phylogenetic signal. Most of the sequence analyses fall between two extremes: identical sequences and sequences which have become so divergent as to become randomized in relation to the phylogenetic history. The former case dictates no further analysis. The latter will result in an inferred phylogeny, though the randomness of the resulting phylogeny may not be worth the effort. Those sequence alignments that fall in between will have a mixture of conserved and random positions and will be the most useful in phylogenetic inference (Hillis 1993).

Once the alignment is complete, the next steps in phylogenetic inference are to decide the most appropriate tree-building method for a specified data set followed by choosing a strategy to find the best tree under the selected optimality criterion. Finally, the tree obtained must be scrutinized to determine the level of confidence that can be placed on the results (Hillis 1993).

One of the most complex issues faced during the process of phylogenetic inference is choosing the tree-building method.

Tree-building methods can be classified in two ways (Swofford 1996, Hershkovitz 1998).

The first way to classify these methods is to define them as **either algorithm-based or criterion-based.**

Though the procedure involved in each of these methods is different, the same algorithm could potentially be used in either method. An algorithm-based method generates a tree by following a series of steps, whereas criterion-based methods define an optimality criterion for comparing alternative phylogenies to one another and deciding, which one is better. Therefore, there is a big advantage when working with criteria-based methods because scores are assigned to every examined tree and can be used to rank the resultant phylogenies in order of preference. This provides the user with immediate knowledge about the strength of support for that tree. Strictly algorithmic methods are computationally much faster than the criteria-based methods, because they do not require evaluation of a large number of competing trees. Due to the large number of possible solutions, criteria-based methods do not produce exact results for data sets with more than 8-20 taxa.

Alternatively, **tree-building methods** can be classified into *distance-based versus character-based methods*.

A distance-based method computes pair wise distances according to some measure. Then, the actual data is discarded and the fixed distances are used in the derivation of trees. Trees derived by way of a character-based method have been optimized according to the distribution of actual data patterns in relation to a specified character.

Cluster analysis and neighbor joining are examples of methods defined solely on the basis of an algorithm or of methods that are unable to separate the task of finding an optimal tree from that of evaluating a specific tree, unlike the criteria-based methods. Cluster analysis constructs trees by linking the least distant pairs of taxa, followed by successively more distant taxa, or groups of taxa. Once two taxa are linked, they lose their individual identities and are subsequently referred to as a single cluster. Neighbor joining is related to this traditional cluster analysis except it removes the assumption that data are ultrameric. The tree is constructed by linking the least distant pairs of nodes as defined by a modified matrix. The modified distance matrix is constructed by adjusting the separation between each pair of nodes on the basis of the average divergence from all other nodes (Swofford 1996, Hershkovitz 1998).

There are three common types of optimality criteria that will be briefly discussed including parsimony, likelihood, and pair wise distance. Both maximum parsimony and maximum likelihood use the original data set for inference. Maximum parsimony falls under the philosophy of "the simpler hypotheses are preferable to the complicated ones" (Swofford 1996). It works in such a way as to choose from the alternative trees, the one with the fewest character-state transformations, thus minimizing homoplasy (e.g. convergence, reversal). Thus, this optimality criterion operates by selecting trees that minimize the total tree length. This method tends to yield numerous trees with the same score, which is not characteristic of other methods such as distance or maximum likelihood. Parsimony is less dependent upon assumptions about the sequence evolution than some other methods and amenable to weighting in order to accommodate any substitution bias.

The drawbacks for parsimony include slowed computation with weighting and poor performance when there is substantial among-site rate heterogeneity. Though there are several modifications that can correct for heterogeneity, such as modifying the data set or reweighting positions according to their propensity to change (successive approximation), this could potentially lead to errors in a prior step if the preliminary tree contains any errors.

An area of trouble using maximum parsimony is referred to as the Felsenstein zone. This zone is created when there exists strongly unequal rates of change along different branches of a tree or even with equal rates of change in cases of long-branch attraction. Long-branch refers to a lineage that evolved so much between nodes in the phylogeny that its character states have been effectively randomized with respect to the other taxa. Once in the Felsenstein zone misleading inferences are produced. At the ends of these long branches, character states are exhibited that no longer retain genealogical information leading to a distortion in the inference. Particularly deceptive are taxa on long branches that have converged on character states present in other taxa within the analysis. This appears as a false phylogenetic signal, obscuring the true signal (Lyons-Weiler 1997). There are several ways to fix this problem including weighted parsimony, the use of Relative Apparent Synapomorphy Analysis (RASA), or using maximum likelihood that incorporates models of evolutionary change (Swofford 1996, Lyons-Weiler1997).

Parsimony once took the lead as the most favored method; however, maximum likelihood appears to be replacing parsimony, particularly as this method becomes better defined. The critical difference between these two methods is that parsimony minimizes the amount of evolutionary change required for data explanation, while maximum likelihood attempts to estimate the actual amount of change according to the evolutionary model in place. Maximum likelihood works with a prior nucleotide substitution model to compute a likelihood score for each tree given the original data. Before beginning, either an evolutionary model must be specified that can account for the conversion of one sequence into another or parameters must be selected that can be estimated from the data. Then the maximum likelihood approach evaluates the probability that the selected evolutionary model will have generated the observed sequences. The trees yielding the highest likelihoods are used to infer phylogeny. The substitution model should be optimized to fit the observed data as modifying the substitution parameters modify the likelihood of the data associated with particular trees.

The greatest drawback to using maximum likelihood is the vast amount of computation time required (Swofford 1996, Hershkovitz 1998).

Maximum likelihood is not always available for use. An alternative method that also minimizes the impact of the underestimation problem present in parsimony is the pair wise distance method. It works on the idea that corrected distances to account for superimposed changes can be obtained by estimating the number of unseen events using the same models used with maximum likelihood. The corrected distances are estimates of the true evolutionary distance. The drawback for this method is the loss of data during the process (Swofford 1996).

Because many of the more complex models require an enormous amount of time to complete the computations, heuristic methods are often selected in place of the alternative search methods (Swofford 1996, Lewis 1998, Mau 1999). A heuristic method does not guarantee finding the optimal solution, but does provide a large increase in speed. Such is the case with maximum likelihood. Likelihood has several advantages including consistency, lower variance in estimation, and its robustness to violations of its assumptions, so many attempts have been made to incorporate maximum likelihood into a heuristic method that will simultaneously optimize the substitution model and the tree for a given data set.

In applying any of these methods, there are two key ideas that have been emphasized in the literature throughout the development of phylogenetics. The importance of the starting data cannot be stressed enough. The type of data not only determines which method to choose for analysis, but also determines the validity of the results obtained from a selected method (Cavilla-Sforza 1967, Swofford 1996, Hershkovitz 1998).

It follows, then, that the validity of the resulting tree is dependent upon the appropriateness of the model used in tree generation. Phylogenetic inference methods are under continual evaluation and improvement upon the accuracy and speed of computation in these methods is a continual process. In several cases, it has been determined that trees obtained from the simpler methods produce as good results as those obtained by more sophisticated methods. Though this may be an accurate assessment, the more complex methods have the advantage of producing several alternatives, which allow for the different topologies to be evaluated for statistical significance (Russo 1996, Nei 1998). There is no agreement, yet, on which method is the best method, and more than likely there never will be as the best method is dependent upon the type of data with which one begins. As long as the method has a theoretical justification, then it is more important to choose a good gene or a large number of amino acids than it is to choose a particular tree-building method (Russo 1996).

7
Phylogenetic Prediction

7.1 Tree of Life

On one level, it is interesting to understand and study how the evolution of species has occurred. There are many different resources discussing the evolution of species. This includes the NCBI taxonomy web sites, and the University of Arizona's tree of life project.

7.2 Evolutionary Trees

An evolutionary tree is a two-dimensional graph showing the evolutionary relationship among a set of items being compared. This set can be organisms, genes, or DNA sequences. Consider for the moment that each of the units in the set are referred to as a taxon. Each taxon will be defined by a distinct unit on the tree.

An evolutionary tree is composed of outer branches or leaves that represent the taxa and nodes and branches representing the relationships among the taxa. Two taxa that are derived from the same common ancestor will share a node in the graph. In general, approaches to designing evolutionary trees attempt are made to define the length of each branch to the next node according to the number of sequence level changes that occurred. One thing to be careful of in phylogenetic analysis is that this distance may not be in direct relation to evolutionary time. Analyses that prescribe to the theory of a uniform rate of mutation are known as the molecular clock hypothesis.

7.3 Rooted Trees

In a rooted tree topology, one sequence (the root) is defined to be the common ancestor of all of the other sequences. A unique path leads from the root node to any other node, and the direction of the path indicates evolutionary time. The root is chosen by including a sequence from an organism that is thought to have branched off earlier than the other sequences. If the molecular clock hypothesis holds, it is also possible to predict a root. As the number of sequences increase, the number of possible rooted trees increases very rapidly. In some cases, a bifurcating binary tree is the best model to simulate evolutionary events in which case one species branches off into two separate species.

Example of a rooted tree : (Fig. 7.1)

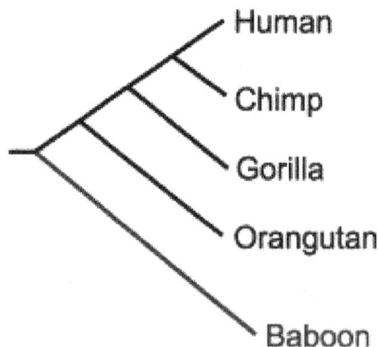

Fig. 7.1 Example of a rooted tree.

7.4 Star Topology (Unrooted Trees)

An unrooted tree (sometimes referred to as a star topology) shows the evolutionary relationship among sequences, without revealing the location of the oldest ancestry. There are fewer choices for an unrooted tree than a rooted tree.

Example of an unrooted tree : (Fig. 7.2)

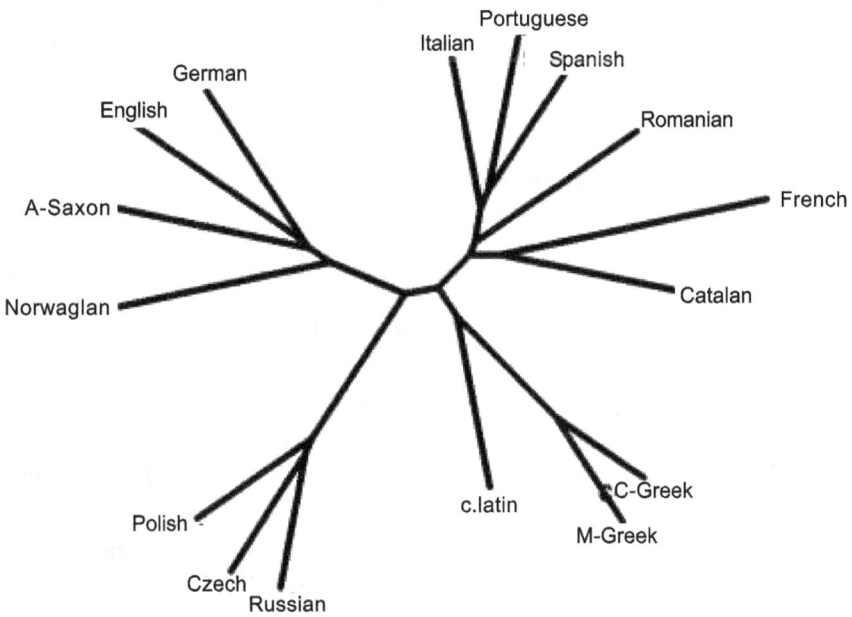

Fig. 7.2 Example of an unrooted tree.

7.5 Methods for Determining Evolutionary Trees

There are three methods used to calculate the tree(s) that best account for the observed variation in a set of sequences. These methods are Maximum Parsimony, Distance, and Maximum likelihood.

(i) *Maximum Parsimony*

Maximum parsimony methods predict the evolutionary tree that minimizes the number of steps required to generate the observed variation in the sequences. In order to construct a tree using maximum parsimony, a multiple sequence alignment must first be obtained. For each aligned position, phylogenetic trees that require the smallest number of evolutionary changes to produce the observed sequence changes are identified. This continues for each position in the alignment. Those trees that produce the smallest number of changes overall for all sequence positions are identified. This is a rather time consuming algorithm that only works well if the sequences have a strong sequence similarity.

```
              5     7     9
1  A A G A G T G C A
2  A G C C G T G C G
3  A G A T A T C C A
4  A G A G A T C C G
```

Fig. 7.3 Multiple Alignment for phylogeny

Consider the example above. There are a total of four sequences, (Fig. 7.3), which gives a possibility of three different unrooted trees as shown in Fig. 7.4. In this case some sites are informative, and other sites are not. An informative site has the same sequence character in atleast two different sequences. Only the informative sites need to be considered.

Possible trees :

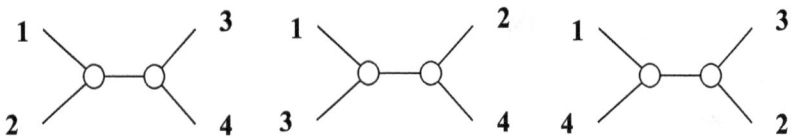

Fig. 7.4 Possible trees from four sequences.

In this case, adding the number of changes at each informative site for each tree, and picking the tree requiring the least total number of changes obtain the optimal tree.

For a large number of sequences the number of trees to examine becomes so large that it might not be possible to examine all possible trees. Some programs, such as PAUP, add features that will allow the user to invoke a heuristic that will keep representative trees that best fit the data.

The informative sites in the example of alignment are position 5, 7, and 9 in Fig. 7.3.

Let's go through the possible trees and figure out the number of rearrangements for each in the informative sites.

One problem with determining evolutionary distance between sequences is that columns representing greater variation dominate the analysis. In order to overcome this problem of determining long branch lengths is to look only at transversion events, which are the most significant base changes (i.e. changes a purine to a pyrimidine or vice versa). This is referred to as Lake's method of invariants.

(ii) *Distance Methods*

The distance method for construction of phylogenetic trees looks at the number of changes between each pair in a group of sequences to produce a phylogenetic tree of the group. The goal of distance methods is to identify a tree that positions neighbors correctly and that also has branch lengths, which reproduce the original data as closely as possible.

CLUSTALW uses the neighbor-joining method as a guide to multiple sequence alignments. The PHYLIP suite of programs employs neighbor-joining methods.

Phylip http://evolution.genetics.washington.edu/phylip.html

Distance analysis programs in PHYLIP :

FITCH : estimates a phylogenetic tree assuming additivity of branch lengths using the Fitch-Margoliash method.

KITSH : same as FITCH, but under the assumption of a molecular clock.

NEIGHBOR : estimates phylogenies using the neighbor joining (no molecular clock assumed) or unweighted pair group method with arithmetic mean (UPGMA) (molecular clock assumed).

For phylogenetic analysis, the distance score counted as either the number of mismatched positions in the alignment or the number of sequence positions that must be changed to generate the other sequence is used.

The success of distance methods depends on the degree to which the distances among a set of sequences can be made additive on a predicted evolutionary tree.

Consider the alignment :

A ACGCGTTGGGCGATGGCAAC

B ACGCGTTGGGCGACGGTAAT

C ACGCATTGAATGATGATAAT

D ACACATTGAGTGATAATAAT

The distances between these sequences can be shown as a table :

Table Showing distances between the above sequences

	A	B	C	D
A	-	3	7	8
B	-	-	6	7
C	-	-	-	3
D	-	-	-	-

Note : Distances are nothing but the number of changes in bases/aminoacids between any two sequences under comparision.

Using this information, an unrooted tree showing the relationship between these sequences can be drawn as shown in Fig. 7.5.

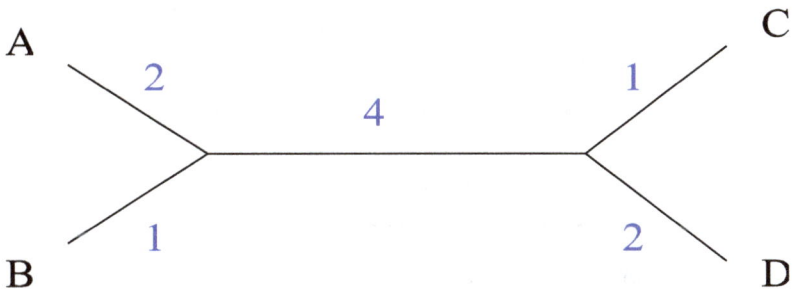

Fig. 7.5 Unrooted tree resulting from the above four sequences.

(iii) *Fitch and Margoliash Method*

The Fitch and Margoliash method uses a distance table. The sequences are combined in threes to define the branches of the predicted tree and to calculate the branch lengths of the tree.

Example using three sequences :

1. Draw an unrooted tree with three branches originating from a common node and label the ends as in Fig. 7.6.

Fig. 7.6 Representing the initial step of Margoliash method.

2. Calculate the lengths of tree branches algebraically. Tree will be generated as shown in Fig. 7.7.

	A	B	C
A	—	22	39
B	—	—	41
C	—	—	—

Distance from A to B = a + b = 22   (1)

Distance from A to C = a + c = 39   (2)

Distance from B to C = b + c = 41   (3)

Subtracting (3) from (2) yields :

$$b + c = 41$$

$$-a - c = -39$$
_____

$$b - a = 2 \qquad (4)$$

Adding (1) and (4) yields 2b = 24; b = 12

So   a + 12 = 22; a = 10

                       10 + c = 39; c = 29

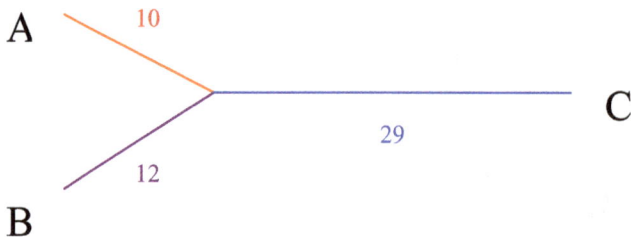

Fig. 7.7 Representing the final tree using Fitch Margoliash method.

(iv) *Example of Fitch-Margoliash Using Five Sequences*

The Fitch-Margoliash algorithm can be extended to three or more sequences. Consider the following table of distances between five separate sequences :

	A	B	C	D	E
A	—	22	39	39	41
B	—	—	41	41	43
C	—	—	—	18	20
D	—	—	—	—	10
E	—	—	—	—	—

Suppose that the initial tree is as follows : In Fig. 7.8.

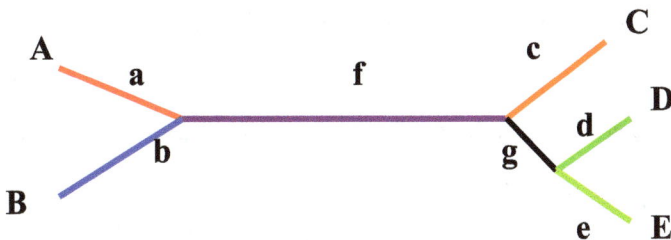

Fig. 7.8 (Tree constructed using five sequences)

1. The first step is to locate the most closely related sequences in the distance table. In this case, that would be sequences D and E.

2. Now create a new table by combining the remaining sequences. For the distance from D to A, B, C takes the average distance of each of these to D ((39 + 41 + 18) / 3 = 32.7). For the distance from E to A, B, C, takes the average distance of each of these to E ((41+43+20)/3 = 34.7). The resulting table is as follows :

	D	**E**	**AVG ABC**
D	—	**10**	**32.7**
E	—	—	**34.7**
AVG ABC	—	—	—

3. The average distances from D to ABC and E to ABC could also be found by averaging the sum of the appropriate branch lengths:

D to E : $d + e = 10$ (1)

D to ABC : $d + m = 32.7$ (2)

where $m = g + (c + 2f + a + b) / 3$

E to ABC: $e + m = 34.7$ (3)

By subtracting the third equation from the second equation we get:

$d - e = -2$

Adding this result to (1) we get :

$2d = 8; d = 4$

Substitute back in to get $e = 6$

4. Now treat D and E as a single sequence, and create a new distance table. The distance to DE is taken as the average of sequence A to D and A to E. The other distances are calculated in a similar fashion. The resulting distance table is :

	A	**B**	**C**	**(DE)**
A	—	22	39	40
B	—	—	41	42
C	—	—	—	19
(DE)	—	—	—	—

5. Identify the closely related sequences in the table. In this case, it is C to DE. Using algebra, the distance c can be calculated to be 9, and g is calculated to be 5.

6. Repeat the process until all lengths have been identified, in which case there is only single composite node left.

(v) *Summary of Fitch-Margoliash Algorithm*

1. Find the most closely related pairs of sequences (A, B).

2. Treat the rest of the sequences as a composite. Calculate the average distance from A to all others; and from B to all others.

3. Use these values to calculate the length of the edges a and b.

4. Treat A and B as a composite. Calculate the average distances between AB and each of the other sequences. Create a new distance table.

5. Identify next pair of related sequences and begin as with step 1.

6. Subtract extended branch lengths to calculate lengths of intermediate branches.

7. Repeat the entire process with all possible pairs of sequences.

8. Calculate predicted distances between each pair of sequences for each tree to find the best tree.

7.6 Neighbour-Joining Algorithm

The neighbour-joining method is very similar to the Fitch-Margoliash method. The sequences that should be joined are chosen to give the best least-squares estimates of the branch lengths that most closely reflect the actual distances between the sequences.

The neighbour-joining method begins by creating a star topology in which no neighbours are joined (Fig. 7.9 below).

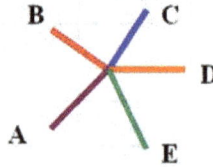

Fig. 7.9 Star topology of neighbour join method

The tree is modified by joining pairs of sequences. The pair to be joined is chosen by calculating the sum of the branch lengths for the corresponding tree. The sum of the branch lengths is calculated as follows :

$$S_{mn} = \frac{\sum d_{im} + d_{in}}{2(N-2)} + \frac{d_{mn}}{2} + \frac{\sum d_{ij}}{N-2}$$

Where i,j represent all sequences except m and n, and i < j.

For example, consider the tree when A and B are joined: See Fig. 7.10 below.

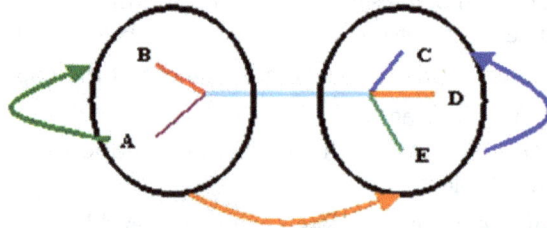

Fig. 7.10 Modified tree after joining pairs of sequences

The pair that results in the smallest branch length is then chosen to be the pair that is joined. Based on this choice, the Fitch-Margoliash algorithm is used to compute the actual branch lengths.

After the pair has been joined, a new distance table is created with the recently joined sequences now entered as a composite. The neighbor-joining algorithm chooses the next pair of sequences to join, and the F-M algorithm computes the branch lengths.

The process continues until the correctly branched tree and distances have been identified.

7.7 Unweighted Pair Group Method with Arithmetic Mean (UPGMA)

Works by clustering the sequences, starting with more similar sequences and working towards more distant sequences.

The process assembles a tree upwards, with each node being added above the others, and the edge lengths being determined by the difference in the heights of the nodes.

The distance d_{ij} between two clusters Ci and Cj are no. of sequences in clusters i and j is defined to be the average distance between pairs of sequences from each cluster :

$$d_{ij} = \frac{1}{|C_i||C_j|} \sum_{p \in C_i, q \in C_j} d_{pq}$$

Where $|C_i|$ and $|C_j|$ are the number of sequences in clusters i and j, respectively

The algorithm for UPGMA clustering (Durbin p 166) is as follows:

1. Assign each sequence i to its own cluster C_i
2. Define one leaf of the tree T for each sequence, and place it at height 0.
3. Determine the two clusters, i and j for which d_{ij} is minimal
4. Define a new cluster k by $C_k = C_i \cup C_j$, and define d_{kl} for all l
5. Define a node k with daughter nodes i and j, and place it at height $d_{ij}/2$.
6. Add k to the current clusters and remove i and j.
7. Continue steps 3-6 until only two clusters i and j remain, and place the root of the tree at height $d_{ij}/2$

Example of UPGMA

Consider the case where there are five sequences represented by dots on a graph. See Fig. 7.11, the spacing between each of these is representative of the distance between them :

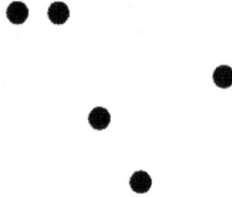

Fig. 7.11 Five sequences represented by dots.

The first step is to assign each of the sequences to their own cluster, which now gives a number to each of these. In addition, the tree can be constructed at the base, where each sequence is a leaf of the tree see Fig. 7.12.

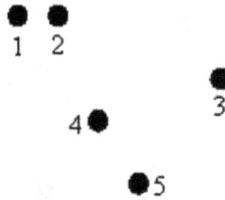

Fig. 7.12 Sharing assignment of sequences to their own cluster

Now select the two clusters that are closest to each other. These are the sequences 1 and 2. Create a single cluster for these two sequences, and create a parent node in the tree at height $d_{12}/2$ see Fig. 7.13.

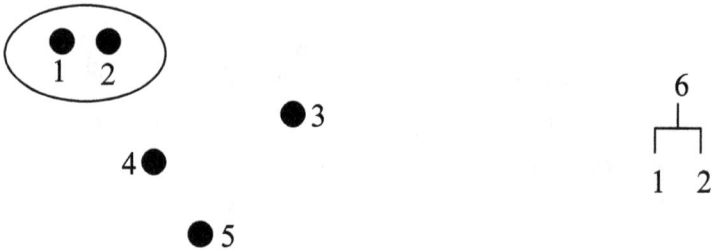

Fig. 7.13 Clumping of close clusters to create a single cluster

Continue on, selecting the two clusters that are closest: in this case, it is 4 and 5. Combine into a single cluster, and update the tree, see Fig. 7.14.

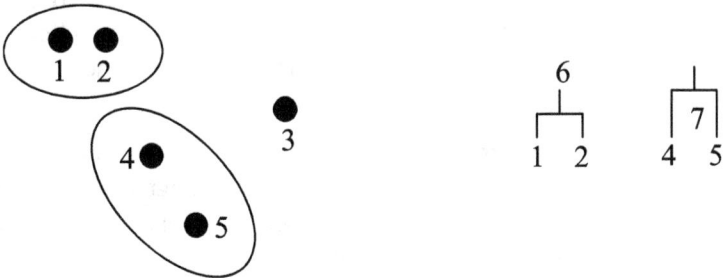

Fig. 7.14 Clustering process being extended

The next two clusters are the one containing 4 and 5, and the one containing 3, see Fig. 7.15.

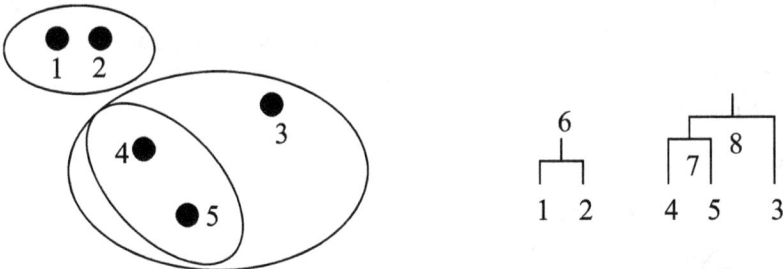

Fig. 7.15 Clustering further extended

There are now only two clusters left, so join them to complete the tree, see Fig. 7.16.

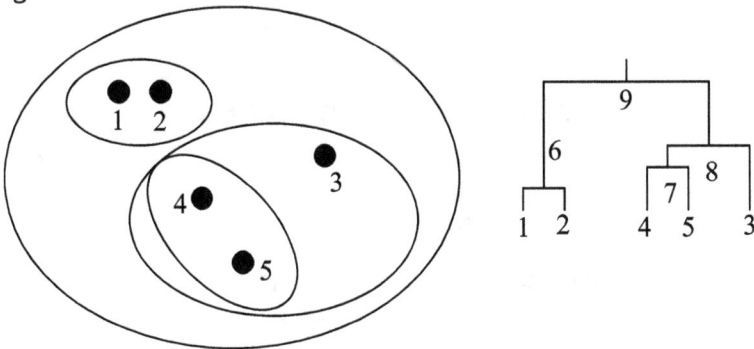

Fig. 7.16 Completion of clustering

7.8 Difficulties with Phylogenetic Analysis

Phylogenetic analysis would be easier if evolution occurred in a vertical fashion. However, horizontal or lateral transfer of genetic material (for instance through viruses) occurs, which makes it difficult to determine the phylogenetic origin of some evolutionary events.

If *a gene is under selective pressure* in different organisms, it can be *rapidly evolving*. Such an evolution can mask earlier changes that had occurred phylogenetically. In addition, different regions of a genome are under different pressures, and therefore different sites within two comparative sequences may be evolving at different rates.

Rearrangements of genetic material can also lead to false conclusions with phylogenetic analysis, especially if two sequences of different evolutionary origins are place next to each other.

Gene duplication events also cause problems with phylogenetic analysis, since the duplicated genes can evolve along separate pathways, leading to different functions.

PAUP (Maximum Parsimony)

MacClade (Maximum Parsimony)

CONSENSE

PHYLIP – (Distance — neighbor joining)

CLUSTALW – distance-based tree

Consider the following list of Globin sequences:

>gamma_A

MGHFTEEDKATTISLWGKVNVEDAGGETLGRLLVVYPWTQRFFDSFGNLSSASAIMGNPKVKAHGKKVLT
SLGDAIKHLDDLKGTFAQLSELHCDKLHVDPENFKLLGNVLVTVLAIHFGKEFTPEVQASWQKMVTAVAS
ALSSRYH

>alfa

VLSPADKTNVKAAWGKVGAHAGEYGAEALERMFLSFPTTKTYFPHFDLSHGSAQVKGHGK
KVADALTNAVAHVDDMPNALSALSDLHAHKLRVDPVNFKLLSHCLLVTLAAHLPAEFTPA
VHASLDKFLASVSTVLTSKYR

>beta

VHLTPEEKSAVTALWGKVNVDEVGGEALGRLLVVYPWTQRFFESFGDLSTPDAVMGNPKV

KAHGKKVLGAFSDGLAHLDNLKGTFATLSELHCDKLHVDPENFRLLGNVLVCVLAHHFGK

EFTPPVQAAYQKVVAGVANALAHKYH

>delta

VHLTPEEKTAVNALWGKVNVDAVGGEALGRLLVVYPWTQRFFESFGDLSSPDAVMGNPKV

KAHGKKVLGAFSDGLAHLDNLKGTFSQLSELHCDKLHVDPENFRLLGNVLVCVLARNFGK

EFTPQMQAAYQKVVAGVANALAHKYH

>epsilon

VHFTAEEKAAVTSLWSKMNVEEAGGEALGRLLVVYPWTQRFFDSFGNLSSPSAILGNPKV

KAHGKKVLTSFGDAIKNMDNLKPAFAKLSELHCDKLHVDPENFKLLGNVMVIILATHFGK

EFTPEVQAAWQKLVSAVAIALAHKYH

>gamma_G

MGHFTEEDKATTTSLWGKVNVEDAGGETLGRLLVVYPWIQRFFDSFGNLSSASAIMGNPKVKAHGKKVLT

SLGDAIKHLDDLKGTFAQLSELHCDKLHVDPENFKLLGNVLVTVLAIHFGKEFTPEVQASWQKMVIGVAS

ALSSRYH

>myoglobin

MGLSDGEWQLVLNVWGKVEADIPGHGQEVLIRLFKGHPETLEKFDKFKHLKSEDEMKASEDLKKHGATVL

TALGGILKKKGHHEAEIKPLAQSHATKHKIPVKYLEFISECIIQVLQSKHPGDFGADAQGAMNKALELFR

KDMASNYKELGFQG

>teta1

ALSAEDRALVRALWKKLGSNVGVYTTEALERTFLAFPATKTYFSHLDLSPGSSQVRAHGQ

KVADALSLAVERLDDLPHALSALSHLHACQLRVDPASFQLLGHCLLVTLARHYPGDFSPA

LQASLDKFLSHVISALVSEYR

>zeta

SLTKTERTIIVSMWAKISTQADTIGTETLERLFLSHPQTKTYFPHFDLHPGSAQLRAHGS

KVVAAVGDAVKSIDDIGGALSKLSELHAYILRVDPVNFKLLSHCLLVTLAARFPADFTAE

AHAAWDKFLSVVSSVLTEKYR

Create a phylogeny from these.

Hint : Explore the below mentioned sites. I hope you will do it.

2. Examples using a phlogenetic program:

http://bioweb.pasteur.fr/seqanal/phylogeny/phylip-uk.html

TreeTop http://www.genebee.msu.su/services/phtree_reduced.html

Phylodendron http://iubio.bio.indiana.edu/treeapp/treeprint-form.html

ATV (A Tree Viewer) http://www.genetics.wustl.edu/eddy/atv/

How to make a phylogenetic tree http://hiv-web.lanl.gov/content/hiv db/tree_tutorial/Tree-tutorial.html

A Brief Review of Common Tree Making Methods

http://bioinfo.mbb.yale.edu/mbb452a/projects/Patricia-M-Strickler.html

NCBI Primer on Phylogenetics http://www.ncbi.nlm.nih.gov/About/primer/phylo.html

List of Phylogeny Programs http://evolution.genetics.washington.edu/phylip/software.html

TreeViewer http://www.avl.iu.edu/projects/DNAml/

Phylip http://evolution.genetics.washington.edu/phylip.html

7.9 How to Make a Phylogenetic Tree

7.9.1 Methods to build a tree

    (i)   Genetic distances

    (ii) Phylogenetic analysis programs and where to get them

    (iii) Our interface

    (iv) Common mistakes in making trees

    (v) what to do when your tree looks funny

        • Tree 'reliability'

First of all, it is important to realize that all tree-building methods assume that the alignment is correct; errors in the alignment can lead to a very misleading tree. Once the alignment is optimal, there are many different methods to create phylogenies. ***Roughly, the methods can be divided into distance-based and character-based methods.*** Character-based methods use the individual substitutions among the sequences to determine the most likely ancestral relationships, while distance-based methods first calculate the overall distance between all pairs of sequences, and then calculate a tree based on those distances. Maximum parsimony (MP) and maximum likelihood (ML) are the most important character-based methods. In most comparative studies, ML seems to be the method that yields the best trees (Leitner, 1996).

The most important drawback of ML is that it is very computationally intensive; it is almost unusable with more than a few dozen sequences. MP is much faster than ML, but still slow compared to most distance-based methods. Both these programs calculate large numbers of trees and compare them by either the likelihood or the parsimony score. There are programs available which speed up the process considerably, such as FastDNAml (Olsen, 1994) but for large numbers of sequences the computational burden is still a major hurdle.

The ***distance-based methods are generally much faster than the character-based ones***. In this group, Neighbor Joining (NJ) is by far the most popular method. It is very fast and generally quite good, although there are conditions under which it systematically produces a wrong tree (bias). NJ is not the only biased method: in fact, under the right conditions (mostly when evolutionary rates are different for different sites, which is frequently the case for HIV) any method is biased, i.e. systematically produces the wrong tree (Kuhner & Felsenstein, 1994). The importance of the bias for the everyday tree is a matter of fierce debate.

Weighbor (short for "weighted Neighbor-Joining") is a new method by Bruno, Socci, and Halpern, which gives less weight to the longer distances in the distance matrix. The resulting trees are less sensitive to specific biases than NJ and MP, and negative branch lengths are avoided. The method is much faster than ML and usually faster than MP, but much slower than NJ.

To some extent the choice between methods can be based on the purpose of the tree. For subtyping sequences, an NJ tree based on a matrix of genetic distances is generally good enough. It is not vital that the tree is correct in every branch, only that the sequence of interest is clustered with the right subtype. Almost any method will solve this problem correctly. However, when more detailed information on the evolutionary relationships is important, for instance in forensic analyses, or when studying rates of evolution or trying to resolve key relationships (for example, short domains and potential recombination), more realistic models of evolution and unbiased tree reconstruction methods should be used.

(i) *Genetic distances*

The simplest way to calculate a distance between two sequences is to count the number of differences. This measure is often called the Hamming distance. It reflects the difference between sequences, but ignores their evolutionary relationship. The most intuitive way to show how this can be misleading to think of superimposed or reversed mutations: a nucleotide in a sequence, say an A, gets mutated and becomes a G. This results in a difference of 1. Many replication rounds later the same site gets mutated again. If it becomes an A, the difference now goes down, even though the genetic distance (the number of mutational events) has gone up. If it becomes a T or a C, the differences doesn't change, but the evolutionary distance should increase, because there have now been two evolutionary events.

The oldest attempt to adjust the number of differences between two sequences for the chances of a parallel or back mutation was designed by Jukes and Cantor (1969). They proposed the corrective formula $D=-3/4\ln(1-(4p/3))$, where D = Distance, ln = Leen, P = Base frequency. First, the effect of the correction increases with the difference between the sequences, and is negligible with very homologous sequences. Second, the effect of saturation can be seen beyond a certain number of differences (75%), it becomes impossible to tell what the true genetic distance is.

Since this formula was first proposed in 1969, and especially in the 1980s, many different models have been proposed to accurately estimate the underlying evolutionary distance from the observed number of differences between the sequences, taking into account new knowledge about the behavior of DNA, such as different transition/ transversion rates, different base frequencies, and non-uniform substitution rates between sites. Not all of these sophisticated methods are easily available (Dnadist, for example, only offers Jukes-Cantor, Kimura 2-parameter, Jin-Nei, and the F84 model Phylip uses for its maximum likelihood trees; Mega also offers Tamura and Tamura-Nei and a set of Gamma distribution-based distances).

A relatively new development is the use of models that incorporate variable evolutionary rates across sites. This is an important extension of the existing models, especially for HIV, which is well known to show dramatically different evolutionary rates (e.g. under the influence of immune escape) over the length of the genome. Gary Olsen has a program called **DNA rates**, which can estimate the rates of evolution in different sites, given an initial tree. The number of categories for the rates can be specified by the user. Using the DNA rates program can quite dramatically increase the quality of the resulting trees.

Many simulations show that the importance of using a realistic substitution model for estimating the genetic distance depends very much on the divergence of the sequences. If the expected number of substitutions per site is small (below 0.2), the resulting tree will not change much when different substitution models are used. If the sequences are highly diverged, however, and especially when the number of substitutions per site rises above 1, the differences become marked, the choice of the substitution model is very important.

(ii) *Tree-building programs available*

Probably the most widely used program suite is Felsenstein's PHYLIP. It offers a large array of methods, including ML, MP and NJ. The choice of genetic distance is fairly limited, and learning to use the programs requires some time investment, but their versatility makes them very popular. Most allow input of user trees, jumbling (randomizing input orders), and out-group designation.

MEGA is a nifty little program for DOS/Windows. It offers NJ and MP (although in a quirky implementation) and the sophisticated Tamura-Nei genetic distance estimation. MEGA is able to build trees on the basis of silent or non-silent mutations only, and has a fast bootstrapping option built in. It is available for minimal cost from the authors. Downsides are that the program is fairly unstable and has memory problems with large sets of sequences, and the printing of the trees often gives problems.

PHYLOWIN is a UNIX/Linux based program with a very nice graphical user interface. It does ML, MP and NJ, allows selection of sequences (rows) and position (columns) and bootstrapping. It allows the user to define subsets of sequences and positions and save them. It is available free of charge for academic users.

FastDNAml computes fast(er) ML trees. It is not very easy to use, but is often the only option if one wants to calculate ML trees for more than 20 sequences. It uses input file or command line parameters to specify the trees. The C source code for the program and an executable for Powermac are available by ftp.

PAUP* is a very versatile program that does maximum likelihood tree building in addition to parsimony, and allows incorporation of variable rates per site. It is presently distributed as a beta version, and costs around $100. The Mac version is entirely menu-driven, but the user interface is very clumsy. There are no user interfaces for the Windows and Unix versions.

(iii) *The HIV-WEB Treemaker interface*

This interface is just that: it interfaces between the user and the phylogenetic programs Dnadist, Neighbor and Drawtree/Drawgram from Joe Felsenstein's PHYLIP suite. The interface can only be used to make Neighbor-Joining trees, which may not be optimal for all circumstances, but usually form a good starting point for more sophisticated analysis; and as mentioned above, if the inferences made from the tree need not be very exact, for example for subtyping a small region or for a quick contamination check, this tree can suffice. Please note that the interface does not do bootstrapping.

The interface takes a sequence alignment in several formats, allows the adjustment of a few parameters (transition/transversion ratio, outgroup, and the shape of the tree). It uses the F84 genetic distance estimate (i.e. the option called 'ML' in Dnadist).

(iv) *Common mistakes in making a tree*

1. *Presenting the output from PHYLIP's Consense program as the final tree.*

This tree gives only a branching order. The 'branchlengths' are not true branch lengths, but rather reflect the % bootstrap values. For this reason, the Treefile that Consense produces does not contain branch lengths, and when printed, all branches in the tree have the same length.

REMEDY : If you want to include bootstrap values in a tree created with PHYLIP, the simplest method is to simply paste the values into the non-bootstrapped tree with valid branchlengths. The better way is to use the tree you get from the Consense program as input for another run of the tree-building program to have the branch lengths estimated for that particular tree. This also solves the (infrequent) problem where the topology of the consensus tree doesn't exactly match the one of the original tree.

2. *Visible alignment errors and/or unrecognized hypermutation*

When one sequence protrudes far out beyond all the others and there is no inherent reason for it to be so different, further inspection is needed. Frequently the cause is an alignment error or a hypermutated sequence.

REMEDY :

(a) Visually check the alignment of your sequences. There are many alignment editors available that make it very easy to do this.

(b) Check your sequence for hypermutation. Hypermutation, a relatively common phenomenon in HIV, means a very high incidence of G -> A mutations, usually resulting in a non-viable sequence. An interface that was designed to detect hypermutation: HYPERMUT.

3. *Unrecognized recombination*

When an isolate branches off close to the root between two subtypes, especially if it has a long branch or if it is not from a particularly old isolate, there is a chance that it is a recombinant. In this case the MAL isolate, an A/D/I recombinant. Similarly, when a sequence branches off between two clusters from one patient isolate, it can be a within-patient recombinant. In this case it can be the result of a real recombination event, or a PCR artifact.

REMEDY : If you suspect your sequence may be a recombinant, there are a multitude of ways to look at this more closely. On this we have RIP, which produces an alignment and an easy-to-read plot that shows the similarity of your sequence to a set of reference sequences over the entire length of the sequence. If there are major changes in what the most similar sequence is over the length of your sequence, this suggests recombination. There are many more methods to detect recombination; a good collection of links is maintained by David Robertson.

4. Assuming a molecular clock

1. The graphical representation of this assumption is that all branches end on one vertical line, representing the present day.

   This assumption is not realistic for HIV, and it is very uncommon for other organisms. The most commonly used method that produces these trees is UPGMA; the Kitsch (which explicitly assumes a molecular clock) program from the PHYLIP suite also results in this type of tree.

REMEDY : Use a different tree reconstruction method. Neighbor joining, Maximum Parsimony and Maximum Likelihood all produce trees that do not assume a strict molecular clock.

(v) *What to do when your tree looks funny*

If none of these errors describe your situation, but you still think your tree is off, there are a few things you can do.

1. Try a different method, or a different distance estimate. In rare cases (when there are many equivalent trees) even the input order of the sequence can make a difference; use the Jumble option provided in DNAML, or rearrange your input file.

2. Try using a different program that uses the same tree reconstruction method and compare the results.

3. Use a different outgroup: although the outgroup does not affect the structure of the tree, it can sometimes make it easier to interpret.

4. Split your sequences in half and see if the resulting trees are different. This suggests either recombination or dramatic evolutionary rate differences. In some cases (an example is the Rev-responsive element or RRE in HIV) two adjacent regions can be under such different constraint that they evolve very differently; building a tree from a sequence that spans both regions can give confusing results.

(vi) *Tree 'reliability'*

By far the most popular test for trees is the bootstrap. Contrary to what many people think, this is not a test of how accurate your tree is; it only gives information about the stability of the tree topology (the branching order), and it helps assess whether the sequence data is adequate to validate the topology. The bootstrap randomly resamples columns from your alignment, so that some positions will not be used and others will be used more than once, and builds a new tree from this dataset. This is done as many times as you specify. The bootstrap value is a count or percentage of how often each branch was present in exactly the same topology in all the resampled trees, so it gives an impression of how much the tree topology could change if, for example, you'd reconstruct it using a different gene. There are many rules of thumb about how to interpret the bootstrap. It is known to be a conservative measure, so a bootstrap of 95% gives more than 95% confidence in that branch. The number of 70% is often cited as a cut-off for a 'reliable' branch (see also Hillis & Bull, 1993).

7.10   Sequence Alignments and Tree Building

Alignment tools and methods for building Phylogenetic trees

Objectives :

1. Gain a basic appreciation of phylogenetics.
   - Know the difference between phylogeny and taxonomy
   - Explore phenetic and cladistic approaches
   - Examine criteria of data selection and analysis
2. Become familiar with on-line resources helpful in studying the phylogeny of organisms.
   - Explore and use sites, such as Phylodendron Web and PHYLIP servers
   - Examine phylogenetic literature on-line
3. Learn to use alignment and tree building tools, and to analyze the results.
   - BLAST2 and ALIGN for selected pair wise alignments
   - Clustalw and ClustalX for multiple sequence alignments
   - Build trees using DRAWTREE and DRAWGRAM

(i)   *An excellent resource for this unit is below :*

If you intend to use these methods in your work or research, this following practical is highly recommended to extend beyond the basic introduction in this exercise. It contains both basic information and guided tutorials in the use of a variety of tools.

(ii) *Pre-Exercise :*

1. Review basic background on evolution. It is well explained in the next chapter of this book, review it thoroughly before proceeding further. Dr. Jasper's site, which has excellent notes and interesting, links is also good for your cause. The site is mention below:

   http://www.zo.utexas.edu/faculty/sjasper/bio304/syl304.html

2. Jargon, and the associated concepts, you need to know:
- Phylogenetics vs. taxonomy
- Cladistic vs. phenetic
- Clustering
- Parsimony vs. maximum likelihood

Exercise :

(iii) **Part A :** Multiple sequence alignments [MSA] and pairwise alignments

1. You have already tried using Clustalw to do multiple sequence alignments. It is now time to dust off the cobwebs ['tis the season!] and get back to it. Recall that you need to start with sequences in FASTA format, or have files in Biology Workbench. For this exercise, please use the following set of accession numbers to obtain some protein sequences of glutamate synthase. These were chosen because they have similar enzymatic function and are therefore conserved, while being drawn from five kingdoms as shown in Table below.

A38596	Maize	Plant
CAC05496	Arabidopsis	Plant
AAC08261	Porphyra	Algae
CAA76602	Plasmodium	Protozoa
AAF49409	Drosophila	Animal
CAB92626	Neurospora	Fungi
CAA61505	Saccharomyces	Fungi
BAB05447	Bacillus	Bacteria
AAA58014	E. Coli	Bacteria
AAK94787	Klebsiella	Bacteria
CAB64595	Nostoc	Bacteria
AAG44102	Staphylococcus	Bacteria

These numbers can be used to obtain the protein sequences from NCBI. FASTA format is recommended for easy transfer into your log and uploading into Biology Workbench or elsewhere.

2. In your log, you need to **remove the spaces on the line preceding "> gi|xxx..."** for each entry. [Don't disturb the sequence lines.] This is necessary when running Clustal, because any extra spaces will terminate the alignment for all entries beyond those spaces.

3. At this point, you have two options. Choose the one you like. [You can always return to try another option.]

    (a) You can use ClustalW at EBI. You need to be careful when you paste in your sequences that you remove any spaces at the beginning of lines. You may leave a blank line between sequence entries.

    http://www.ebi.ac.uk/clustalw/ or

    http://www.ebi.ac.uk/clustalw/

    Explore the site. You can read about the windows by clicking on them. [For the next steps, see 4b.] Once you have an alignment, you can save it, or transfer it to another application or to Biology Workbench.

    (b) You can upload your sequences directly into Biology Workbench before aligning them. Be sure to check each sequence entry for inadvertent spaces at the beginning of lines. If you find any, remove them. Within Workbench, you can use ClustalW in either Protein Tools or Nucleotide Tools [see 4c], and then use other applications in Alignment Tools for analysis.

4. Follow the directions according to the option you selected in 3 above.

    (a) Paste your grouped FASTA sequences into the text box. For your first run, use the defaults. The alignments will take a few minutes. You may want to enter your e-mail to retrieve the report. If your run fails, the first check to see if the FASTA format and the left-hand spaces are OK. If a run seems to take too long, try "off-hours", keeping in mind that this is a European site, or try making your alignment request smaller. You can do this by selecting only 4-6 sequences.

Alternatively, you may want to focus on just one region or domain of your sequences. In that case, you can select portions of the FASTA reports. After using the defaults, try changing some of the settings after reading about them in the support pages. For report viewing, see 5 below.

Note : When running Clustal on a set of sequences, you may need to edit your sequences before you get reasonable alignments. It doesn't hurt to try a test run first. As you work through the following, consider what might be some of the causes of misalignments.

(b) Select the sequences you want to compare by checking the boxes. Choose ClustalW. Initially accept the defaults. On repeated runs, try changing some of the settings [Go to the EBI site for documentation support]. Try running subgroups of sequences and try changing the order of sequences. You can change order by selecting a sequence and choosing a menu item, then return. The selected sequence is at the top of the list. You can easily scramble your list by randomly selecting and copying different sequences. You can also create edited sequences to select a region or to remove nonstandard characters. To save alignments, select "Import alignments". Then you can use the Alignment Tools. [See 6 below. You should skip 5.]

5. **For option b only.** [Option b, skip to 6 below.] Once you have the report, browse to see what you have. Click on **Jalview** for a graphical display. Wait for the calculations and color assignment to be complete before trying to navigate. For your convenience, consensus notations and colors used in Jalview are assigned as follows :

Consensus line notations :

* = identical or conserved residues in all sequences in the alignment

: = indicates conserved substitutions

. = Indicates semi-conserved substitutions.

Characteristics :	Amino acids:
red: small & hydrophobic R groups	AVFPMILW
blue: acidic	DE
magenta: basic	RHK
green: hydroxyl + X	STYHCNGQ
gray: other	Symbols for amino acids

Compare the results of your different runs. Which parameters did you change? What was the effect? Record for future reference. Upload some alignments into Biology Workbench.

6. At this point, everyone should have some aligned sequences in Biology Workbench. To check, select Alignment Tools after selecting the appropriate session. You should see blocks of sequences listed. If that is not true, go back and continue working on alignments and/or uploads until you do.

   (a) Use Boxshade and Textshade to easily view conserved and non-conserved regions. Note that these are similar, but not identical to Jalview. These can be saved and used as graphic inserts in reports and manuscripts. Use one of these to browse your alignments and to make comparisons between your different alignments.

   (b) Make note of conserved regions.

(iv) *Part B : Tree building*

1. Neighbor joining [NJ] is a clustering method to group pair wise distances. It is the favored distance calculation method because equal rates of evolution are not assumed, as in the arithmetic approach. In Biology Workbench's Alignment Tools, try the following:

   (a) Use Clustaldist to obtain a set of distance calculations.

(b) Choose either DNAdist or Protdist, depending on whether you have nucleotide or protein alignments. Run the same alignments again to obtain a second set of distance results. How do these results differ from the first set? Which application appears to be more sensitive to differences?

(c) Sketch a tree based on distance calculations obtained from Clustaldist. Sketch another tree based on the calculation results obtained from DNAdist or Protdist.

(d) Use Drawtree to produce a PHYLIP unrooted tree. Compare this tree to your sketches.

2. Parsimony [also known as max pars, for maximum parsimony, and as MP] is a method, which looks for the minimum number of changes, which satisfy the data. It examines sequence comparisons rather than a numerical result, as in NJ.

   Use DNAPars or ProtPars to generate a tree, which maximizes parsimony. How many calculation steps were required to obtain the tree? Do different alignment runs affect the outcome of the final tree? If so, how?

3. Next try using Drawgram, a PHYLIP rooted tree tool. This allows you to build a variety of tree types from the same alignment. You can generate a phenogram, based on neighbor joining, which can then be compared to your Drawtree result. You can generate a cladogram, based on parsimony, which can then be compared to both the phenogram and to the tree obtained using DNAPars or ProtPars. If you are feeling adventurous, try out some of the other tree types.

4. OK, now you are at the point where computational intensity increases considerably. To try running maximum likelihood [ML] or Bayesian analysis on your alignments, it is recommended that you download suitable software, along with any server-stored alignments of interest and run them on your PC. This is required if you want to examine protein alignments.

For nucleotide alignments, you can use WebPHYLIP's DNAML to do maximum likelihood. This is a good site to explore for other programs within PHYLIP. Try it now, or come back while you are working on the project:

http://sdmc.krdl.org.sg:8080/~lxzhang/phylip/

(v)   *Summary Questions :*

Try to limit your answers to 2-3 typed pages [12 pt font]. This length should be sufficient for your comments and any appropriate copy/ pasted examples. [You need not retype or copy/paste the questions as part of your responses.]

1. Summarize one of your MSA results. Give the following information :

     (a) Which option did you use? ClustalW at EBI or ClustalW in Workbench?

     (b) Were mutations evenly distributed or were there regions relatively free of them? What might be the reason for conserved regions? How could you test this?

2. Summarize the results obtained using distance calculations. How did your sketched trees compare to the computer-generated tree(s) in Drawtree?

3. Summarize the results obtained using parsimony. How did the maximum parsimony tree(s) compare with the NJ-based trees?

4. Summarize your explorations of Drawgram, especially between creating phenograms and cladograms. After exploring the other types of trees, which one did you like best overall? Why? In considering the available choices for a tree displayed in a publication aimed at a general scientific readership, which type would you choose? Why? [If you enjoyed playing with trees, try out Tree View, which you can download. See below.]

5. *Optional :* If you ran maximum likelihood [ML] on your alignments, summarize how the results compared to NJ and MP.

(vi) *Further exploration :*

1. More information on PHYLIP can be found at these related sites:

http://evolution.genetics.washington.edu/phylip.html

http://evolution.genetics.washington.edu/phylip/phylipweb.html

2. A wide variety of phylogenetic software can be downloaded from collections. The following is very easy to use:

http://evolution.genetics.washington.edu/phylip/software.html

The cross-reference list is useful, although you should check elsewhere for possible updates:

http://evolution.genetics.washington.edu/phylip software.xref.html

3. **PUZZLE** is a good program to download for maximum likelihood analysis of nucleotide and protein sequence alignments. This program has several cool features worth exploring:

http://www.tree-puzzle.de/

Warning : While running ML, your computer will be dedicated to running this program. Forget playing games or checking your mail. Go for a run or take a nap if you are running a large set of sequences.

4. **MrBayes** is freeware to download for Bayesian analysis:

http://morphbank.ebc.uu.se/mrbayes/

Warning : While running Bay, your computer will be dedicated to running this program. Although not as bad as ML for large sets, it is slower than ML for fewer sequences [roughly, less than 40]. For exploration purposes, use a small set, and then go enjoy a leisurely cup of hot chocolate.

5. **Tree View**, software download for drawing quality trees using a variety of file formats:

http://taxonomy.zoology.gla.ac.uk/rod/treeview.html

6. Another tree drawing program is Phylodenron. It can be downloaded from the U. Washington site in 2 above, or it can be accessed from a server:

http://iubio.bio.indiana.edu/treeapp/treeprint-form.html

7. Additional access to lots of cool applications:

http://bioweb.pasteur.fr/intro-uk.html

Access to good documentation on many applications: [left-hand frame- index]

http://www.molbiol.ox.ac.uk/

There are **summary questions** at the end of this section. Read them through before you start browsing. You can answer them as you go, or answer them after browsing the above mentioned sites.

8
Genetic Engineering

- GENETIC ENGINEERING Techniques
  - o Restriction Enzymes/DNA Ligase
  - o Vectors/Plasmids
  - o Gene Transfer
  - o Genetic Markers
  - o PCR
  - o DNA probes
  - o Electrophoresis
  - o DNA Sequencing
  - o Applications
  - o Gene Products
  - o New Phenotypes
  - o Gene Therapy

8.1 Genetic Engineering

Genetic engineering, also known as *recombinant DNA technology*, means altering the genes in a living organism to produce a Genetically Modified Organism (GMO) with a new genotype. Various kinds of genetic modification are possible: inserting a foreign gene from one species into another, forming a *transgenic organism*; altering an existing gene so that its product is changed; or changing gene expression so that it is translated more often or not at all.

8.2 Techniques of Genetic Engineering

Genetic engineering is a very young discipline, and is only possible due to the development of techniques from the 1960s onwards. These techniques have been made possible from our greater understanding of DNA and how it functions following the discovery of its structure by Watson and Crick in 1953. Although the final goal of genetic engineering is usually the expression of a gene in a host, in fact most of the techniques and time in genetic engineering are spent isolating a gene and then cloning it. This table lists the techniques that we'll look at in detail.

TECHNIQUE	PURPOSE
Restriction Enzymes	To cut DNA at specific points, making small fragments
DNA Ligase	To join DNA fragments together
Vectors	To carry DNA into cells and ensure replication
Plasmids	Common kind of vector
Genetic Markers	To identify cells that have been transformed
PCR	To amplify very small samples of DNA
cDNA	To make a DNA copy of mRNA
DNA probes	To identify and label a piece of DNA containing a certain sequence
Gene Synthesis	To make a gene from scratch
Electrophoresis	To separate fragments of DNA
DNA Sequencing	To read the base sequence of a length of DNA

8.3 Restriction Enzymes

These are enzymes that cut DNA at specific sites. They are properly called restriction endonucleases because they cut the bonds in the middle of the polynucleotide chain. Most restriction enzymes make a staggered cut in the two strands, forming sticky ends. As shown in Fig. 8.1.

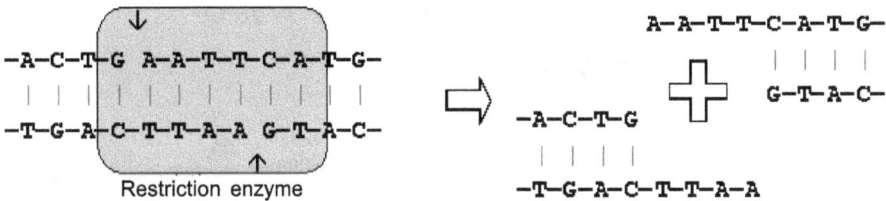

Fig. 8.1 Action of restriction enzyme on DNA seq.

The cut ends are "sticky" because they have short stretches of single-stranded DNA. These sticky ends will stick (or anneal) to another piece of DNA by complementary base pairing, but only if they have both been cut with the same restriction enzyme. Restriction enzymes are highly specific, and will only cut DNA at specific base sequences, 4-8 base pairs long.

Restriction enzymes are produced naturally by bacteria as a defence against viruses (they "restrict" viral growth), but they are enormously useful in genetic engineering for cutting DNA at precise places ("molecular scissors"). Short lengths of DNA cut out by restriction enzymes are called restriction fragments. There are thousands of different restriction enzymes known, with over a hundred different recognition sequences. Restriction enzymes are named after the bacteria species they came from, so *Eco*R1 is from E.coli strain.

DNA LIGASE

This enzyme repairs broken DNA by joining two nucleotides in a DNA strand. It is commonly used in genetic engineering to do the reverse of a restriction enzyme, i.e. to join together complementary restriction fragments.

The sticky ends allow two complementary restriction fragments to anneal, but only by weak hydrogen bonds, which can quite easily be broken, say by gentle heating. The backbone is still incomplete.

DNA ligase completes the DNA backbone by forming covalent bonds. Restriction enzymes and DNA ligase can therefore be used together to join lengths of DNA from different sources. See Fig. 8.2.

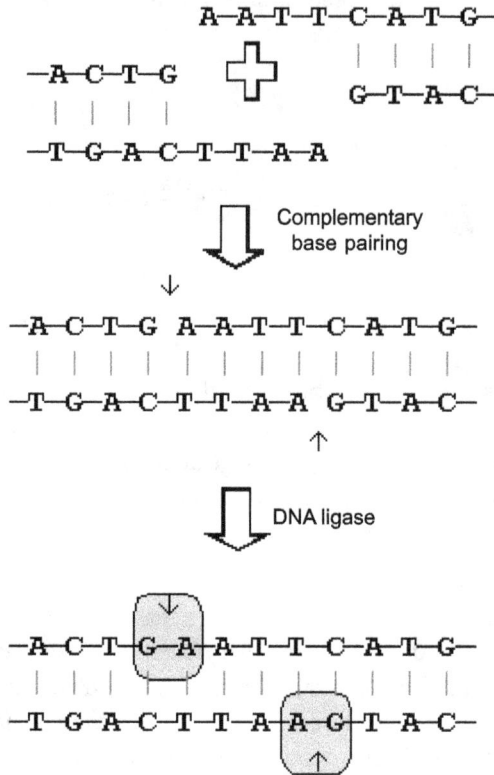

Fig. 8.2 Representing the work of DNA ligase.

8.4 Vectors

In biology a vector is something that carries things between species. E.g. the mosquito is a vector that carries the malaria parasite into humans. In genetic engineering a vector is a length of DNA that carries the gene we want into a host cell. A vector is needed because a length of DNA containing a gene on its own won't actually do anything inside a host cell. Since it is not part of the cell's normal genome it won't be replicated when the cell divides, it won't be expressed, and in fact it will probably be broken down pretty quickly.

A vector gets round these problems by having these properties:

- It is big enough to hold the gene we want
- It is circular (or more accurately a closed loop), so that it is less likely to be broken down
- It contains control sequences, such as a transcription promoter, so that the gene will be replicated or expressed.
- It contains marker genes, so that cells containing the vector can be identified.

TYPE OF VECTOR	MAX LENGTH OF DNA INSERT
Plasmid	10 kbp
Virus or phage	30 kbp

8.5 Plasmids

Plasmids are by far the most common kind of vector, so we shall look at how they are used in some detail. Plasmids are short circular bits of DNA found naturally in bacterial cells. A typical plasmid contains 3-5 genes and there are around 10 copies of a plasmid in a bacterial cell. Plasmids are copied when the cell divides, so the plasmid genes are passed on to all daughter cells. They are also used naturally for exchange of genes between bacterial cells (the nearest they get to sex), so bacterial cells will take up a plasmid. Because they are so small, they are easy to handle in a test tube, and foreign genes can quite easily be incorporated into them using restriction enzymes and DNA ligase.

The R plasmid

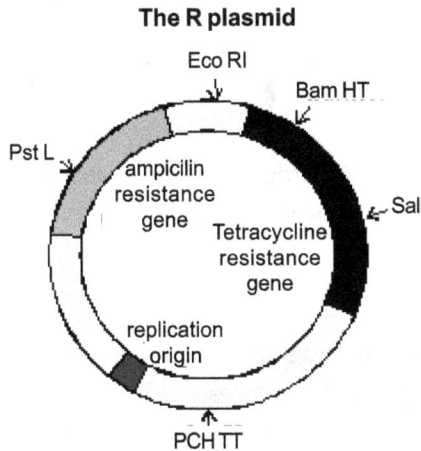

Fig. 8.3 Plasmid as a vector

One of the most common plasmids used is the R-plasmid (or pBR322). This plasmid contains a replication origin, several recognition sequences for different restriction enzymes (with names like *EcoRI*), and two marker genes, which confer resistance to different antibiotics (ampicillin and tetracycline). See Fig. 8.3.

The diagram below shows how DNA fragments can be incorporated into a plasmid using restriction and ligase enzymes. The restriction enzyme used here (*PstI*) cuts the plasmid in the middle of one of the marker genes (we'll see why this is useful later). The foreign DNA anneals with the plasmid and is joined covalently by DNA ligase to form a hybrid vector (in other words a mixture or hybrid of bacterial and foreign DNA). Several other products are also formed: some plasmids will simply re-anneal with themselves to re-form the original plasmid, and some DNA fragments will join together to form chains or circles. Theses different products cannot easily be separated, but it doesn't matter, as the marker genes can be used later to identify the correct hybrid vector. See Fig. 8.4.

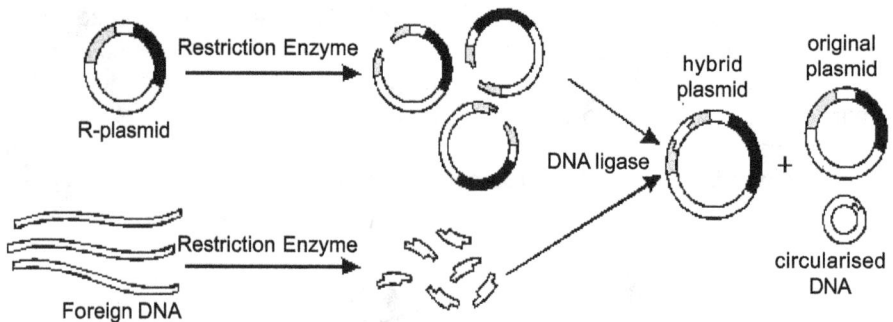

Fig. 8.4 Incorporation of DNA fragments into a plasmid. Using restriction and ligase enzymes.

8.6 Gene Transfer

Vectors containing the genes we want must be incorporated into living cells so that they can be replicated or expressed. The cells receiving the vector are called host cells, and once they have successfully incorporated the vector they are said to be transformed. Vectors are large molecules, which do not readily cross cell membranes, so the membranes must be made permeable in some way. There are different ways of doing this depending on the type of host cell. The most important one have the → symbol the others are less commonly used

- → **Heat Shock.** Cells are incubated with the vector in a solution containing calcium ions at 0° C. The temperature is then suddenly raised to about 40° C. This heat shock causes some of the cells to take up the vector, though no one knows why. This works well for bacterial and animal cells.

- → **Electroporation.** Cells are subjected to a high-voltage pulse, which temporarily disrupts the membrane and allows the vector to enter the cell. This is the most efficient method of delivering genes to bacterial cells.

- → **Viruses.** The vector is first incorporated into a virus, which is then used to infect cells, carrying the foreign gene along with its own genetic material. Since viruses rely on getting their DNA into host cells for their survival they have evolved many successful methods, and so are an obvious choice for gene delivery. The virus must first be genetically engineered to make it safe, so that it can't reproduce itself or make toxins. Three viruses are commonly used :

Plant Tumors : This method has been used successfully to transform plant cells, which are perhaps the hardest to do. The gene is first inserted into the plasmid of a soil bacterium, and then plants are infected with the bacterium. The bacterium inserts the plasmid into the plant cells' chromosomal DNA and causes a "crown gall" tumour. These tumour cells can be cultured in the laboratory.

Gene Gun : This technique fires microscopic gold particles coated with the foreign DNA at the cells using a compressed air gun. It is designed to overcome the problem of the strong cell wall in plant tissue.

Micro Injection : A cell is held on a pipette under a microscope and the foreign DNA is injected directly into the nucleus using an incredibly fine micro-pipette. Used where there are only a very few cells available, such as fertilised animal egg cells. See Fig. 8.5.

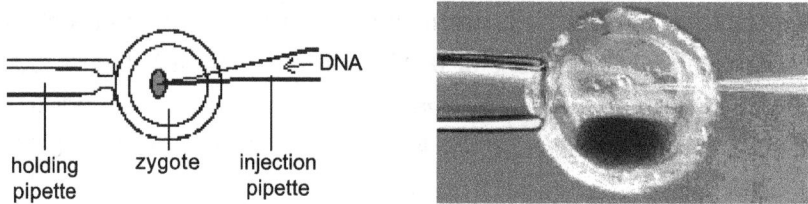

Fig. 8.5

Liposomes : Vectors can be encased in liposomes, which are small membrane vesicles. The liposomes fuse with the cell membrane (and sometimes the nuclear membrane too), delivering the DNA into the cell. This works for many types of cell, but is particularly useful for delivering genes to cell *in vivo* (such as in gene therapy). See Fig. 8.6.

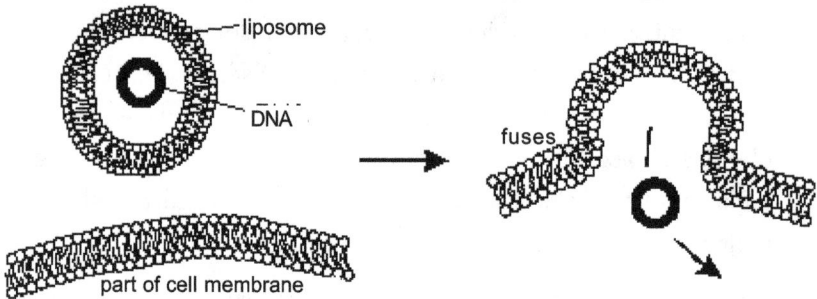

Fig. 8.6 Action of Liposomes, delivering the DNA.

8.7 Genetic Markers

These are needed to identify cells that have successfully taken up a vector and so become transformed. With most of the techniques above less than 1% of the cells actually take up the vector, so a marker is needed to distinguish these cells from all the others. A common marker, used in plasmids, is a gene for resistance to an antibiotic such as tetracycline. Bacterial cells taking up this plasmid are resistant to this antibiotic. So if the cells are grown on a medium containing tetracycline all the normal untransformed cells (99%) will die. Only the 1% transformed cells will survive, and these can then be grown and cloned on another plate. See Fig. 8.7.

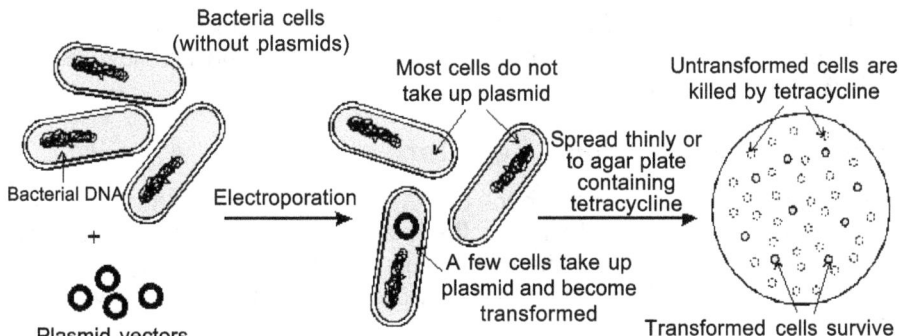

Fig. 8.7 Figure representing confirmation of transformation.

Replica Plating : Replica plating is a simple technique for making an exact copy of an agar plate. A pad of sterile cloth the same size as the plate is pressed on the surface of an agar plate with bacteria growing on it. Some cells from each colony will stick to the cloth. If the cloth is then pressed onto a new agar plate, some cells will be deposited and colonies will grow in exactly the same positions on the new plate. This technique has a number of uses, but the most common use in genetic engineering is to help solve another problem in identifying transformed cells. See Fig. 8.8. This problem is to distinguish those cells that have taken up a hybrid plasmid vector (with a foreign gene in it) from those cells that have taken up plasmids without the gene. This is where the second marker gene (for resistance to ampicillin) is used. If the foreign gene is inserted into the middle of this marker gene, the marker gene is disrupted and won't make its proper gene product. So cells with the hybrid plasmid will be killed by ampicillin, while cells with the normal plasmid will be immune to ampicillin. Since this method of identification involves killing the cells we want, we must first make a master agar plate and then make a replica plate of this to test for ampicillin resistance.

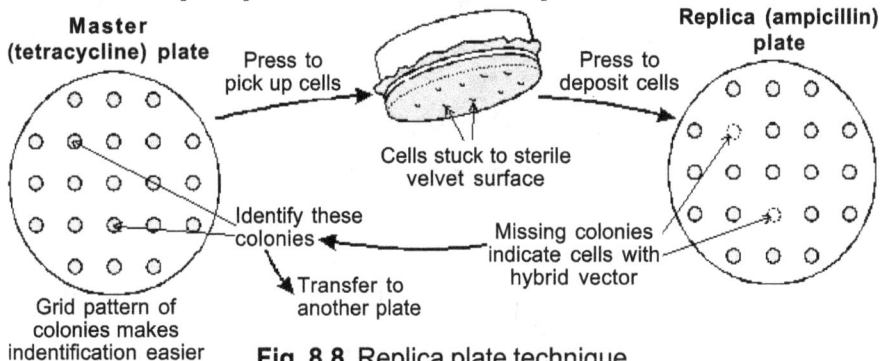

Fig. 8.8 Replica plate technique.

Once the colonies of cells containing the correct hybrid plasmid vector have been identified, the appropriate colonies on the master plate can be selected and grown on another plate.

8.8 Polymerase Chain Reaction

Genes can be cloned by cloning the bacterial cells that contain them, but this requires quite a lot of DNA in the first place. PCR can clone (or <u>amplify</u>) DNA samples as small as a single molecule. It is a newer technique, having been developed in 1983 by Kary Mullis, for which discovery he won the Nobel prize in 1993. The polymerase chain reaction is simply DNA replication in a test tube. If a length of DNA is mixed with the four nucleotides (A, T, C and G) and the enzyme DNA polymerase in a test tube, then the DNA will be replicated many times. See Fig. 8.9.

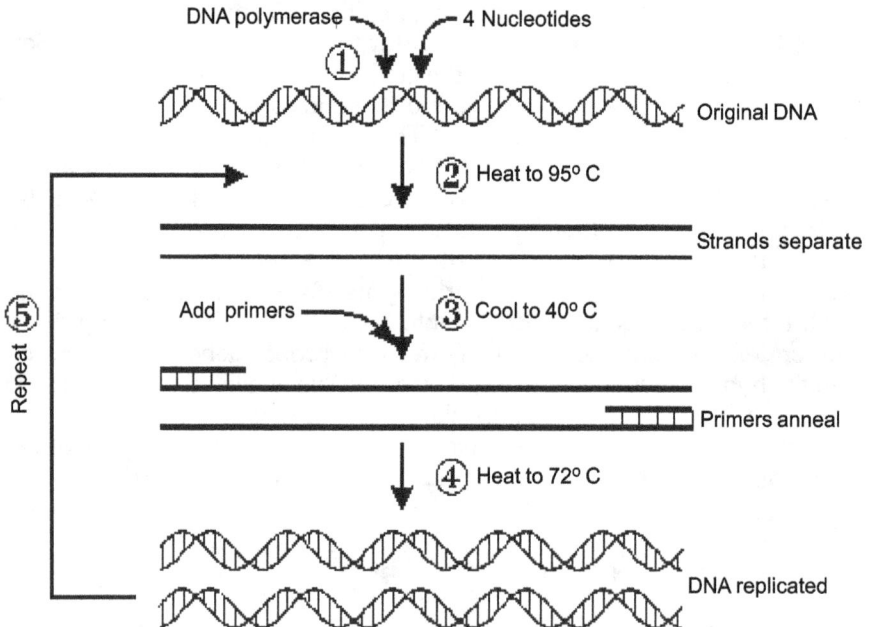

Fig. 8.9 Polymerase chain reaction.

1. Start with a sample of the DNA to be amplified, and add the four nucleotides and the enzyme DNA polymerase.

2. Normally (*in vivo*) the DNA double helix would be separated by the enzyme helicase, but in PCR (*in vitro*) the strands are separated by heating to 95° C for two minutes. This breaks the hydrogen bonds.

3. DNA polymerisation always requires short lengths of DNA (about 20 bp long) called <u>primers</u>, to get it started. *In vivo* the primers are made during replication by DNA polymerase, but *in vitro* they must be synthesized separately and added at this stage. This means that a short length of the sequence of the DNA must already be known, but it does have the advantage that only the part between the primer sequences is replicated. The DNA must be cooled to 40° C to allow the primers to anneal to their complementary sequences on the separated DNA strands.

The DNA polymerase enzyme can now extend the primers and complete the replication of the rest of the DNA. The enzyme used in PCR is derived from the thermophilic bacterium *Thermus aquaticus*, which grows naturally in hot springs at a temperature of 90° C, so it is not denatured by the high temperatures in step 2. Its optimum temperature is about 72° C, so the mixture is heated to this temperature for a few minutes to allow replication to take place as quickly as possible.

Each original DNA molecule has now been replicated to form two molecules. The cycle is repeated from step 2 and each time the number of DNA molecules doubles. This is why it is called a chain reaction, since the number of molecules increases exponentially, like an explosive chain reaction. Typically PCR is run for 20-30 cycles. See Fig. 8.10

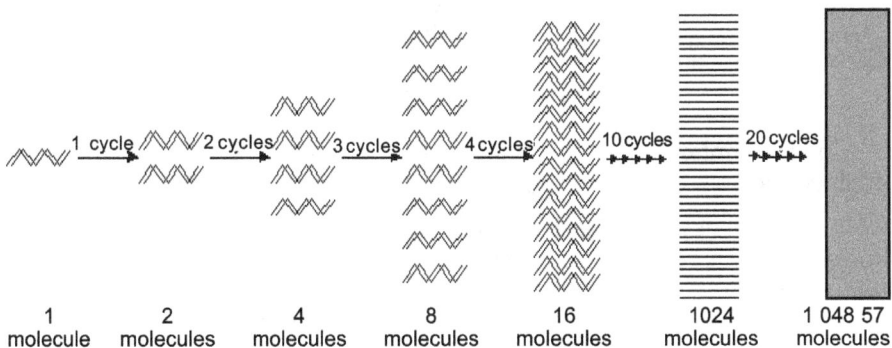

Fig. 8.10 Cycle process of PCR.

PCR can be completely automated, so in a few hours a tiny sample of DNA can be amplified millions of times with little effort. The product can be used for further studies, such as cloning, electrophoresis, or gene probes. Because PCR can use such small samples it can be used in forensic medicine (with DNA taken from samples of blood, hair or semen), and can even be used to copy DNA from mummified human bodies, extinct woolly mammoths, or from an insect that's been encased in amber since the Jurassic period. One problem of PCR is having a pure enough sample of DNA to start with. Any contaminant DNA will also be amplified, and this can cause problems, for example in court cases.

Complementary DNA : Complementary DNA (cDNA) is DNA made from mRNA. This makes use of the enzyme reverse transcriptase, which does the reverse of transcription: it synthesises DNA from an RNA template. It is produced naturally by a group of viruses called the retroviruses (which include HIV), and it helps them to invade cells. In genetic engineering reverse transcriptase is used to make an artificial gene of cDNA as shown in this diagram 8.11.

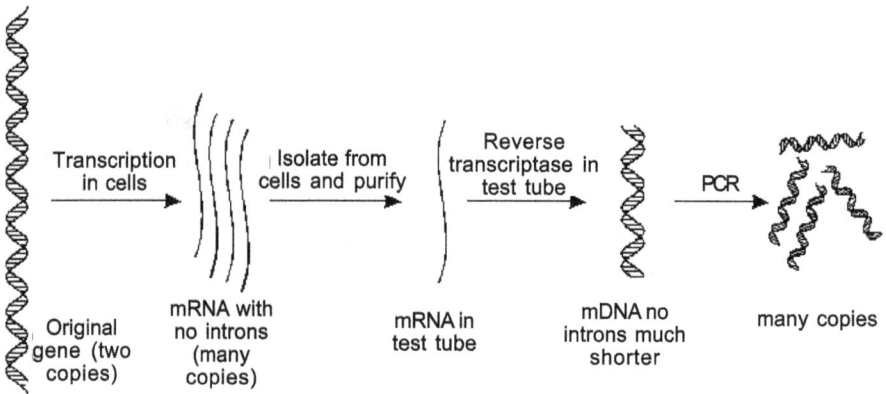

Fig. 8.11 cDNA formation.

Complementary DNA has helped to solve different problems in genetic engineering:

It makes genes much easier to find. There are some 70 000 genes in the human genome, and finding one gene out of this many is a very difficult (though not impossible) task. However a given cell only expresses a few genes, so only makes a few different kinds of mRNA molecule. For example the b cells of the pancreas make insulin, so make lots of mRNA molecules coding for insulin. This mRNA can be isolated from these cells and used to make cDNA of the insulin gene.

8.9 DNA Probes

These are used to identify and label DNA fragments that contain a specific sequence. A probe is simply a short length of DNA (20-100 nucleotides long) with a label attached. There are two common types of label used:

- A radioactively labelled probe (synthesized using the isotope ^{32}P) can be visualized using photographic film (an <u>auto radiograph</u>).

- A fluorescently labelled probe will emit visible light when illuminated with invisible ultraviolet light. Probes can be made to fluoresce with different colours.

Probes are always single-stranded, and can be made of DNA or RNA. If a probe is added to a mixture of different pieces of DNA (e.g. restriction fragments) it will anneal (base pair) with any lengths of DNA containing the complementary sequence. These fragments will now be labelled and will stand out from the rest of the DNA. DNA probes have many uses in genetic engineering:

- To identify restriction fragments containing a particular gene out of the thousands of restriction fragments formed from a genomic library. This use is described in shotguning below.

- To identify the short DNA sequences used in <u>DNA fingerprinting</u>.

- To identify genes from one species that are similar to those of another species. Most genes are remarkably similar in sequence from one species to another, so for example a gene probe for a mouse gene will probably anneal with the same gene from a human. This has aided the identification of human genes.

- To identify genetic defects. DNA probes have been prepared that match the sequences of many human genetic disease genes such as muscular dystrophy, and cystic fibrosis. Hundreds of these probes can be stuck to a glass slide in a grid pattern, forming a <u>DNA microarray</u> (or <u>DNA chip</u>). A sample of human DNA is added to the array and any sequences that match any of the various probes will stick to the array and be labelled. This allows rapid testing for a large number of genetic defects at a time.

Shotguning : This is used to find one particular gene in a whole genome, a bit like finding the proverbial needle in a haystack. It is called the shotgun technique because it starts by indiscriminately breaking up the genome (like firing a shotgun at a soft target) and then sorting through the debris for the particular gene we want. For this to work a gene probe for the gene is needed, which means at least a short part of the gene's sequence must be known.

Antisense Genes : These are used to turn off the expression of a gene in a cell. The principle is very simple: a copy of the gene to be switch off is inserted into the host genome the "wrong" way round, so that the complementary (or antisense) strand is transcribed. The antisense mRNA produced will anneal to the normal sense mRNA forming double-stranded RNA. Ribosomes can't bind to this, so the mRNA is not translated, and the gene is effectively "switched off".

8.10 Electrophorises

This is a form of chromatography used to separate different pieces of DNA on the basis of their length. It might typically be used to separate restriction fragments. The DNA samples are placed into wells at one end of a thin slab of gel (usually made of <u>agarose</u>) and covered in a buffer solution. An electric current is passed through the gel. Each nucleotide in a molecule of DNA contains a negatively charged phosphate group, so DNA is attracted to the anode (the positive electrode). The molecules have to diffuse through the gel, and smaller lengths of DNA move faster than larger lengths, which are retarded by the gel. So the smaller the length of the DNA molecule, the further down the gel it will move in a given time. At the end of the run the current is turned off. (See Fig. 8.12).

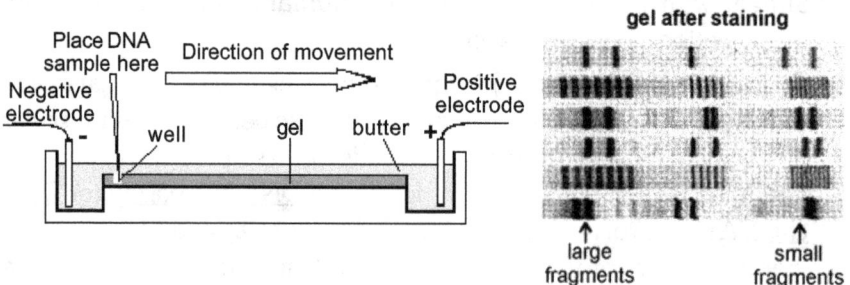

Fig. 8.12 Electrophorises

Unfortunately the DNA on the gel cannot be seen, so it must be visualized. There are three common methods for doing this:

- The gel can be stained with a chemical that specifically stains DNA, such as ethidium bromide. The DNA shows up as blue bands.

- The DNA samples at the beginning can be radiolabelled with a radioactive isotope such as ^{32}P. Photographic film is placed on top of the finished gel in the dark, and the DNA shows up as dark bands on the film. This method is extremely sensitive. The DNA fragments at the beginning can be labelled with a fluorescent molecule. The DNA fragments show up as colored lights when the finished gel is illuminated with invisible UV light. As shown in Fig. 8.13.

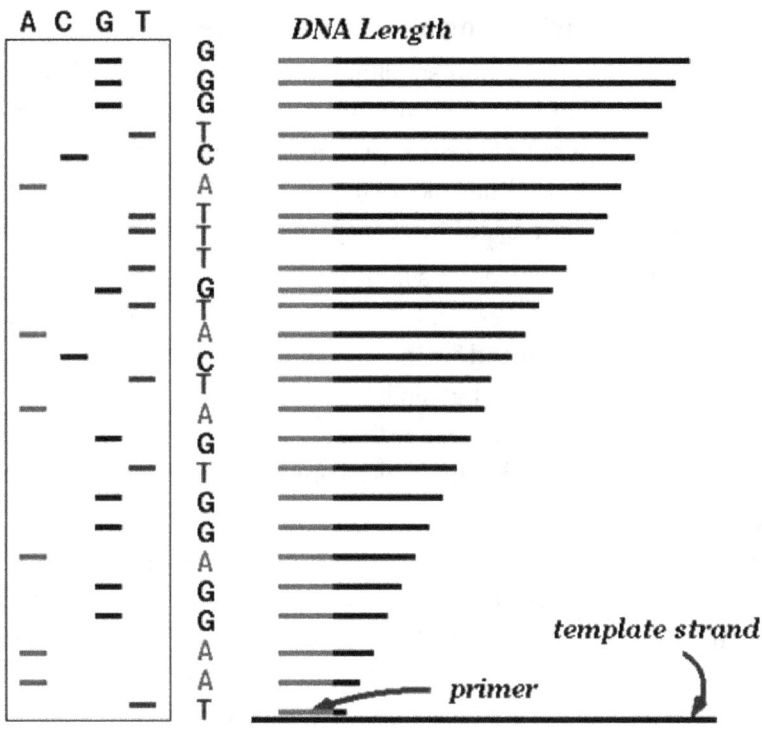

Fig. 8.13 Showing flouscent labelled / radio labelled DNA bands.

8.11 DNA Sequencing

This means reading the base sequence of a length of DNA. Once this is known the amino acid sequence of the protein that the DNA codes for can also be determined, using the genetic code table. The sequence can also be compared with DNA sequences from other individuals and even other species to work out relationships.

DNA sequencing is based on a beautifully elegant technique developed by Fred Sanger method.

- Label 4 test tubes labelled A, T, C and G. Into each test tube add: a sample of the DNA to be sequenced (containing many milli radioactive primer (so the DNA can be visualized later on the gel), the four DNA nucleotides and the enzyme DNA polymerase.

- In each test tube add a small amount of a special modified <u>dideoxy</u> nucleotide that cannot form a bond and so stops further synthesis of DNA. Tube A has dideoxy A (A*), tube T has dideoxy T (T*), dideoxy C (C*) and tube G has dideoxy G (G*). The dideoxy nucleotides are present at about 1% of the concentration of the normal nucleotides.

- Let the DNA polymerase synthesise many copies of the DNA sample. From time to time at random a dideoxy nucleotide will be added to the growing chain and synthesis of that chain will then stop. A range of DNA molecules will be synthesized ranging from full length to very short. The important point is that in tube A, all the fragments will stop at an A nucleotide. In tube T, all the fragments will stop at a T nucleotide, and so on.

- The contents of the four tubes are now run side by side on an electrophoresis gel, and the DNA bands are visualized by autoradiography. Since the fragments are now sorted by length the sequence can simply be read off the gel starting with the smallest fragment (just one nucleotide) at the bottom and reading upwards. See Fig. 8.14.

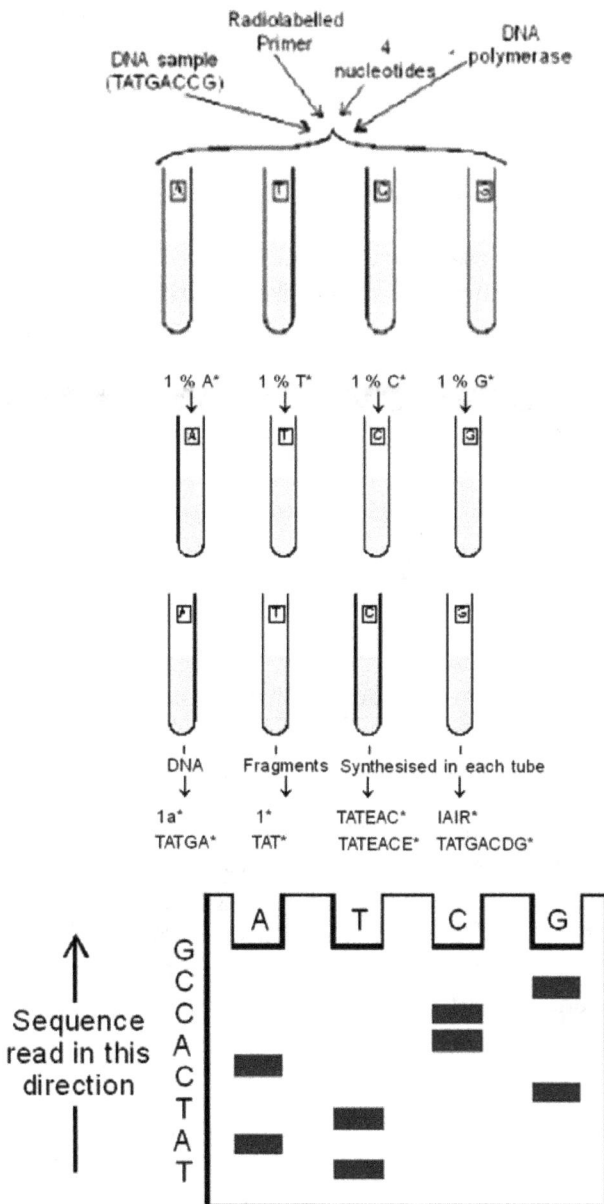

Fig. 8.14 DNA sequencing in a notshell.

There is now a modified version of the Sanger method called <u>cycle sequencing</u>, which can be completely automated. The primers are not radiolabelled, but instead the four-dideoxy nucleotides are fluorescently labelled, each with a different colour (A* is green, T* is red, C* is blue and G* is yellow). The polymerisation reaction is done in a single tube, using PCR-like cycles to speed up the process. The resulting mixture is separated using <u>capillary electrophoresis,</u> which gives good separation in a single narrow gel. The gel is read by a laser beam and the sequence of colours is converted to a DNA sequence by computer program (like the screenshot below Fig. 8.15). This technique can sequence an amazing 12 000 bases per minute.

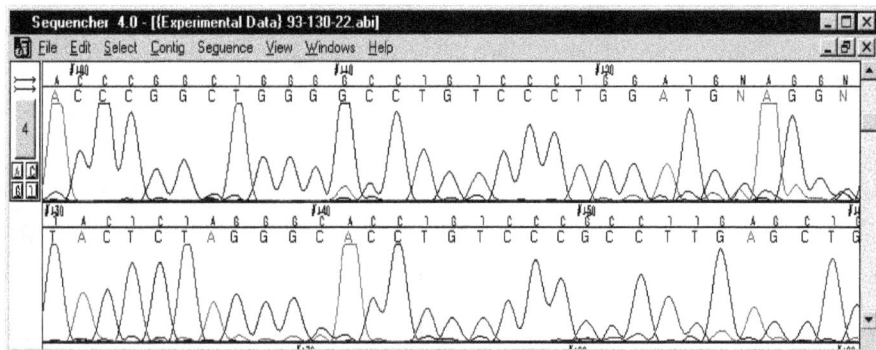

Fig. 8.15 Screen shot

Thousands of genes have been sequenced using these methods and the entire genomes of several organisms have also been sequenced. A huge project is underway to sequence the <u>human genome</u>, and it delivered a draft sequence in June 2000. The complete 3 billion base sequences should be complete by 2004. This information will give us unprecedented knowledge about ourselves, and is likely to lead to dramatic medical and scientific advances.

8.12 DNA Sequencing Problem

The goal is to find the complete sequence of nucleotides (i.e. A, C, T, G) in a given sample of DNA. Unfortunately, a machine that can receive a long DNA sample as input and output its complete sequence does not currently exist. Current DNA sequencing technology can only directly sequence approximately 500 nucleotides at a time. (Fig. 8.16).

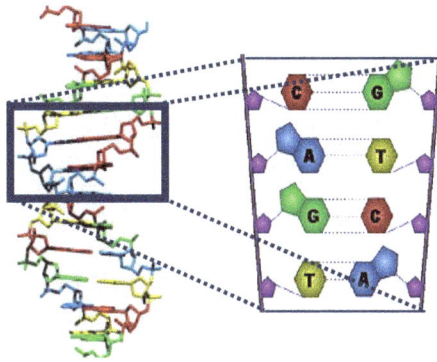

Fig. 8.16 DNA Structure

8.13 Similarity of the Human Genome

- In undertaking the monumental task of sequencing the entire human genome, deciding which particular individual's genome to sequence seems important. Although Craig Venter was the subject of Celera's sequencing effort, the actual genomic variation between individual humans is negligibly minimal. One-hypothesis suspects that *Homo sapiens* arose in Africa where a small population interbred, reducing overall genetic variation. Dispersal from Africa of an even smaller subset of this population approximately 100,000 years ago across the rest of the world, further reducing genetic variation. Can be Seen in Fig. 8.17.

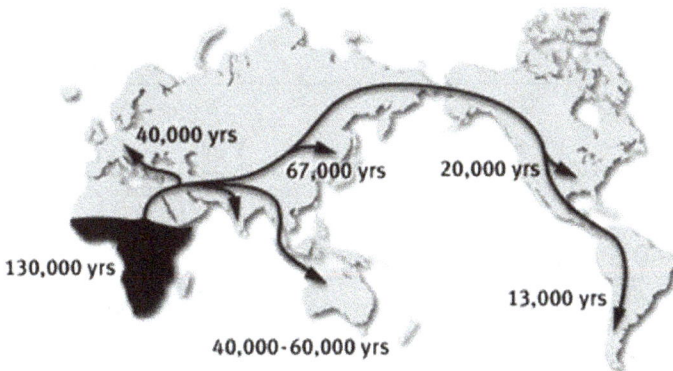

Fig. 8.17 Process of reducing genetic variation.

- *Polymorphism rate* is defined as the number of nucleotide base changes between two different members of species. This occurs at an average rate of 1 in 1,000 bases in humans; therefore, the nucleotide sequences of any two humans are roughly 99.9% identical. The polymorphism rate may be substantially higher in other species. Additionally, bases possessing the highest polymorphism rates are typically least important, often falling in non-functional DNA where mutations in the nucleotide sequence have least impact on the organism's survival. Thus, similarity is preserved.

8.14   Tools of DNA Sequencing

- ***Vectors :*** small circular pieces of DNA.

  o Using restriction digest enzymes, the sample DNA is cleaved into shorter ($\sim 10^3$ bases) fragments. These restriction enzymes only cleave at specific recognition sequences in the DNA. The vector is then cleaved using the same restriction enzymes, allowing the DNA fragments (inserts) to incorporate into the vector. See Fig. 8.18.

Vectors and their respective sizes

Vector	Size of Insert Kb
Plasmid	2,000-10,000 (Can control size)
Cosmid	40,000
BAC (Bacterial Artificial Chromosome)	70,000-300,000
YAC (Yeast Artificial Chromosome)	> 300,000 (Not used much recently)

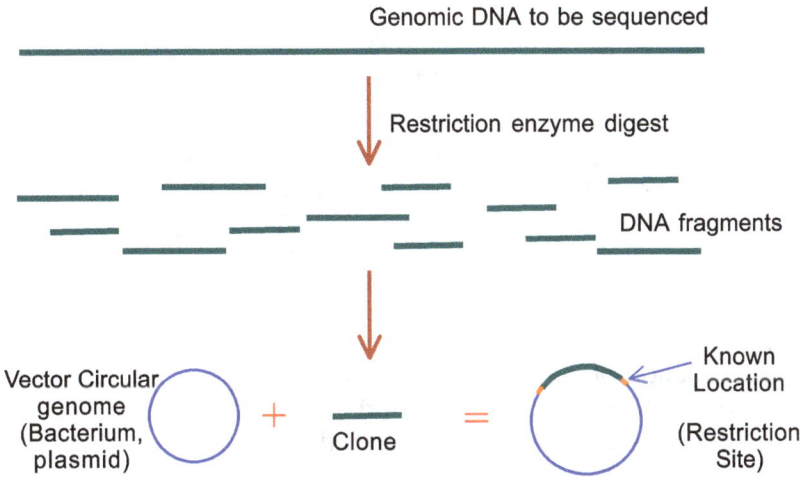

Fig. 8.18 Representing recombinant DNA technology.

8.15 Gel Electrophoresis

Separation of DNA fragments by electric field induced migration through a gel matrix, which causes longer fragments to move more slowly than shorter fragments.

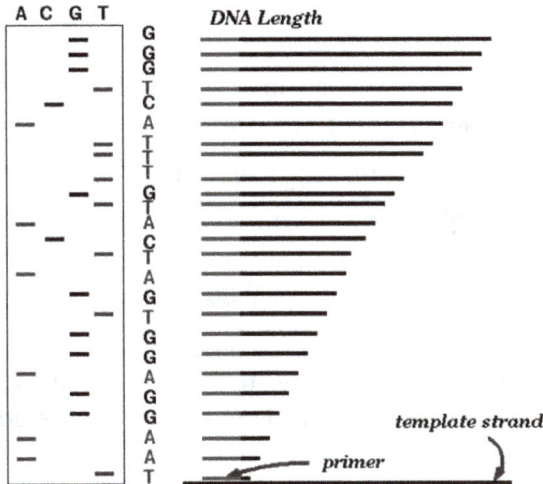

Fig. 8.19 Showing flouscent labelled / radio labelled DNA bands (Gel Electrophoresis).

o The vectors are now mixed with primers in solution. These primers will recognize the restriction sites marking the beginning and end points of the incorporated sample fragment and initiate synthesis of new DNA strands at those points.

o During this synthesis reaction, one species (either A, C, T, or G) of fluorescent dideoxynucleoside is added to the reaction mixture of regular nucleosides. Anytime a modified nucleoside is added to a growing DNA strand, extension of that strand will halt. This stops the synthesis reaction at all possible points.

o The reaction products are then separated by gel electrophoresis. The resolution of gel electrophoresis decreases with increasing length of the DNA strands. This is the primary factor that limits the length of DNA that can be directly sequenced.

• *Electropherogram :* output of gel electrophoresis that orders fragments by length and distinguishes among terminating nucleotides of each fragment.

    o **PHRED** (**PH**il's **R**ead **ED**itor by Phil Green): popular dynamic programming method used to read the sequence from an electropherogram following filtering, smoothing, and correction for length compressions.

    o *Read :* A read is a 500-700 nucleotide sequence from the leftmost or rightmost ends of an insert that is output by PHRED. Each nucleotide is accompanied by a quality score defined as

$$-10 \times \log_{10} \text{Prob(Error)}$$

The quality score corresponds to the probability that a given nucleotide is correctly reported. A quality score of 40 corresponds to an error probability of 0.001, which is considered the gold standard.

    o *Double-barreled Sequencing :* Sequencing from both the leftmost and rightmost ends of a clone; this is done because it is impossible to tell whether the forward or backward strand is being sequenced.

8.16 Shotgun Sequencing

- The method most commonly used for genomic DNA sequencing is called *Shotgun*. The sample DNA is first randomly cleaved multiple times into several thousand base pair segments. Each segment provides one or two reads or approximately 500 base pairs from the leftmost and rightmost ends. Enough reads are obtained to cover the region to be sequenced with seven to ten-fold redundancy to ensure complete tiling. Coverage C is defined as

$$C = \frac{n \cdot l}{L}$$

L = length of genomic segment

n = number of reads

l = length of each read.

Assuming a uniform distribution of reads, the Lander-Waterman model predicts coverage of 10 to result in 1 gapped region per 10^6 nucleotides. Overlaps among the reads are detected and extended to reconstruct the original genomic sequence as shown in Fig. 8.20.

Genomic segment

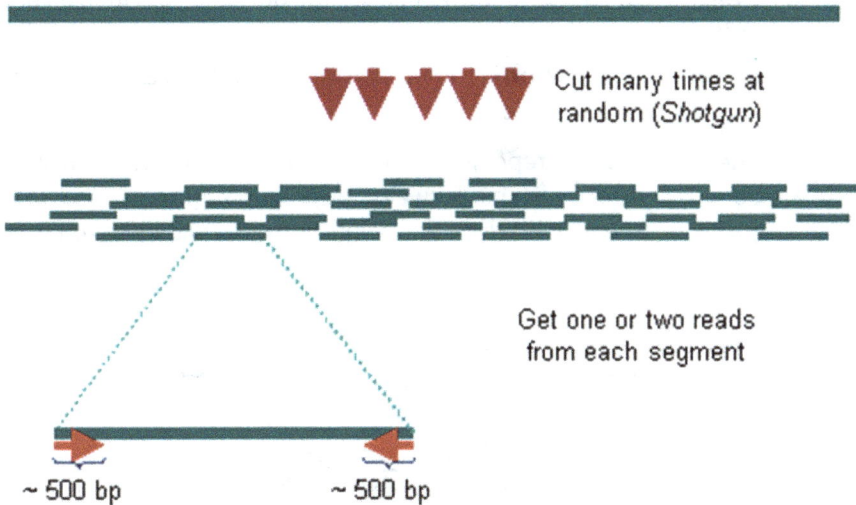

Cut many times at random (*Shotgun*)

Get one or two reads from each segment

~ 500 bp   ~ 500 bp

Fig. 8.20 Shotgun sequencing.

- Sequencing errors typically occur in 1-2% of all bases.
- Repeated genomic sequences account for approximately 5% of bacterial and 50% of mammalian genomes. Many of these repeated sequences are considered selfish DNA, which have no functional purpose but have evolved to replicate themselves within the genome. Repeat types include:

  o *Low-Complexity DNA* : simple repeated nucleotide sequences (e.g. ATATATATATACATA...).

  o *Microsatellite Repeats* : repeated short motifs of the form $(a_1...a_k)^N$ where k ~ 3-6 (e.g. CAGCAGTAGCAGCACCAG).

  o *Transposons* :

    - **SINE** (**S**hort **I**nterspersed **N**uclear **E**lements): most common repeat type; roughly 300 base pairs long with approximately 10^6 copies in the genome (e.g. ALU).

    - **LINE** (**L**ong **I**nterspersed **N**uclear **E**lements): roughly 500-5,000 base pairs long with approximately 200,000 copies in the genome.

    - **LTR Retroposons** (**L**ong **T**erminal **R**epeats): approximately 700 base pairs at each end of the genome.

  o *Gene Families* : genomic sequences that duplicate and then diverge to become *paralogs*.

  o *Recent Duplications* : approximately 100,000 base pairs long with very similar copies.

  The existence of repeats creates the problem of distinguishing between true overlaps between adjacent segments and false overlaps generated by clone endpoints occurring within two different copies of a repeated sequence. See Fig. 8.21.

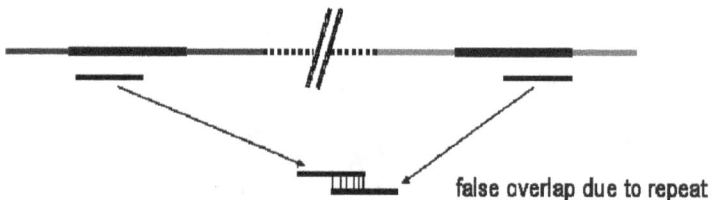

Fig. 8.21 Representing overlapping.

8.17 Sequencing Strategies

(i) **Hierarchical Sequencing :** A large collection (coverage of 10-20) of roughly 100,000 base pair BAC clones is obtained. These clones are physically mapped relative to each other onto the genome. The map is used to select a minimum tiling path of clones to be sequenced. Each clone in the path is sequenced by shotgun and reassembled. The clone sequences are then assembled into the complete genome. This strategy fundamentally assumes that 100,000 base pair segments will contain fewer repeats than the complete genome. (See Fig. 8.22).

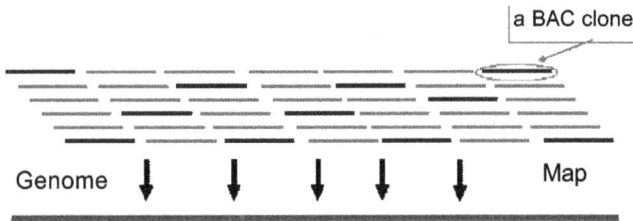

Fig. 8.22

Physical mapping can be accomplished by *hybridization* or *digestion*.

o Hybridization utilizes many DNA probes $(p_1, p_2, ..., p_n)$ each consisting of short words that attach to complementary sequences in the set of clones. Each clone C_i is treated with all probes, and all attachments (C_j, p_i) are recorded. If the same probes attach to clones X and Y, it can be assumed that these clones overlap.

- Overlap between clones can be determined using a matrix of m probes by n clones. Cell (i, j) equals 1 if p_i hybridizes to C_j and 0 otherwise. The probes of the filled matrix are then reordered to put the matrix in consecutive-ones form where all 1's are consecutive in each row and column. This can be solved with time complexity $O(m^3)$ where m > n.

The ordering and overlap of the clones can be easily deduced from the consecutive-ones matrix as shown in Fig. 8.23.

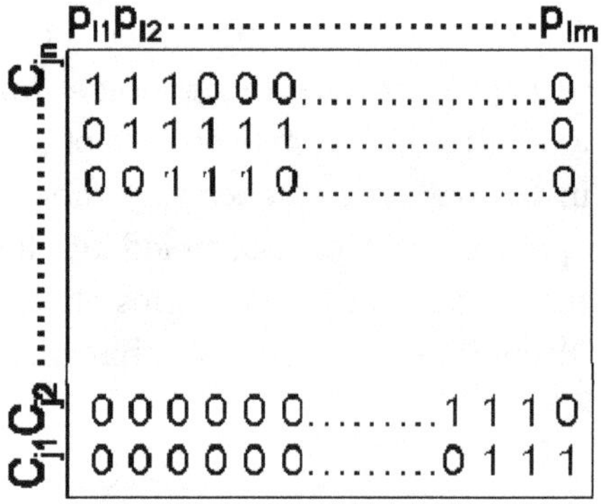

Fig. 8.23 Matrix of m probes by n clones.

- An additional computational problem results from the possibility of a probe hybridizing in multiple places in the genome, generating a false overlap. Incomplete tiling by the clones may also introduce gaps in the reordered matrix. Thus, the parsimonious sequence of probes implying minimal probe repetition must be found. Or in other words, find the shortest string of probes such that each clone appears as a sub string. This problem is APX-hard; solutions are typically greedy, probabilistic, and require significant manual curation.

  o Digestion uses restriction enzymes to cut each clone where specific words appear. After each clone has been cut separately with an enzyme, the fragments are run on a gel to measure their lengths. Clones C_a and C_b that produce a set of fragments of identical lengths $\{l_i, l_j, l_k\}$ following enzymatic digestion can be assumed to overlap.

- ***Double Digestion :*** The process can be repeated digesting with enzymes A and B individually and then with both enzymes simultaneously.

(ii) **The Walking Method**: This method sequences the genome clone-by-clone without following an initial physical map. First, a very redundant library of BAC clones with sequenced clone-ends is built. Several "seed" clones are randomly selected from this library and sequenced. Sequencing continues by "walking" off the seeds using clone-ends to choose library clones that extend left and right. Optimally, clones having the least overlap should be selected to sequence in each ensuing step. If a selected clone turns out to be a false overlap, it can be used as a new seed instead. See Fig. 8.24.

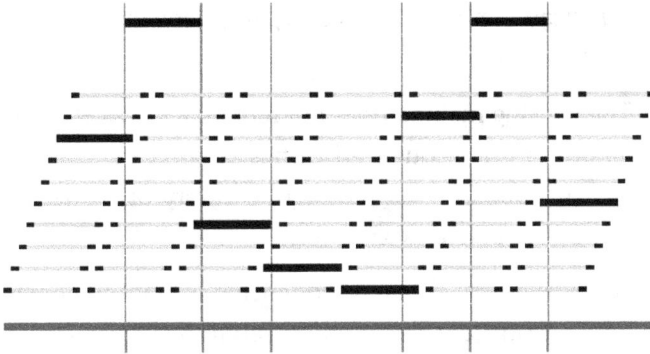

Fig. 8.24 Walking method.

o Although walking off a single seed would minimize redundant sequencing, it would be very impractical, requiring almost 15,000 walking steps. By walking off several seeds in parallel, a genome can be sequenced in approximately 5 walking steps with less than 20% redundancy.

o Most inefficiency results from redundant sequencing in which a small gap is closed using a much larger clone. This inefficiency can be minimized by integrating the use of a second library of shorter clones. See Fig. 8.25.

Efficient   Inefficient

Fig. 8.25 Shorter clones.

(iii) *Advantages & Disadvantages*

- o Hierarchical sequencing provides the advantage of ease of assembly. But building the required library and initial physical map is time-consuming. Additionally, the minimum tiling path may demand significantly redundant sequencing depending on the distribution of clones in the genome.

- o The walking method does not require a physical map. Building the library of end-sequenced clones is relatively cheap. The process can be optimized using a second library of shorter clones to close small gaps in later walking steps.

- o Whole genome shotgun sequencing will not be discussed until the next lecture, but this method requires no physical mapping and results in very little redundant sequencing. However, assembly is challenging due to the difficulty in resolving repeats.

8.18 Applications of Genetic Engineering

We have now looked at some of the many techniques used by genetic engineers. What can be done with these techniques ? By far the most numerous applications are still as research tools, and the techniques above are helping geneticists to understand complex genetic systems. Despite all the hype, genetic engineering still has very few successful commercial applications, although these are increasing each year. The applications so far can usefully be considered in three groups.

- *Gene Products :* Using genetically modified organisms (usually microbes) to produce chemicals, usually for medical or industrial applications.

- *New phenotypes :* using gene technology to alter the characteristics of organisms (usually farm animals or crops).

- *Gene therapy :* Using gene technology on humans to treat a disease.

8.19 Gene Products

The biggest and most successful kind of genetic engineering is the production of gene products. These products are of medical, agricultural or commercial value. This table shows a few of the examples of genetically engineered products that are already available.

PRODUCT	USE	HOST ORGANISM
Insulin	human hormone used to treat diabetes	bacteria /yeast
Factor VIII	human blood clotting factor use to treat hemophiliacs	bacteria
AAT	enzyme used to treat cystic fibrosis and emphysema	sheep
Rennin	enzyme used in manufacture of cheese	bacteria /yeast

The products are mostly proteins, which are produced directly when a gene is expressed, but they can also be non-protein products produced by genetically engineered enzymes. The basic idea is to transfer a gene (often human) to another host organism (usually a microbe) so that it will make the gene product quickly, cheaply and ethically. It is also possible to make "designer proteins" by altering gene sequences, but while this is a useful research tool, there are no commercial applications yet.

Since the end product is just a chemical, in principle any kind of organism could be used to produce it. By far the most common group of host organisms used to make gene products are the bacteria, since they can be grown quickly and the product can be purified from their cells. Unfortunately bacteria cannot always make human proteins, and recently animals and even plants have also been used to make gene products. In neither case it is appropriate to extract the product from their cells, so in animals the product must be secreted in milk or urine, while in plants the product must be secreted from the roots. This following page shows some of the advantages and disadvantages of using different organisms for the production of genetically engineered gene products.

Prokaryotes (i.e. Bacteria)

Advantages : no nucleus so DNA easy to modify; have plasmids; small genome; genetics well understood; asexual so can be cloned; small and fast growing; easy to grow commercially in fermenters; will use cheap carbohydrate;

Disadvantages : few ethical problems. Can't splice introns; no post-translational modification; small gene size.

Eukaryotes

Advantages : Can do post-translational modifications; can accept large genes

Disadvantages : Do not have plasmids (except yeast); often diploid so two copies of genes may need to be inserted; control of expression not well understood

Fungi (yeast, mould)

Advantages : Asexual so can be cloned; haploid, so only one copy needed; can be grown in vats.

Disadvantages : can't always make animals gene products

Plants

Advantages : photosynthetic so don't need much feeding; can be cloned from single cells; products can be secreted from roots or in sap.

Disadvantages : cell walls difficult to penetrate by vector; slow growing; must be grown in fields; multicellular.

Animals (pharming)

Advantages : most likely to be able to make human proteins; products can be secreted in milk or urine.

Disadvantages : multicellular; slow growing.

We'll look at some examples in detail :

Insulin is a small protein hormone produced by the pancreas to regulate the blood sugar concentration. In the disease insulin-dependent diabetes the pancreas cells don't produce enough insulin, causing wasting symptoms and eventually death. The disease can be successfully treated by injection of insulin extracted from the pancreases of slaughtered cows and pigs. However the insulin from these species has a slightly different amino acid sequence from human insulin and this can lead to immune rejection and side effects.

The human insulin gene was isolated, cloned and sequenced in the 1970s, and so it became possible to insert this gene into bacteria, which could then produce human insulin in large amounts. Unfortunately it wasn't that simple. In humans, pancreatic cells first make pro-insulin, which then undergoes post-translational modification to make the final, functional insulin. Bacterial cells cannot do post-translational modification. Eventually a synthetic cDNA gene was made and inserted into the bacterium *E. coli*, which made pro-insulin, and the post-translational conversion to insulin was carried out chemically. This technique was developed by Eli Lilly and Company in 1982 and the product; "humulin" became the first genetically engineered product approved for medical use.

In the 1990s the procedure was improved by using the yeast *Saccharomyces cerevisiae* instead of *E. coli*. Yeast, as a eukaryote, is capable of post-translational modification, so this simplifies the production of human insulin. However another company has developed a method of converting pig insulin into human insulin by chemically changing a few amino acids, and this turns out to be cheaper than the genetic engineering methods. This all goes to show that genetic engineers still have a lot to learn.

(i) ***Bovine Somatotrophin (BST)*** : This is a growth hormone produced by cattle. The gene has been cloned in bacteria by the company Monsanto, who can produce large quantities of BST. In the USA cattle are often injected with BST every 2 weeks, resulting in a 10% increase in mass in beef cattle and a 25% increase in milk production in dairy cows. BST was tested in the UK in 1985, but it was not approved and its use is currently banned in the EU. This is partly due to public concerns and partly because there is already overproduction of milk and beef in the EU, so greater production is not necessary.

Renin : Renin is an enzyme used in the production of cheese. It is produced in the stomach of juvenile mammals (including humans) and it helps the digestion of the milk protein casein by solidifying it so that is remains longer in the stomach. The cheese industry used to obtain its rennin from the stomach of young calves when they were slaughtered for veal, but there are moral and practical objections to this source. Now an artificial cDNA gene for rennin has been made from mRNA extracted from calf stomach cells, and this gene has been inserted into a variety of microbes. The rennin extracted from these microbes has been very successful and 90% of all hard cheeses in the UK are made using microbial rennin. Sometimes (though not always) these products are labelled as "vegetarian cheese".

(ii) *AAT (alpha-1-antitrypsin) :* AAT is a human protein made in the liver and found in the blood. As the name suggests it is an inhibitor of protease enzymes like trypsin and elastase. There is a rare mutation of the AAT gene (a single base substitution) that causes AAT to be inactive, and so the protease enzymes to be uninhibited. The most noticeable effect of this in the lungs, where elastase digests the elastic tissue of the alveoli, leading to the lung disease emphysema. This condition can be treated by inhaling an aerosol spray containing AAT so that it reaches the alveoli and inhibits the elastase there. AAT for this treatment can be extracted from blood donations, but only in very small amounts. The gene for AAT has been found and cloned, but AAT cannot be produced in bacteria because AAT is a glycoprotein, which means it needs to have sugars added by post-translational modification. This kind of modification can only be carried out by animals (because they have a golgi body), and AAT is now produced by genetically modified sheep. In order to make the AAT easy to extract, the gene was coupled to a promoter for the milk protein b-lactoglubulin. Since this promoter is only activated in mammary gland cells, the AAT gene will only be expressed in mammary gland cells, and so will be secreted into the sheep's milk. This makes it very easy to harvest and purify without harming the sheep. The first transgenic sheep to produce AAT was called Tracy, and she was produced in Edinburgh in 1993. This is how Tracy was made :

A female sheep is given a fertility drug to stimulate her egg production, and several mature eggs are collected from her ovaries. (See Fig. 8.26).

The eggs are fertilized *in vitro*.

A plasmid is prepared containing the gene for human AAT and the promoter sequence for b-lactoglobulin. Hundreds of copies of this plasmid are microinjected into the nucleus of the fertilized zygotes. Only a few of the zygotes will be transformed, but at this stage you can't tell which.

The zygotes divide *in vitro* until the embryos are at the 16-cell stage.

The 16-cell embryos are implanted into the uterus of surrogate mother ewes. Only a few implantations result in a successful pregnancy.

Test all the offspring from the surrogate mothers for AAT production in their milk. This is the only way to find if the zygote took up the AAT gene so that it can be expressed. About 1 in 20 eggs are successful.

Collect milk from the transgenic sheep for the rest of their lives. Their milk contains about 35 g of AAT per litre of milk. Also breed from them in order to build up a herd of transgenic sheep.

Purify the AAT, which is worth about Rs. 4,00,000 per gm.

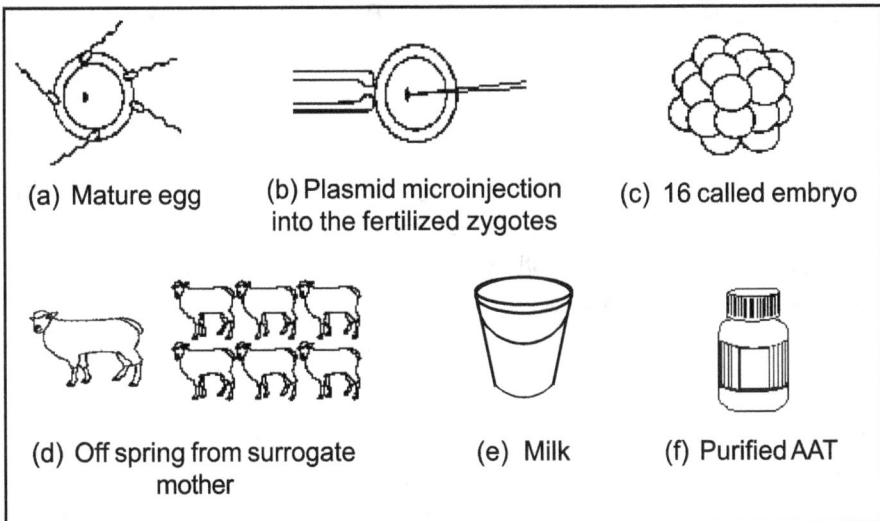

(a) Mature egg   (b) Plasmid microinjection into the fertilized zygotes   (c) 16 called embryo

(d) Off spring from surrogate mother   (e) Milk   (f) Purified AAT

Fig. 8.26 Squence involved in production of AAT.

8.20 New Phenotypes

This means altering the characteristics of organisms by genetic engineering. The organisms are usually commercially important crops or farm animals. It can be seen as a high-tech version of <u>selective breeding</u>, which has been used by humans to alter and improve their crops and animals for at least 10 000 years. Nevertheless GMOs have turned out to be a highly controversial development. We don't study any of these in detail, but the following description gives an idea of what is being done.

Long life tomatoes : There are two well-known projects, both affecting the gene for the enzyme (PG), which softens the fruits as they ripen. Tomatoes that make less PG ripen more slowly and retain more flavour. The American "Flavr Savr" tomato used antisense technology to silence the gene, while the British Zeneca tomato disrupted the gene. Both were successful and were on sale for a few years, but neither is produced any more.

Insect Resistant Crops : Genes for various powerful protein toxins have been transferred from the bacterium *Bacillus thuringiensis* to crop plants including maize, rice and potatoes. These <u>Bt toxins</u> are thousands of times more powerful than chemical insecticides, and since they are built-in to the crops, insecticide spraying (which is non-specific and damages the environment) is unnecessary.

Nitrogen Fixing Crops : This is a huge project, which aims to transfer the 15-or-so genes required for nitrogen fixation from the nitrogen-fixing bacteria *Rhizobium* into cereals and other crop plants. These crops would then be able to fix their own atmospheric nitrogen and would not need any fertiliser. However, the process is extremely complex, and the project is nowhere near success.

Tick Resistant Sheeps : The gene for the enzyme chitinase, which kills ticks by digesting their exoskeletons, has been transferred from plants to sheep. These sheep should be immune to tick parasites; this is perhaps the most significant, and most controversial kind of genetic engineering. It is also the least well developed. And may not need sheep dip.

Gene Therapy : The idea of gene therapy is to genetically alter humans in order to treat a disease. This could represent the first opportunity to cure incurable diseases. Note that this is quite different from using genetically engineered microbes to produce a drug, vaccine or hormone to treat a disease by conventional means. Gene therapy means altering the genotype of a tissue or even a whole human.

8.21 The Future of Gene Therapy

Gene therapy is in its infancy, and is still very much an area of research rather than application. No one has yet been cured by gene therapy, but the potential remains enticing. Gene therapy need not even be limited to treating genetic diseases, but could also help in treating infections and environmental diseases:

- White blood cells have been genetically modified to produce tumour necrosis factor (TNF), a protein that kills cancer cells, making these cells more effecting against tumours.

- Genes could be targeted directly at cancer cells, causing them to die, or to revert to normal cell division.

- White blood cells could be given antisense genes for HIV proteins, so that if the virus infected these cells it couldn't reproduce.

  It is important to appreciate the difference between <u>somatic cell therapy</u> and <u>germ-line therapy</u>.

- Somatic cell therapy means genetically altering specific body (or somatic) cells, such as bone marrow cells, pancreas cells, or whatever, in order to treat the disease. This therapy may treat or cure the disease, but any genetic changes will not be passed on their offspring.

Germ-line therapy means genetically altering those cells (sperm cells, sperm precursor cell, ova, ova precursor cells, zygotes or early embryos) that will pass their genes down the "germ-line" to future generations. Alterations to any of these cells will affect <u>every</u> cell in the resulting human, <u>and</u> in all his or her descendants.

Germ-line therapy would be highly effective, but is also potentially dangerous (since the long-term effects of genetic alterations are not known), unethical (since it could easily lead to eugenics) and immoral (since it could involve altering and destroying human embryos). It is currently illegal in the UK and most other countries, and current research is focussing on somatic cell therapy only. All gene therapy trials in the UK must be approved by the Gene Therapy Advisory Committee (GTAC), a government body that reviews the medical and ethical grounds for a trial. Germ-line modification is allowed with animals, and indeed is the basis for producing GMOs.

9
DNA Sequencing

9.1 Fragment and Map Assembly and Combinational Approaches to Sequencing

Determination of order of nucleotides in DNA molecule (this definition is not restricted to DNA, this is same for RNA and proteins also) is called as sequencing

The central dogma of molecular biology tells how genes encoded by DNA sequences are copied to mRNA, which are then translated into functional proteins. DNA sequence contains the instructions for everything a cell does, from the moment of conception until death. Knowing complete DNA sequence facilitates to understand the molecular components of the cell and their interactions.

The two important techniques for DNA sequencing are the enzymatic chain termination method (Sanger method) and the chemical degradation method (Maxam and Gilbert method). Both will generates a nested set of single stranded DNA fragment, which are separated by size on an acryl amide gel. As compared to Maxam Gilbert method, the Sanger chain termination method generates more easily interpreted raw data and has become the most widely used. An important step towards large-scale sequencing was the development of automated DNA sequencers.

The preferable approach for sequencing of large genomes is still under discussion. Obviously, directed strategies can only be considered if a physical map has been or will be constructed. The approach for many sequencing efforts on large eukaryotic genomes including S.cerevisiae and C. elegans has been construction of overlapping arrays of large insert clones, followed by complete sequencing of these clones one at a time, either by shotgun or directed strategies. Similar strategies have also been applied for smaller bacterial genomes like M.pneumoniae.

In these cases, genome sequencing has been initiated after the construction of a physical map. Shotgun sequencing of whole genomes was first applied at the institute of Genome Research (TIGR) then headed by Craig Venter. In 1995, the 1.83 Mb genome of Haemophilus influenzae was completely determined by assembly of 24,000 random sequence reads from plasmid with 1.62 ± 2.0 kb inserts followed by directed approaches on lambda clones and PCR products to fill the remaing gaps. The overall redundancy was 6.3 and the quality was estimated to 1 error in 5000 ± 10000 bases. Very similar emphasis was put into end sequencing of lambda clones with large inserts (16kb) in parallel to the Plasmid sequencing. By including these sequences in the assembly process the lambda clones were automatically ordered and thus, a physical map was obtained as a result of the assembly. Several other genomes of bacteria and archaea have been sequenced using the whole genome shotgun approach. Sequencing of the human genome has for many years awaited the experiences from the model organisms, but is now completed to the extent of draft sequence. This involved both clone-by-clone approach as well as short gun approach.

9.2 cDNA sequencing

The ultimate goal for sequencing of whole genome is to decode all the genetic information carried in the genome. However, there is a drastic variation in the amount of useful information between different organisms. Bacterial genome shotgun approaches also carry compact genetic information with upto 88% coding sequence (M.genetalium). In addition, the sequence is easily interpreted due to lack of intron. Sequencing of larger eukaryotic genomes is less rewarding. The coding sequence in the human genome only represents approximately 3% of the total DNA and for some plant genomes, the figure is even lower. Eukaryotic gene identification by whole genome sequencing is therefore slow and coding regions are difficult to predict due to the introns. A more efficient method for gene identification in eukaryotic genomes is sequencing of ESTs. ESTs are partial sequences of cDNA, reversibly transcribed from mRNA, and represent a direct supply of coding intron free sequences of genes. Even if techniques for enrichment of full-length clones have been adapted, many transcripts lack sequence in the 5-prime end due to internal priming or due to internal restriction sites. To specifically determine missing 5-prime or 3-prime sequences, a variety of methods based on the polymerase chain reaction have been developed. Rapid amplification of cDNA ends (RACE) was first described closely followed by the very similar anchored PCR (A-PCR) technique. To find missing 3-prime ends the first strand synthesis is performed with an oligo (dT) tail and a gene specific primer, designed from the partial cDNA sequence selected (i.e., ESTs or fragments selected by differential approaches). For isolation of the 5-prime end PCR can be performed with the specific primer and a primer annealing to the new primer site. Originally the new primer site was introduced by homopolymer tailing using terminal transferase, but greater success have been obtained by using anchor oligonucleotides and T4 RNA LIGASE. Biotin capture of the gene-specific first strand fragments has also been used.

The throughput in full-length sequencing does not match the speed for which new gene candidates are produced by EST efforts or differential expression techniques. Yet full length and high quality sequences can potentially provide more accurate database comparisons as well as enhance the ability for different computer programs to predict gene function and structure. Each selected clone is usually sequenced by primer walking, which is a well established but slow technique. As an alternative concatenation cDNA sequencing (CCS) has been suggested.

9.3 Assembly

Sequence assembly is a process that involves comparison of sequences, finding overlapping fragment pairs, merging as many fragments as possible and creating a consensus sequence from the merged fragments. Accurate assembly algorithms are essential for reconstruction of the original DNA sequence (cosmid, BAC, prokaryotic genome, cDNA clone) in shotgun sequencing and for grouping of ESTs in expression profiling. The challenges for assembly programs are to allow potential sequence ambiguities and still discriminate between repetitive regions, members of gene families or genes sharing the same motif. There are several assembly algorithms available, including auto assembler (ABI), sequencer, GAP 4 and the TIGR assembler.

A commonly used program for cosmid scale assembly is GAP 4, which is one of several programs in the Staden package. It has a highly interactive graphical interface with several tools for manipulation and display of data. The phrap assembly program has been successfully used to assemble larger DNA fragments. It works specially well in concert with phred, which is an improved lane tracking and base calling software, and consead, which is the graphical interface. The TIGR assembler was developed to manage a whole genome shotgun assembly, i.e., to assemble genomes of 0.5 ± 4 Mb. Such large assemblies means a dramatic increase in the number of pair wise comparisons required, an increased likelihood to encounter repetitive regions and a higher probability to obtain false overlaps due to chimeric clones. The TIGR assembler algorithm has been used for assembly of several prokaryotic genomes as well as for grouping of ESTs for gene indexing purposes. Assembly algorithms are applied on ESTs sequences to generate clusters of sequences deriving from the same transcript. It is a way to reduce the large quantity of EST data to a number of groups with overlapping sequences representing unique genes. Among the efforts to form such gene indexes can be mentioned,

Unigene, TIGRs, human gene index (HGI) and Gene Express. The strategies for grouping of the sequences differ in stringency. The TIGR Assembler used HGI, has a stringent gene-matching criterion, which prevents chimerism. On the other hand, the strictness results in a more fragmented representation, which disallows divergent ESTs, that represents alternative form of the same gene to fold into the same index class. Splice variants are only accepted if they match fully sequenced genes with known isoform in the expressed gene anatomy database (EGAD), which is a database with well-characterized human genes. Unigene and gene express represent looser gene indices. Sequences are grouped into common classes if they share overlap over a certain threshold, using BLAST, FASTA and Smith-Waterman methods for comparisons. A single index class can then contain several splice forms of the same gene but chimeras and other artifacts may be incorrectly included. There are several aspects that challenge a successful assembly. First, the error frequency in sequence raw data, which depends on experimental aspects like template, sequencing enzyme, sequencing chemistry and instrumentation, but also on aspects, like tracking and base calling software. A general estimate for the quality of raw data can be obtained from EST sequences, which represents poorly edited, single-pass sequence reads. The over all accuracy for ESTs is usually about 97%. The error types include additions, deletions and substitutions of bases and are usually more abundant in the end of sequence. Other problems that occur are chimeric clones and lane tracking errors and for EST assembly, splice variants, clone reversals and internal priming errors. In the assembly of ESTs genes belonging to the same gene family can be hard to distinguish. This is especially difficult in plants where as many as 20%(Arabidiopsis) of the genes belong to gene families. The higher sequence diversity in the 3-prime UTR of the transcripts is best used to distinguish between gene family members. Assembly of genomic clones however meets problems in repetitive regions. This is especially difficult for organisms with very high GC content like Deinococcus radiodurans (68% GC) or high AT content like Plasmodium Falciparum (82% AT). A correct assembly over long repetitive regions has to be performed with careful respect to the physical map or PCR fragments spanning the regions.

9.4 Genome Sequence Assembly Using Trace Signals and Additional Sequence Information

(i) *Introduction*

Today large-scale genome sequencing efforts produce enormous quantities of data each day. They are now nearly all based on the chain termination dideoxy method published by Sanger et al. (1977) in one way or another. But the gel or capillary electrophoresis used can determine only about a maximum of 1000 to 1500 bases. The high quality stretch with low error probabilities for the called bases often being around the first 400 to 500 bases. Current sequencing strategies for a contiguous DNA sequence (contig) ranging anywhere between 20 kilo bases (kb) and 200 kb. These will therefore basically boil down to fragment the given contig in hundreds or thousands of overlapping sub clones. [Durbin and Dear, 1998], analyze these by electrophoresis and subsequently assemble the subclones back together in one contig.

They extensively studied reconstruction of the unknown, correct contiguous DNA sequence by inferring it through the help of a number of representations, (also called fragments, see Myers (1995). It is called the assembly problem. The devil is in the details, however. If the collected readings (reads) were 100% error free, then a multiplicity of problems would not occur. In reality, the extraction of data by gel electrophoresis is a physical process in which errors due to chemical artifacts like compressions show up quite often. Ewing et al. (1998); Ewing and Green (1998) showed that together with errors occurring in the subsequent signal analysis current laboratory technologies total an error rate that might be anywhere between 0.1% for good parts in the middle of a read and more than 10% in bad parts of a read at the very beginning and at the end. This error rate, combined sometimes with exacerbating fact that DNA tends to contain highly repetitive stretches with only very few bases differing across different repeat locations, impedes the assembly process in an awesome way.

The above mentioned error rates and repetitive properties of DNA lead to the necessity of using fault tolerant and alternatives seeking algorithms. Wang and Jiang (1994) showed that the assembly problem even using error free representations (fragments) of the true sequence is incomplete. This means that the volume of data can only be assembled by approximating strategies, relying on algorithms that are well behaved in time and space complexity.

(ii) Assembly strategies

Referring to Dear et al. (1998), a "sequence assembly is essentially a set of contigs, each contig being a multiple alignment of reads". A number of different strategies have been proposed to tackle the problem, ranging from simple greedy pair wise alignments sometimes using additional information [Peltola et al., 1984], sometimes using a whole set of refinements [Huang, 1996] to weak AI methods like genetic algorithms [Parsons et al., 1993; Notredame and Higgins, 1996; Zhang and Wong, 1997].

There are nowadays mainly two different existing approaches for assembling sequences: (i) the iterative and (ii) the 'all in one step' approach. The first type of assembly is essentially derived from the fact that the data analysis and reconstruction approximation algorithms can be parameterized differently, ranging from very strict assembly of only the highest quality parts to very 'bold' assembly of even lowest quality stretches. An assembly starts with strictest parameters, having the output edited manually (by highly trained personnel) or by soft ware and then the process is reiterated with less strict parameters until the assembly is finished or the parameters become too lax. The second approach has been made popular by the PHRAP assembler presented by Phil Green (http://www.phrap.org/). This assembler uses low and high quality sequence data from the start and generates a consensus by puzzling its way through an assembly using the highest quality parts as reference, giving the result to a human editor for finishing.

A common characteristic to all existing assemblers is that they rely on the quality values with which the bases have been attributed by a base caller. Within this process, an error probability is computed by the base caller to express the confidence with which the called base is thought to be the true base. The positive aspect is the possibility for assemblers to decide in favour of the best, most probable bases when a discrepancy occurs. The negative aspect of current base callers is their inability to write confidence values for optional, uncalled bases at the same place. This could improve the search for alternative assemblies substantially.

Researchers therefore implemented a third type of assembler, trying to combine and substantially extend the strengths of both approaches mentioned above and copying assembly analysis strategies done by human experts. An important criterion in the design of their assembler is the quality aspect of the final result: the assembler works only with the stretches of DNA sequences marked as 'high' or 'acceptable' quality, from which it selects the best to start an assembly. These high confidence regions (HCR) ensure a firm base and good building blocks during the assembly process. Lower quality parts (low confidence regions, LCR) can be used later on if needed.

But the main difference of their approach is that they combined the assembler with some capabilities of an automatic editor. Both the assembler and the automatic editor are separate programs and run separately, but they view the task of assembly and finishing to be closely related enough for both parts to include routines from each other. In this process, the assembler gains the ability to perform signal analysis on partly assembled data, which helps to reduce misassembles especially in problematic regions like repeats (ALUS, REPT etc.), where simple base qualities alone could not help. Analyzing trace data at precise points with a given hypothesis 'in mind' there is a substantial advantage of a signal analysis aided assembler compared with a 'sequential base caller and assembler' strategy, especially while discriminating alternative solutions during the assembly process. In return, the automatic finisher gains the ability to use alignment routines provided by the assembler

(iii) *Methods and Algorithms*

They worked out a multiphase concept to have their assembler perform the difficult task of shotgun sequence alignments. Different authors have proposed different sets of acceptance criteria for the optimality of an alignment [Chan et al., 1992]. Traditionally [Myers, 1995], "the objective of this (assembly) problem has been to produce the shortest string that contains all the fragments as sub strings, but in case of repetitive target sequences this objective produces answers that are over compressed." As a result to this, they conceived the strategy of the 'least number of unexplainable errors' present in an assembly to be optimal.

To demonstrate their working principles, they will use a toy project of six reads of which they assume to have an overall fair base quality as example.

(iv) *Data preprocessing*

A high confidence region (HCR) of bases within every read is to be selected as an anchor point for the next phases. Existing base callers (ABI, PHRED and others) detect bases and rate their quality quite accurately and keep increasing in their performance, but bases in a called sequence always remain afflicted by increasing uncertainty towards the end of a read. This additional information, potentially worthful, can nevertheless constitute an impeding moment in the early phases of an assembly process, bringing in too much noise or preventing the correct determination of true, long range repeats.

Another important factor is sequencing vector, which will invariably be found at the start of each read. This earliest part of any cloned sequence must be marked or removed from the assembly. In analogy to the terms used in the GAP 4 package, they will refer to LCR also as 'hidden' data [Staden et al. 1997] whereas sequence marked as being part of the sequencing vector is 'marked' data.

This is the information the assembler will work with, any of which can be left out (except sequence and vector clippings) but will reduce the efficiency of the assembler:

1. The initial trace data, representing the gel electrophoresis signal
2. The called DNA sequence
3. Position specific confidence values for the called bases of the DNA sequence
4. A stretch of DNA in each sequence marked as HCR
5. General properties like name of the sequencing template etc.
6. Special DNA properties in different regions of a read (like sequencing vector, standard repeat sequence etc.,) that have been tagged or marked

The data preprocessing step has been taken out of the actual assembler as almost every laboratory has its own means to define 'good' quality within reads and already use existing programs to perform this task. For example, quality clipping, sequencing vector and cosmid vector removal are controlled by the PREGAP script provided with the GAP4 package or can be done with cross match 4 provided by PHRAP.

(v) *Read scanning*

A common start for an assembly is to compare every read with every other read (and its reversed complement) using a fast and fault tolerant algorithm to detect potential overlaps. Researchers developed an algorithm based on the Shift AND text search algorithm introduced by Wu and Manber (1992a); Wu and Manber (1992b) which extended ideas of BaezaYates and Gonnet (1992). The Shift AND algorithm allows with a configurable error threshold two sequences to be recognized as partly identical only by shifting bit vectors. The type of errors within the partial identity is irrelevant as insertions, deletions and mismatches in sequences are equally recognized. Originally, the complexity of the Shift AND algorithm allowing errors is $O(cmn)$ where c is a constant depending of the number of errors allowed in the match, m being the length of the pattern and n is the length of the sequence to be compared with. Our modified implementation of the algorithm has the complexity $O(cn)$ as we are able to have $O(m) = 1$ by using a limited number 5 of small patterns that fit into single machine registers.

The efficiency of the algorithm has been demonstrated by testing it on simulated shotgun data sets of real world DNA sequences and comparing results with previously published ones by Huang (1996). They found that fast scanning method is especially well suited for finding weak overlaps or overlaps in error rich regions. For example, the DNASAND algorithm was always able to find potential overlaps with a false positive rate below 0.5 and with less than 2% of missed overlaps, even in data sets with an artificially introduced high error rate of 10%. Although the DNASAND algorithm does not specify the overall type of global relationship of two sequences (total correspondence, containment and overlapping, see Huang (1994)), any type of this relationship is recognized. As result of this first scan, a matrix containing information on potential overlaps of all the fragments is generated and the direction of the potential overlap (forward—forward or forward—complement) is generated.

(vi) *Systematic match inspection*

In the next fundamental step, potential overlaps found during the scanning phase are examined with a Smith Waterman based algorithm for local alignment of overlaps. SW alignment algorithm takes into account the fact that today's base caller have a low error rate, the block indel model [Giegerich and Wheeler, 1996] does not apply to the alignment of shotgun sequencing data. This means that long stretches of mismatches or gaps in the alignment are less probable than small, punctual errors. We also assume a 'mismatch' of a base against a 'N' (symbol for aNy base) to have no penalty as in many case the base caller rightfully set 'N' for a real existing base (and not an erroneous extra one) that could not be resolved further.

Quality criteria like the score of the expected length of the overlap, the overall computed score of the overlap etc. are calculated for each overlap. Every candidate pair whose computed score is within a configurable threshold of the expected score and where the length of the overlap is not too small is accepted as 'true' overlap, candidate pairs not matching these criteria often due to spurious hits in the scanning phase are identified and rejected from further assembly. The aligned dual sequences (ADS) along with complementary data (like orientation of the aligned reads, overlap region etc.) that passed the Smith Waterman test are stored to facilitate and speed up the next phases. Good alternatives are also stored to enable alternative alignments to be found later on in the assembly.

All the ADS form one or several weighted graphs which represent the totality of all the assembly layout possibilities of a given set of shotgun sequencing data. The nodes of the graph are represented by the reads. An edge between two nodes indicates that these two reads are partially overlapping. The weights of the edges themselves are computed from the squared quality of the alignment multiplied with the length of the overlap. This emphasizes the quality aspect of the alignment and also takes the length of the overlap into account.

(vii) *Building contigs*

The overlaps found and verified in the previous phases must then be assembled into contigs. This is the most fundamental and intricate part of the process, especially in projects containing many repetitive elements. Several basic approaches to the multiple alignment problems have been devised to tackle this problem. Although algorithms for aligning multiple sequences at once have been used with increasing success lately for up to about 10 to 15 sequences [Stoye, 1998], the amount of time needed to perform this alignment is still too unpredictable to be used in sequence assembly.

Researchers decided to use iterative pair wise sequence alignment and devise new methods for searching overlap candidates and for empowering contigs to accept or reject reads presented to them during the contig building. The algorithm consists mainly of two objects, which interact with each other: a pathfinder module and a contig building module.

(viii) *Pathfinder and contig interaction*

Because they use an iterative approach to aligning the multiple alignment problem, this means always successively aligning an existing consensus against the next read the results of the alignment sensitively depends on the order of pair wise alignments [Morgenstern et al. 1996]. We have to make sure that we start at the position in the contig where we mostly have many reads with almost no errors, the pathfinder will thus in the beginning will search for a node in the weighted graph having a maximum number of highly weighted edges to neighbors. The idea behind this behaviour is to take the read with the longest and qualitatively best overlaps with as many other reads as possible. This ensures a good starting point: the 'anchor' for this contig.

They first tried a simple greedy algorithm to determine the next overlap candidate to a contig, but on occasions especially in highly repetitive parts of a genome this algorithm fails. With their current algorithm, the number of misalignments could be substantially reduced: the pathfinder designates the next read to add to an existing contig by making an in-depth analysis 7 of the weights to neighboring reads, taking the edge leading to the first node that is contained in the best partial path found so far. It then presents this read (and its approximate position) to the contig object as potential candidate for inclusion into the existing consensus.

A contig is represented by a collection of reads that have been arranged in a certain order with given offsets to form an alignment that is as optimal as possible, i.e., an alignment where the reads forming it have as few unexplained errors as possible but still form the shortest possible alignment. To serve this purpose, a contig object has been provided with functions that analyze the impact of every newly added read (at a given position) on the existing consensus. Our assumption is now that as the assembly started with the best overlapping reads available the bases in the consensus will be right at almost every position. Should the newly added read integrate nicely into the consensus, perhaps extending it, and then the contig object will accept this read as part of the consensus. In cases representing a chance alignment, the read differs in too many places from the actual consensus (thus differing in many aspects from reads that have been introduced to the consensus before). The contig will then reject the read from its consensus and tell the pathfinder object to search for alternative paths through the weighted overlap graph. The pathfinder object will eventually try to add the same read to the same contig but at a different position or by skipping it or trying other reads.

Once the pathfinder has no possibilities left to add unused reads to the actual contig, it will again search for a new anchor point and use this as starting point for a new contig. This loop continues until all the reads have been put into contigs or else if some reads could not be assembled anywhere to form single read contigs.

(ix) *Consensus approval methods*

As mentioned briefly above, each contig object has the possibility to reject a read being introduced into its consensus. This is one of the most crucial points in the development of assembler: allowing presumably good building blocks, i.e. reads with high quality, to start an assembly is a decisive step in the ongoing assembly process. It allows to use implicit and explicit knowledge available in reads that are known to be good.

The simplest behaviour of a contig could be to simply accepting every new read that is being presented as part of the consensus without further checks. In this case the assembler would thus rely only on the weighted graph, the method with which the weighted edges were calculated and the algorithm which traverses this graph.

However, using additional information that is available at the time of assembly might prove useful. For example, known standard repetitive elements have been tagged in the data-preprocessing step of the assembly. It is therefore possible to apply much stricter control mechanisms in those stretches of a sequence known to be repetitive, because they might really differ, but only in a few bases and are thus dangerous in the assembly.

In a new assembly repetitive elements must be checked, because they will induce errors. Reads with errors will be rejected from the already existing contigs as the pathfinder tried to enter them. In an automatic assembly process contig object failed to find a valid explaination to this problem when calling the signal analysis function provided by the automatic editor. Automatic editor will resolve the uncertainties by investigating probable alternatives at the fault site.

Highly trained personnel normally execute this labour intensive task although in a significant number of cases it is fairly easy to adjudicate between conflicting readings by analyzing the trace data. A previous suggestion on incorporating electrophoresis data into the assembly process promoted the idea of cap turning intensity and characteristic trace shape information and provide these as additional data to the assembly algorithm [Allex et al., 1996]. They decided against such an approach as essentially, all the assembler and with it the consensus finding algorithm of a contig needs to know is if yes or no the signal analysis reveals enough evidence for resolving a conflict within reads by changing the bases incriminated. Signal analysis is therefore treated as a black box decision formed by an expert system only called during the assembly algorithm when conflicts arise. It provides nevertheless more information than the one contained in quality values extracted from the signal of one read only (compare to Durbin and Dear (1998)): there is a reasonable suspicion deduced from other aligned reads on the place and the type of error where the base caller could have made a mistake.

There is not enough evidence found in the conflicting reads to allow a base change to resolve the discrepancies arising. There is also the additional knowledge that these non resolvable errors occur in an area tagged as 'ALUrepeat', which leads to a highly sensitive assessment of the errors. Consequently, the reads 4 and 5 containing repetitive sequence which the first contig object could not make match to its consensus form a second contig.

(x) *Read extension*

As the initial assembly used only high quality parts of the reads, further information can be extracted from the assembly by examining the end of the reads that were previously unused because the quality seemed too low. Although the signal to noise in read traces quickly degrades toward the end, the data is not generally useless. These 'hidden' parts of the reads can now be uncovered in two ways: (i) by uncovering parts of the reads that align to the already existing consensus and (ii) by uncovering hidden stretches of reads at the end of the contigs that are not confirmed by a consensus.

Intracontig extension is used to uncover reads and 'beef up' areas of low coverage within a contig and is a straight forward process. Mainly used, as a method to get more data confirmation than is available using only high quality parts, the hidden sequence is aligned step by step to the existing consensus. In most cases, the discrepancies found between the HCRs forming the existing consensus and the unaligned LCR will be decided in favour of the HCR. But in some cases, especially in regions with very low coverage, one or more reads with LCR data can correct an error in the HCR stretch, e.g. when there is a local drop in the confidence values and signal quality of bases in the HCR stretch whereas signal quality and confidence values of the same bases in the LCR stretch seem better.

Extracontig read extension, the second possibility, uncovers LCR at the ends of contigs and is used to extend the consensus to the left or to the right of a contig. LCR data present at the end of probably each read is not directly bad quality, but it is treated as hidden data: a region where the base caller calculated lower quality for the bases because it depended on the trace data of a single read. However, once reads have been aligned in their HCR, two or more stretches of lower quality can be used to uncover each other. The main purpose for this is to enable potential joins between contigs to be made.

The iterative enlargement procedure enables the assembler to redefine step by step the HCR of each read by comparing it with supporting sequences from aligned reads. This use of information in collateral reads is the assembler's major advantage over a simple base caller, which has only the trace information of one read to call bases.

(xi) *Contig linking and editing*

As last step of the assembly, the extended contigs are linked together where possible and the result is passed to the automatic finisher to correct errors in the assembly. Depending on the number and type of errors found in the assembled data by the finisher, the contigs can be dismantled and reassembled, taking into account the corrections made to the individual reads by the auto finisher and therefore refining the overall assembly.

By cycling through the previous steps, the assembler iteratively corrects errors like misassembled repetitive repeats that were made during previous steps and thus ensures the resulting contigs contain as few unexplainable errors as possible.

9.5 Genome Sequencing

Outline:

Methods for DNA Sequencing

(i)   Maxam-Gilbert Chemical DNA Sequencing

(ii) Sanger dideoxy DNA Sequencing

(iii) Automated DNA Sequencing with Fluorescent Labels

(iv) Genome Sequencing

    1. Sequencing is limited to 500-700 bp

    2. DNA Sequence Assembly - Contigs

    3. Methodologies for DNA Sequence Assembly

        (a) Shotgun Sequencing

        (b) Clone Contig Assembly

        (c) Directed Shotgun Assembly

Methods for DNA Sequencing

(i) **Maxam-Gilbert Chemical sequencing** no in vitro DNA polymerase reaction

    1. Use DNA, ds or ss, with radioactive label at one end ONLY

    2. In at least 4 separate reactions, treat the DNA with **Base specific chemicals** that result in cleavage of the DNA strand at that base Example: DMS (di methyl sulfate) for G's, hydrazine for pyrimidines.

    3. Get a **nested set** of labeled DNA fragments.

    4. Analyze as a ladder on a **DNA sequencing gel**:

        (a) Polyacrylamide denaturing gel resolution of short ssDNA fragments

        (b) Denaturing gel: 8 M urea keep DNA denatured during electrophoresis

        (c) Analyze **only** the **labeled** DNA fragments via Auto radiography or Fluorescence analysis

    5. Read the **DNA sequence** from bottom of gel to top by examination or "reading" of the **ladder** of **DNA bands** gives sequence 5' to 3' (5' -> 3')

(ii) *Sanger Dideoxy DNA Sequencing*

    1. Comes from DNA Polymerase properties:

        1. Have a DNA template and a DNA primer

        Cloning vehicles often have **universal primers** for sequencing into DNA cloned into one of the MCS (Multiple Cloning Sites) sites or Polylinkers

2. Execute 4 separate polymerization reactions containing each of the 4 dNTPs and one each of the four **dideoxynucleoside TPs:** ddGTP, ddATP, ddTTP, ddCTP.

    To assay the product DNA, one of the 4 dNTPs is radioactively labeled,

    or the Primer is labeled, radioactively or fluorescently,

    or the ddNTP is labeled fluorescently (see below).

    Dideoxy means 3'-H as well as 2'-H

    When a ddNTP is incorporated, it acts as a **Chain Terminator**:

    DNA synthesis stops since the DNA primer no longer has a 3'-OH Primer Terminus

3. Thus, get as reaction products, a **nested set** of fragments, each terminated at one of the four bases: G in the ddGTP reaction, A in the ddATP reaction, ...

4. When "run" on a **DNA sequencing gel** (polyacrylamide, with DNA denatured),
    the "nested set" of fragments forms a **ladder** of DNA bands corresponding to the positions of the bases.

5. Read the DNA sequence by reading the 4 lanes, one for each base, from bottom up, to correspond to 5' -> 3' sequence

(iii) Automated DNA Sequencing with Fluorescent Labels : use Sanger dideoxy sequencing. But with either fluorescent **primers** or fluorescent dideoxy chain **terminators**

Use different fluor for each of the four nucleotide types. This permits analysis of all four nucleotide reactions for a given DNA sample in one lane of the sequencing gel => 4-fold increase in analysis capability per gel run.

Most recently : Capillary gel electrophoresis is used in the Perkin Elmer - ABI 3700 automated sequencing machines rather than slab gel electrophoresis thus, have separate thin capillary gel for each DNA sample.

Advantages :

1. Better resolution, no running over from one lane toanother,

2. Separation of bands occurs much faster => 10- to 15-fold increase in speed.

   Both advantages are very important for Celera sequencing of the human genome.

(iv) Genome Sequencing

1. The major problem in DNA sequencing :

Can only Sequence 500-700 nucleotides from a given DNA sample (!)

This is due to **convergence** of the DNA bands. That is, the **percent size difference** between bands of 9 and 10 nucleotides is 10%.

But this percent size difference between bands of 99 and 100 nucleotides is only 1% !! Thus: bands corresponding to 99 and 100 nucleotides are 10-fold closer to each other than the bands corresponding to DNA fragments of length 9 and 10 nucleotides.

Thus, in **Genome Sequencing** or sequencing of DNA molecules much longer than 500-700 nucleotides, one must obtain sequence of **many, overlapping sets of ~500 bp fragments** and then join these together by determining how they overlap each other.

2. DNA sequence assembly - joining of overlapping sequences to form contigs

When overlapping sequences are properly joined to form a single sequence, this single sequence is called a **Contig.** In sequence assembly for an entire genome, ultimately one should end up with a single contig for each chromosome, since each chromosome is composed of a single DNA molecule.

In practice, this is **Very** difficult; due to **repetitive DNA sequences.** Repetitive DNA sequences present **two major problems** for sequence assembly :

1. *Number of Repeat Copies* : If the length of a repetitive DNA sequence region is long compared to the sequenced DNA length of ~500 bp, it is nearly impossible to determine how many copies of the DNA repeat there are,

2. *Correct Assembly* : If such a long repetitive DNA sequence region is **present at several sites** on a genome, then it is nearly impossible to determine what DNA sequences should be properly joined on either side of each repetitive DNA sequence region.

For these reasons (and a few others), in genome sequencing of genomes from higher eukaryotes, sequence is not obtained for much repetitive DNA and a given chromosome sequence will be present in several contigs in the "final assembly".

3. *Methodologies for DNA Sequence Assembly*

There are three main methodologies (with variations on a theme):

(a) *Shotgun sequencing,*

(b) *Clone Contig Assembly,*

(c) *Directed Shotgun Assembly.*

(a) *Shotgun Sequencing* : One obtains a high **redundancy** of sequencing of a given long DNA: 10 - 15 fold. One then uses **computer programs** to find the correct overlaps and join individual sequence **reads** into long **Contigs**. To do this uniquely and correctly, one needs :

1. little repetitive DNA,   and

2. overlaps between reads of 20 - 40 nucleotides such overlaps necessitate the high degree of redundancy.

Closure of Gaps :

One will still have some Gaps that need closing this is done via :

1. *Use of a Second Clone Library* : often using a different **Cloning Vehicle.** This will often yield a clone which will cover the Gap.

2. *Use of Directed Sequencing :* From this Clone, obtain initial ~500 bp of sequence from one end. Then use this sequence to construct an oligonucleotide to use as primer to extend the sequence further into the clone : **Internal Primer.**

Continue doing this until one has **walked across the Gap**, thereby closing the Gap.

(b) *Clone Contig Assembly :*

First generate a collection of **Mapped Clone Fragments:**

1. **Examples :** YACs, BACs, PACs, Cosmids which are mapped relative to each other, forming a set of overlapping large cloned fragments often with a high degree of redundancy: 5 - 15 fold.

2. From among these, choose a **minimum set of overlapping clones** this is sometimes called a **minimum tiling clone set.**

3. For each of these overlapping clones, do **Shotgun Sequencing:** Re-clone or **sub clone** each large overlapping clone as small sequencing fragments.

   Sequence these, ultimately forming a single **contig** corresponding to the sequence of each large clone.

4. Join each contig for each large clone together via overlapping sequence and knowledge of the map of the clones, yielding the final sequence of the entire DNA molecule, e.g. a chromosome.

How is the Collection of Mapped Clone Fragments Generated ?

1. Generate a Genome Library as YACs, BACs, PACs, Cosmids, etc.

   (a) Locate **Markers** to specific clones in the library. These Markers can be Genetic markers, e.g. genes, or physical DNA markers, e.g. R.sites, STSs, RFLPs, etc.

   (b) Identify **Overlapping Clones** by identifying pairs of clones uniquely containing the same **Markers**, e.g., genes or shared R. fragments.

2. When these markers are **STSs**, they can serve as physical **anchors** in the **sequence assembly process** i.e., one knows the position of specific sequence from the position of the STS and the sequence assembly must have this sequence in this position to be correct assembly.

Chromosome Walking : One can also determine **overlapping clones** without specific **markers** by hybridizing one clone DNA to the DNA of other clones.

However, use of STSs to provide anchors is very desirable with very large DNA fragments.

(c) Directed Shotgun Assembly

This is **Shotgun DNA Sequencing and Assembly** of very large genomes, e.g. Drosophila or human **coupled with** use of **anchored DNA markers**, e.g. **STSs**

Example : Celera approach to sequencing the Human Genome

Three genomic DNA libraries are used for sequencing:

1. Plasmid library with ~2 kb inserts

2. Library with ~ 10 kb inserts different Cloning Vehicle used 10 kb is large compared with most Repetitive DNA regions in the human genome, thereby avoiding much of this problem

3. BAC clone library with ~250 kb inserts.

DNA Sequencing is done on **both ends** of the inserts present in each of these clones.

Computerized **Assembly** of sequence into **Contigs** is greatly helped by the fact that the distance between the sequences of each of the two ends is nearly constant, at 2 kb or 10 kb or 250 kb: these are called **Sequence Pairs.**

The sequences from the **BAC clone ends** are used in two ways:

1. They become **STSs**

2. These STSs are used to **map the BACs and the STSs**

3. The mapped STSs become **Anchored Sequences** for the subsequence Assembly into Contigs

Note the difference here from Clone Contig Assembly :

1. In Clone Contig Assembly, mapping is done first, a minimum set of YACs or BACs is determined, and then **each of these YACs or BACs is subjected to Shotgun Sequencing**.

2. Here, in Directed Shotgun Assembly, the **entire genome is subjected to Shotgun sequencing** via the two smaller insert libraries, the 2 kb and 10 kb insert libraries.

These methodologies yield then the **ultimate Physical Map of the Genome:** its **DNA Sequence**

This **DNA Sequence** is then the ultimate foundation information about the organism with this information, one knows completely the enzymatic and molecular capabilities of the organism what it **can** do and what it **can not** do.

10

Genome Mapping

10.1 Cognate Modification Enzymes

Each Type II R.enzyme has a cognate Modification Enzyme: **DNA methylase.** This enzyme recognizes the same nucleotide sequence as does the R.enzyme and methylates specifically one of the bases in each strand in the nucleotide sequence.

Example : **EcoRI methylase** (GAA*TTC) methylates the inner A in both strands

Function : This methylation renders this R.site resistant to cleavage by the R.enzyme.

Hence, a cell encoding a Restriction Enzyme also encodes the Modification Enzyme; the latter will methylate the cell chromosomal DNA, thereby preventing the R.enzyme from digesting the cellular DNA.

10.2   Gel Electrophoresis of DNA Fragments

Digestion of a well-defined DNA molecule, e.g., viral DNA, with a R.enzyme yields a set of well-defined DNA **Restriction Fragments (R.frags).**

Example : EcoRI cleaves Phage Lambda DNA (linear dsDNA, 49 kb) at 5 sites, yielding 6 fragments.

BamHI cleaves Adenoviral DNA at 12 sites, Lambda DNA at 5 sites.

The **sizes** of these R.frags can be determined using **Gel Electrophoresis** and the fragments can often be isolated from each other.

Gel Electrophoresis : When "loaded" as a "band" at top of a gel matrix, and subjected to an electric field, DNA migrates through the gel at rate inversely proportional to its size.

Rough exponential dependence of migration rate with size. Thus,

→ can separate and purify individual R.frags from a gel

→ can analyse for presence and size of R. frags

Use DNA **Markers** for size determination avoid variation between gel runs.

Methodology : "Slab" gels used: several DNA samples in adjacent "lanes" analyzed in same gel

Agarose gels used for R.frags of size 500 bp or larger

Polyacrylamide gels used for smaller fragments, e.g., sequencing gels

"Pulsed gel" electrophoresis used for very large DNA, e.g., entire chromosomes

Visualize the DNA :

1. Using radioactivity: place X-ray film over gel, expose to decaying P^{32}
2. Fluorescence: Ethidium Bromide (EtBr), a dye, which intercalates between bases; EtBr fluorescences is visible when irradiated with UV light

10.3   Physical Map of Genome

Restriction Map as a Physical Map :

Given a large DNA molecule:

- Digest it with R.enzyme, measure sizes via Agarose Gels. Repeat with additional R.enzymes.

  But only get sizes; don't know which fragments are adjacent to each other.

  Do **double digests** with the same enzymes as above, 2 at a time.

  Purify singly digested R.frags and digest with the 2nd R.enzyme (can often avoid this, or purify only a few of the first R.frags).

→ Get Ordering of Both Enzyme set of fragments

  Can also do PARTIAL DIGESTS with single R.enzyme. This is particularly useful for END LABELED DNA assay P^{32} added at 5' ends of DNA with polynucleotide kinase.

  Can also use hybridization of a radioactive 'probe' ssDNA or oligonucleotide to one end or the other of the DNA in a Southern gel nalysis of the partial digests.

  Physical Maps based on R.sites are now available for most "model" organisms. e.g., Kohara map for *E. coli,* Sau3A mapping of *C. elegans* as well as ultimate nucleotide sequence for several bacteria, archae, andyeast. Level of "resolution" depends on 8 vs 6 vs 4 bp "cutter" vs DNA sequence.

10.4   Physical Mapping using Hybridization

Properties of conversion of dsDNA into ssDNA, and the reverse, can also be used for physical mapping and other purposes. These properties have to do with DNA Hybridization.

10.5 DNA Hybridization - Melting Curves

(i) *Denaturation :* conversion of dsDNA to two strands of ssDNA

1. When the H bonds break that join the 2 strands in dsDNA, they all tend to break simultaneously thus, the dsDNA "melts" into two strands This is like a **phase transition** similar to the melting of ice into water.

2. Agents which "denature" DNA:

   (a) Increase the temperature past the "melting" temperature: **Tm**.

   (b) (i) Increase the pH to above about 11.3

   (ii) Decrease the ionic strength to below 10(-5): repulsion of negative charge.

(ii) *Assay or Measurement of Denaturation / Renaturation : UV light Absorption*

1. The bases (mainly Pyrimidines) absorb UV light (260 nm) that impinges **vertically** on the base.

2. Free bases absorb more than ssDNA; ssDNA absorbs more than dsDNA due to this requirement of vertical impingement of the UV light: bases most exposed when free; least exposed when in dsDNA; only partially exposed in ssDNA due to "stacking" of the bases (hydrophobic interactions).

3. Can measure this denaturation via change in UV absorption. This is an **assay**, or measurement method, for this process.

4. The Tm is the "midpoint" in the melting reaction, Tm is proportional to %(G+C), due to 3 H-bonds between C and G but only 2 H-bonds between A and T.

5. The curve of **Assay** (here: UV absorption) **vs Melting Agent** (here: Temperature) is called a **Melting Curve.**

Renaturation :

Joining of two DNA strands of complementary sequence to form dsDNA.

1. *Reverse of Denaturation :* but requires that the two DNA strands have complementary sequence, i.e. permit A joining to T, C joining to G, along the entire length of both DNA strands or chains.

2. Renaturation is also called **Hybridization.**

3. Can also occur between DNA and RNA, to form a **DNA: RNA hybrid**, or between two RNA strands of complementary sequence.

(iii) *DNA Labeling*

DNA probes used in hybridization experiments must be **labeled** in order to **assay** their association with a ssDNA substrate in a hybridization experiment.

DNA labels are most often either **radioactive** labels or **fluorescent** labels.

1. *Radioactive Labeling*

   Radioactive labels used are radioactive isotopes: H^3, C^{14}, P^{32}, or P^{33} the most often used isotopes are H^3 and P^{32}.

   Methods of radioactive labeling :

   - H^3-labeled thymine or thymidine is often used to label DNA uniformly in appropriate thy-mutant organisms.

   - Deoxyribonucleoside triphosphates, the substrates used by DNA polymerase enzymes for DNA synthesis, can be obtained labeled with P^{32} in the alpha-phosphate position. These substrates can then be used with an appropriate DNA polymerase to label DNA, for example, in the E. coli PolI nick tranlsation reaction.

   - Polynucleotide kinase can be used to label the 5'-end of dsDNA with P^{32} using ATP labeled with P^{32} in the gamma-position and a dsDNA substrate with no 5'-phosphates. This is often done for the Maxam-Gilbert chemical method for DNA sequencing, for partial digest restriction mapping, and for other purposes.

2. *Fluorescent Labeling*

   Primarily, radioactive labeling suffers from the obvious problem that people are exposed to radioactivity. This requires specific and special environmental safeguards. Such safeguards do not however solve the problem of long term isotopes: isotopes that take thousands or millions of years to decay away, how does one dispose of these ? This is an unsolved issue.

Second, radioactive labels are not simultaneously of high sensitivity and of high resolution :

High Sensitivity : high signal to noise ratio/decay from the label is high compared with cosmic rays and other background 'noise'

High resolution : ability to pinpoint precisely in the experiment the position of radioactive decay of the radioactive atom.

P^{32} : high sensitivity, low resolution, Beta decay, half-life = 14.2 days (half of the atoms have decayed in two weeks), max energy of the beta particle (high energy electron): $\sim$ 1.3 Mev this is high energy; will pass through one or more cm of human tissue.

H^3 : low sensitivity, high resolution, Beta decay, half life $\sim$ 1100 years, max energy of the beta: $\sim$ 0.01 Mev low energy (low sensitivity), doesn't go far (high resolution).

Other radioisotopes are in between.

Fluorescent labels are by comparison of high sensitity and high resolution.

These are used routinely in **automated DNA sequencing** reactions and now in **DNA microarray** experiments. One can purchase fluorescent labeling nucleotide triphosphates and substrates for oligonucleotide (probe) synthesis.

Fluorescent lables of different wavelengths, green and red particularly, are available and can be used simultaneously in a given experiment, e.g. in DNA microarray experiments

(iv) *Fluorescence In Situ Hybridization - FISH*

FISH is used to detect the position of a marker on a chromosome via fluorescence. The marker is a fluorescent-labeled ssDNA probe of complementary sequence to that of the position on the chromosome.

Methodology - Metaphase chromosomes (or other DNA substrate) is immobilized on a glass slide.

The chromosomes or DNA are denatured, e.g. with formamide.

The fluorescent-labeled probe is hybridized to the denatured DNA.

The DNA is visualized via microscopy or other method and the position of the hybridized fluorescent probe is visualized via its fluorescent signal: **assay**

Example : fly DNA probed with centromeric sequences.

- *Single R.frag Identification :* **Southern Hybridization**
  Often use a short DNA oligonucleotide probe to partially purify R.fragments for further cloning, or to identify a given R.fragment, or other DNA fragment containing Specific DNA sequences.

  One can do this via a combined agarose gel electrophoresis with hybridization against a radioactive probe that has a complementary DNA sequence to the desired specific DNA sequences.

  Named for Ed Southern, famous English molecular biologist.

  Can also use hybridization of a probe to a gene in order to:
  1. Detect DNA spotted and denatured on filter paper : **dot blots**.
  2. Disrupted Lambda phage from a Lambda cDNA library on plates.
  3. Lysed cells on a plate with DNA transferred to a nitrocellulose membrane.

  in situ Hybridization

Methodology :

1. Run DNA fragments out on an Agarose Gel.
2. Float Agarose Gel on an alkaline solution in a trough. Alkali denatures the DNA, yielding ssDNA fragments in the Agarose Gel.
3. Place a Nitrocellulose Membrane on top of the Agarose Gel and then several layers of absorbant paper (towel paper often used) on top of the Nitrocellulose Membrane.
4. Let capillary action transfer DNA to the Nitrocellulose Membrane during transfer of fluid from the trough to the absorbant paper
5. Dry Nitrocellulose Membrane and fix DNA to the Nitrocellulose Membrane: 80 °C, under vacuum.

6. Hybridize the Radioactive Probe to the denatured ssDNA on Nitrocellulose Membrane – hybridization conditions in small liquid volume in a "Seal-a-Meal" sac often used.

7. Dry Nitrocellulose Membrane and expose radioactivity to film.

8. Develop and examine the film.

Such gels can be used **analytically** to provide final information:

1. Identify whether DNA in a lane contains the probe sequences: see hybridization

2. See how many such bands are there

3. Determine their size from position in the gel

Southern gels can also be used **preparatively** to purify DNA fragments :

Cut the band out of the gel and elute the DNA from the gel slice such partially purified fragments that can then be cloned.

10.6 Variants of Southern Gels

Northerns : Same as Southerns but with RNA, e.g. mRNA, run out on the Agarose Gels

Westerns : Proteins run out on a Polyacrylamide gel Polyacrylamide gel Electrophoresis - **PAGE**; generally under protein denaturing conditions, e.g. use of detergent: **SDS gels** (assay presence of a given protein using an antibody to the protein).

Names here are "take-offs" on Southern gels not named for scientist named Northern, etc.

Other variants also exist, e.g. **South-Westerns** run SDS protein gel; attempt to renature proteins in gel; transfer to Nitrocellulose as in Southerns; probe the Proteins so transferred with Radioactive Oligonucleotide probes assay DNA binding Proteins.

10.7 Genome Fragment Identification : DNA Microarrays

One of the profound technological advancements that is a product of this third revolution in Molecular Biology is that of **DNA Microarray** technology.

DNA Microarrays are similar to Southern Gels in that labeled oligonucleotide probes are used to identify specific DNA sequences from among many, e.g. an entire genome.

However :

1. **Southerns** (and Northerns) are one gene at a time technology.
2. **DNA Microarrays** permit simultaneous assay of **all genes** in a genome. DNA Microarrays thus can be thought of as "the Southerns of Genome-based Molecular Biology"

Methodology :

DNA Micro arrays are 2D solid surfaces to which have been immobilized ssDNA molecules. They are used by hybridizing labeled ssDNA molecules to the DNA on the Microarray, and assaying for the labeled ssDNA molecules, thereby determining the positions on the Microarray where hybridization occurred.

Current DNA Microarray technology includes two rather distinct methodologies:

1. Immobilized single-stranded cDNA molecules: long, non-synthetic substrates, at low density
2. Immobilized short oligonucleotide ssDNA: short, synthetic substrates, at high density

cDNA Microarrays : ssDNA from a cDNA library is used and immobilized to a 2D solid surface, usually either a glass slide or a nylon membrane. Individual cDNA species are "spotted" in a 2D-grid on the solid surface. The number of spots is relatively small, at most about 80 x 80 or 6400 spots. These individual cDNA species might for example be obtained from separate Lambda Phage in a lambda cDNA library.

Experimentally, such arrays can be prepared at relatively low expense. They are then used to detect expression of cognate mRNAs (or via cDNAs from these cDNAs) by hybridizing the cDNAs obtained from some given experimental condition to the cDNAs immobilized on the surface. Since each of the 6400 spots represents expression of a different gene, one can assay expression of 6400 genes simultaneously. Further, using different fluors to label the experimental cDNA, e.g. lissamine-labeled vs fluorescein-labeled, one can assay in the same experiment two different experimental conditions.

Example : cDNA microarray and stage-specific gene expression in the malaria parasite *Plasmodium falciparum*

Second Example : cDNA microarray of 10 *Arabidopsis* and 1046 human cDNA species,

Oligonucleotide Microarrays : To get really high densities of substrate ssDNA molecules on DNA micro arrays, companies such as AffyMetrix build DNA microarrays using 'silicon valley' chip technology.

Oligonucleotides (short ssDNA molecules, e.g. 25 bp long) are **synthesized** on the chips. Synthesis technology is similar to that found in the organic chemistry technology associated with Oligonucleotide Synthesizers such as purchased from ABI / Perkin-Elmer via their Gene Chips.

However : Masks are used such that synthesis occurs only with light radiation and light can only pass through regions in the mask where there are spaces this technology permits synthesis of a high density of oligonucleotides (80,000 spots), **each** of a **different** sequence, on a chip much like a silicon chip.

cDNA species or mRNA species are then hybridized to such DNA chips or total DNA from an individual appropriately restriction digested, to determine SNP information about the individual.

Usually, several oligos are used **per gene**, e.g. 5 oligos per gene. Thus, if the gene is expressed, mRNA, or corresponding cDNA, should hybridize to **all 5** oligos. This provides controls: some oligos hybridize better than others one learns which oligos work best, for the next generation of oligo microarrays and at the same time **some** hybridization should occur to all 5 oligos.

This technology then permits **automated** analysis of the type for which DNA microarrays provide information.

For example, one can automate analysis of individual human beings for their heterozygosity as determine by their Single Nucleotide Polymorphisms.

Given that specific SNPs as associated to some degree with a given genetic disease, one can in automated fashion determine the propensity of any given individual for a given genetic disease. The pharmaceutical companies would will you believe that given such knowledge they can better design drugs and treatments for you, taking into consideration **all** of your genetic disease propensities. This includes **when** in your lifetime to start treating you for a disease you might get.

That is : **individual, cradle to grave, prescriptive life care.**

Example of Oligoarray to analyze SNPs (Single Nucleotide Polymorphisms) :

For SNP microarrays, oligos corresponding to the two alleles are placed in two rows, one below the other.

10.8   Genome Fragment Isolation : Cloning and High Resolution Physical Mapping of Genomes

Outline:

I.   Genome Types of Cloning Experiments

   (i)   Gene Isolation - Reverse Genetics

   (ii)   Genome Cloning - Genome Libraries

   (iii)   Mapping from Cloning: Sequence Tagged Sites (STSs)

   (iv)   cDNA Cloning - Expressed Sequence Tags (ESTs)

   (v)   Radiation Hybrids

   (vi)   Mapping from Radiation Hybrids: STSs

II.   Other Types of Cloning Experiments

   (i)   Site Specific Mutagenesis

   (ii)   Protein Production - Bacterial Factories

I.   *Genome Types of Cloning Experiments :*

(i)   *Gene Isolation - Reverse Genetics*

   Assays :

(i)   Complementation of host mutant deficient in gene activity.

(ii)   "Probe" with radioactive short DNA molecule of sequence from the gene.

Obtain short DNA sequence, eg, from amino acid sequence of purified protein.

Thus : go from protein to gene with no previously isolated mutations.

Reverse Genetics – this is the reverse of standard genetics, in which mutants are isolated and characterized (gene -> protein).

Often use such a short DNA oligonucleotide probe to partially purify R.fragments for further cloning :

Southern Gels : Run R.fragments out on a gel transfer DNA from gel to nitrocellulose membrane. Hybridize the fragments in bands on the gel to the probe detect correct bands via radioactivity and film purify R.fragments from this region of the gel to use in cloning.

Characterize gene physically : Restriction Map Sequence

(ii) *Genomic Cloning - Genome Libraries*

Purpose : obtain library of complete genome

Usually use Phage Lambda.

Use of Isoschizomer R. enzymes :

same sticky ends from cleavage

Example : BamHI and Sau3A; Sau3A is a "4-cutter" and hence has many more sites in a genome than does BamHI, which is a "6 cutter". Partial restriction with Sau3A yields large fragments, whose ends are from sites at many locations on the genome thus get **overlapping fragments** – Much less likely to get good overlapping fragment pattern with BamHI due to lack of sufficient restriction sites.

(iii) *Mapping from Cloning :*

Sequence Tagged Sites (STSs) : **Sequence Tagged Sites (STSs)** are short DNA sequences (usually < 500 bp) determined from **unique sequences** in a given genome, and then **mapped** to that genome.

These then provide methodology for **high-resolution physical mapping** of a genome.

* *Sources of DNA for STSs :*

    1. *ESTs - Expressed Sequence Tags*

        These are DNA sequences determined from expressed regions of the genome, or **genes.**

        If a given expressed gene is present **uniquely** on the genome, the sequences of the EST is a good STS sequence.

- *Genomic Sequences*

  Any genomic sequence that is present uniquely on the genome can be used as an STS.

  Good examples of such are DNA sequences previously determined and deposited in a DNA database such as GenBank.

Mapping of STS Sequences :

Once one has a set of DNA sequences to be used as STSs, they must be mapped to the genome.

This can be done in many ways, including the following two general procedures:

Cloning and use of a **Clone Library**.

Radiation Hybrids and use of a **Radiation Hybrid Panel**

The **STS markers**, DNA sequences of length 500 bp or less, are nearly always assayed using Polymerase Chain Reaction (**PCR**) amplification of the STS region. PCR is amenable to automation can be used and hence so-called "High ThroughPut (**HTP**)" methodology (highly automated, robotic methodology).

(iv) cDNA Cloning - Expressed Sequence Tags (ESTs)

Purify a messenger RNA of interest.

"Reverse transcribe" the RNA into DNA, get a "complementary DNA strand":

cDNA

Degrade the mRNA and synthesize the second DNA strand. Clone the DNA so synthesized.

Often use **lambda-cloning vehicles** for cloning cDNA species can thereby maintain an entire cDNA library as lambda phage in liquid at high density: $> 10^{12}$ phage per ml

cDNA library

Same thing but with all mRNAs from given tissue

This provides a library of all mRNA sequences expressed in this tissue.

Such cDNA libraries can provide the DNA for sequencing to map **sequence tagged sites (STSs)** to a given genome or chromosome from a genome.

(v) Radiation Hybrids

Radiation Hybrids provide a methodology for high-resolution mapping of DNA physical markers such as STSs on chromosomes of higher organisms such as human and mouse.

For human chromosomes, **Radiation Hybrid Panels** are created by:

1. Irradiating human cells with x-rays, thereby fragmenting the chromosomes in these cells into fragments. The fragments are smaller when the x-ray dose is higher.

2. Creating a **human-hamster fusion cell** by fusing the irradiated human cells with mutant thymine requiring hamster cells. Fusion can occur between these cells when mediated with chemicals or Sendai virus.

3. Creating a **hybrid cell line** by growing the fused cells in HAT media, selecting for human chromosome fragments containing a thymine gene. Cells in this fused cell line contain the hamster chromosomes plus some human chromosome fragments (as much as about 35% of the human genome).

The **Radiation Hybrid Panel** consists of several such hybrid cell lines, all created in one fusion experiment. Typically, such a Panel has 50-100 different cell lines. Specific Radiation Panels, eg the G3 panel, have been used to construct a high resolution STS map of the human genome.

(vi) Mapping STSs from Radiation Hybrids

Radiation Hybrids can be used similarly to Clones in a Clone Library for **high resolution mapping of STS markers.** The principles for doing this are as follows:

1. Each hybrid cell line in a given radiation hybrid panel contains many fragments of human chromosomes.

2. STSs that are close together will tend to be present together in the same human chromosome fragment in a given hybrid cell line; those that are far apart or on different chromosomes will not tend to be found in the same hybrid cell lines.

3. This tendency is quantitated by recording what percent of the time two markers are found in the same cell line. This is almost always the same as the two markers being present on the same human chromosome fragment.

4. Doing this yields the following type of data:

Data from Human Chromosome 21q:

S16 (8) **S48** (9) **S46** (22) **S4**

With **S16** (19) **S46** and **S48** (29) **S4**

Thus, STS markers S16 and S48 appear on the same human chromosome fragment 92% of the time, i.e., the distance between the markers is 8 units. Similarly, STS markers S16 and S46 appear on the same human chromosome fragment 81% of the time, i.e., the distance between the markers is 19 units.

Note that the distance between S16 and S48, i.e., 8 units, plus the distance between S48 and S46, i.e., 9 units, is close to the distance between S16 and S46, i.e., 19 units.

Radiation Hybrid and Clone mapping of STS markers are widely used to provide high-resolution physical maps of chromosomes and genomes. These STS markers also provide a framework of mixed markers on the genome for complete Genome Sequencing.

II. *Other Types of Cloning Experiments :*

(i) *Site Specific Mutagenesis*

Introduce specific Point Mutations (single base changes) into CloneGene.

Move back into Chromosome via Generalized Recombination.

(ii) *Protein Production*

Overexpress Gene Product, eg Insulin, in Bacteria **(Bacterial Factories).**

10.9 Genome Mapping : Genetic -> Physical

(i) Genetic Maps vs Physical Maps

Comparison of Genetic and Physical Maps :

Genetic Map is colinear with physical placement of Genes on DNA but quantitation is difficult due to variations of Recombination processes between organisms (more rare in eukaryotes than in prokaryotes) and due to dependence on DNA sequence (hot spots for recombination).

Physical Map of Genome : Placement of Genes and Sites on Nucleotide Sequence of DNA, i.e. on the physically real Genetic Material.

The Ultimate Physical Map is the Nucleotide Sequence.

Note : to serve as a **Marker** in either a Genetic Map (genes, map via Recombination Frequency) or a Physical Map (Sites on DNA, map via locating the site on the DNA), a Gene or Site must occur in more than one state. Such states are called **Alleles.**

In classical genetics, the results or manifestations of one state or another, i.e. one Allele or another, of a given Gene are called the **Phenotype** associated with a given Allele. Such might be eye color or pea shape. The differences in the Gene itself associated with a given Allele are called the **Genotype.**

In modern genetics, the Genotype is a change in the DNA sequence encoding the given Gene.

The classical Phenotype such as the examples just given arise from changes in the amino acid sequence of the Protein expressed by the given Gene, resulting in change in activity of the Protein (perhaps no activity for one Allele of the Gene), resulting in change in a metabolic pathway, resulting in change in eye color or pea shape.

In modern genetics, the Phenotype can also be defined at the DNA level. The Phenotype is any measure of the results of one Allele or another. Thus, the Phenotype can also be the change in the DNA sequence associated with the change from one Allele of a Gene to another, because with appropriate sequencing one can determine this change in DNA sequence.

This ability to define the classical genetic concept of **Genotype** in terms of specific molecular changes in the genetic material or DNA molecules, coupled with ability to measure these specific molecular changes via DNA sequencing, bring the concepts of **Genotype** and **Phenotype** into close proximity to each other.

(ii) ***DNA Markers for Genetic Mapping - Polymorphisms :*** Genetic Marker: mutant vs "wild type", compare 2 phenotypes **Alleles** based on mutation eliminating (or creating) a R.site

Polymorphisms : individuals in a population have different **Alleles** or variants of a given Gene Marker.

What is an Allele? Some change in a Gene or Site that can be assayed, that is phenotype.

In principle, any DNA base change is now an Allele, can "assay" any such change via DNA Sequencing.

Uses :

1. *Markers for genetic mapping :* **Pedigree Analysis.**
2. *Markers for physical mapping :* Restriction Mapping.
3. *Genetic disease :* compare diseased vs Non-Diseased individuals.
4. *Forensic purposes :* compare DNA from blood from victim and suspect, compare with blood at "scene of the crime".
5. *Identification purposes :* compare DNA from blood at some site with DNA stock.

   → military, accidents, etc
6. **Parentage** identification "who's the father?" Dogs, Horses, other animals.

(iii) ***Restriction Fragment Length Polymorphisms (RFLPs) :*** **R.sites** as DNA markers can serve as Genome sites for Genetic Mapping

Change in a R.site : assay via cleavage or not by R.enzyme bands on gels.

A change in a Restriction Site : one allele the R.Site can be cleaved another allele the R. Site can NOT be cleaved.

These two alleles yield two different sizes for R.fragments i.e., changes in the Restriction Fragment Length Thus: **Restriction Fragment Length Polymorphisms**

Note : that no Phenotype is associated here with the biology of the organism!! The "phenotype" is defined by Assays in the Lab.

(iv) *Simple Sequence Length Polymorphisms (SSLPs)* : These arise from **Repeated Sequences** present in DNA genomes of higher organisms.

Repeated Sequences are of two general types:

1. *MiniSatellites or VNTRs (Variable Number of Tandem Repeats)* :

   These are regions of DNA containing **tandem repeats** where the repeats are in the size range 25 bp to a few hundred base pairs in length.

2. *MicroSatellite or Simple Tandem Repeats (STRs)* :

   These are also tandem repeat regions of DNA, but where the repeat sizes are smaller, generally 2 to 7 bp in length

Polymorphisms arise in populations of the organism either by variations in :

1. The precise sequence found in each repeat

2. In the **number** of repeats found in a region of the repeat

The latter type of polymorphism is currently used more often than the former. Each such naturally occurring polymorphism in a population of the organism is an **Allele** for the site on the DNA at which the repeat region occurs. Such a polymorphism arising from variations in the number of repeats results in a change in the **length** of the repeated region, and is called an **SSLP.**

Measurement of SSLPs - **Allelic Phenotypes :** – determine the length of the SSLP in a given DNA sample via its size using Gel Electrophoresis

(v) *Single Nucleotide Polymorphisms (SNPs)* : These are **Polymorphisms** or **Alleles** occurring naturally in a population resulting from **point mutations** or **changes in single nucleotides** in the DNA in individuals in the population. They usually are changes within a Gene, resulting in a change in an amino acid of the encoded Protein, resulting in a change in a pathway, yielding a **Phenotype** such as a genetic disease in humans.

Note : That SNPs that occur in a R.site, resulting in Alleles that can be cut or not by the R.enzyme, also result in RFLPs.

Discovery of SNPs :

Unless a SNP happens to fall within a R.site, and therefore also results in an RFLP, the only way to discover naturally occurring SNPs is by way of **DNA sequencing.**

Considerable effort is currently underway in many laboratories and biotech companies to discover SNPs associated with human genetic disease.

It is instructive to have a look at the SNP database at NCBI.

11
Gene Identification

Gene Identification

Gene Identification and functional classification start with the determination of coding sequence. Basically, an open reading frame (ORF) is determined from start codon to a stop codon. This is relatively easy for prokaryotic genomes, where the gene density is high and introns are absent. Usually, ORFs longer than a certain Threshold (300+ 500) are considered a potential genes. Genes that is longer than the threshold and genes on the opposite strand of longer ORF (shadow genes often lead to ambiguities), but can be resolved by analyzing the computational differences between coding regions, shadow genes and non-coding DNA. Predictions of coding sequences in eukaryotes is more difficult. The available gene finding programs generate prediction on the basis of transcriptional signals. (Transcription starts sites, TATA boxes, Poly adenylation sites etc).

Translational signals (transcription initiation and termination sites) and splicing signals (donar and acceptor splice site positions). Among these programs are GENMARK GRAIL, and GENEPARSER.These Programs are continuosly improved and more advanced programs like GENESCAN take into account reading frame compatibility of adjacent exons and compositional properties of introns and exons. Further increase in sensitivity can be obtained by including different sequences similarity functions for comparision to gene and protein sequences in available databases.

As a complement to the gene identification programs, comparison of complete genomic sequence (20 $\pm$ 100) kb of homologus loci between closely related organisms (mouse and human) can reveal most exons and regulatory regions by identifying the regions of particularly high conservation. EST sequences represents spliced genes and are therefore valuable tools for determination of coding sequences in the genomic DNA. Comparision between ESTs and genomic sequences immediately reveals the splice sites. However, among the drawbacks are that inconsistencies might occur due to low quality sequence, alternative splicing presence of pre-mRNA sequences and that the ESTs represents only partial transcript sequences, even after gene indexing by assembly. Gene annotation techniques based on EST and gene prediction algorithm complement each other in the sense that ESTs are often effective in identifying 3- Prime ends of genes where the gene finders often falls, while gene finders relatively well determine the 5-Prime ends which the oligo (dT) primed cDNA clones often fail to reach. This confirms the fact that full understanding of a genome will only be reached by a combination of genomic and cDNA sequencing.

When is a predicted gene a gene? How many encoded in the human genome ? This is a simple question without as yet a straight forward answer. The density of genes in human genome is much lower than for any other genome sequenced so far, making it particularly difficult to predict where genes are. Both Celera and the public sequencing consortium used computational algorithms to model genes and make predictions, but such methods are far from perfect. Not only can the start and end positions of a predicted gene be wrong but exons (the coding parts of a gene) can be missed entirely or wrongly predicted to exist. To reduce this later effect, the public sequencing consortium required the exons of predicted genes to be confirmed, by showing sufficient similarity to a known sequence (DNA or protein) in a database. But this requirement might be too conservative, making it difficult to predict the presence of new gene families. Celera has required similar confirmation of predictions, but its Mouse; Genome sequencing project may have provided evidence for further vertebrate specific genes. Spurious Prediction is also a problem. All genes are expressed by being copied (transcribed) into messenger RNA; Most messenger RNAs are then translated into proteins. But even evidence that a stretch of DNA is transcribed does not definitely show that stretch to be a gene. We do not know how well the cell identifies transcripts that cannot be translated into a functioning protein. Moreover proteins that cannot serve any useful function (for example because they can not fold correctly) could be made, but rapidly removed. To arrive at a true set of protein encoding genes, we cannot rely on computational techniques alone, but must continue to characterize proteins and their functions. These problems provide scope for estimates of human gene to vary widely. Although recent estimates are converging in the 30,000-40,000 range (as opposed to earlier estimates of 100000 or so), it could be in years before we have the final answer.

11.1 Sequence Feature Extraction / Annotation

Because of high throughout sequencing technologies and automated sequencers now biologists are generating huge amount of sequences. The increasing number of availability of this raw sequence constitutes a complex problem for biologist. Without Transcript sequences a genomic sequence can not be directly used and where as the genes is the first of a long list of questions. Further more, the public data release policies force the sequencing centers to deposit as quickly as possible the raw sequences in the databases. To meet the scientific communities expectations together with the massive sequence production the first step is to extract rapidly a maximum of biological information from the sequences to establish a basis for further functional studies. This information has then to be associated with the sequences in order to label the genes, allowing biologist to find sequences of interest. This is the goal of genome annotation.

11.2   Gene Annotation

Annotation is extraction of useful information from raw sequence. Identification of coding regions and genes in a genome and determination of what they do, a combination of comments, notations, references and citations, either in free format or utilizing a controlled vocabulary that together describe all the experimental and inferred information about a gene or a protein.

Classically scientists carry out annotations of sequences by using information linked to experiments. Indeed, in contrast to sequences obtained through individual gene cloning experiments, in turn we should also be able to update annotations and to apply to genes the results of experimental analysis performed later on. This notion of integration is essential from a genomics point of view. Bench work cannot follow the release pace of thousands of new potential genes and experimentally documented genes represent a minor fraction of genes. In order to compensate for this transitional lack of secure data, prediction tools are extensively used to analyse the sequences and extract putative information. By merging statistics, computer science and biological sciences bioinformatics have developed many prediction tools. The analysis of the anonymous sequences combining different prediction programs and the results obtained by bioanalysts are the starting points of the annotation process. For this reason, the annotation work is mostly a predictive work and the result has to be considered as such.

Whole genome annotation should not be taken as definitive and proven, but rather as indication to help biologist in the sequence jungle and to derive future experimental approaches. This point is often forgotten when annotations are used. When in front of a large genomic sequence, the first problem is to localize all the genes on both the strands and more precisely, the different structural elements of these genes. This step is called the structural annotation, to clearly distinguished it from the following one, the Functional annotation, which tries to find signs of function from the deduced protein sequences, as described below, deep and detailed annotation implies numerous complementary analysis and checking. Unfortunately, because of the cost in time and money of this human expertise, genome annotation is generally restricted to the prediction of coding exons to deduce the protein sequence of potential genes and to label it with the functions of the closest homologue. We will compare and discuss the fast high throughout annotation used in the systemic sequencing programmes and the possibilities of a deeper but slower annotation with two objectives to highlight the dangerous traps when automatic annotations are blindly used and to present a few novel approaches and applications in genome annotation.

(i) *Structural annotation* : The very first information needed when analyzing an unknown genomic DNA sequence is where the protein coding regions are located in this sequence. Where are the regulatory sequences? This is very important in genome sequencing projects where a lot of sequences are generated automatically but where only the protein coding sequence may be an interesting to the majority of researchers. Gene structure prediction is not an easy task in prokaryotes, and is an even more difficult task in higher organisms, where genes are split into exons and introns, which can be difficult to detect. Modern gene detection software makes use of very involved artificial intelligence methods, and still far from being completely accurate, even for prokaryotic genes. DNA sequence, which does not code for protein may still be important in the regulation of genes. They may contain recognition sequences for transcription factor. Identifying these patterns may provide a clue to the function of the sequence.

The prediction of the gene elements is a complex problem and its issue is primordial because of its consequences on all the following analysis. Eukaryotic genes with their mosaic structure are more difficult to find than prokaryotic ones, which are simple open reading frames. The presence of introns complicates the problem, although the binding sites of the spliceosomes may be used to predict the exact position of the exon borders. According to the prediction tools, the results of the prediction concern the splice sites, the exons or the whole gene (gene modeling software). These prediction programs are based on two different approaches. The first version is called intrinsic based on the features of the genes and the genomes. Therefore significant and representative sets of only experimentally characterized genes are necessary to develop such efficient prediction programs. Further more, the origin of the training set has to be species specific because each genome has its own features and style. The second approach to find genes and exons, named extrinsic, uses the similarities detected in homologus genes (in general at the protein level to increase the sensibility of the search), or even better, identities with cognate transcript sequences. Only in this ideal last situation is the resulting gene structure asserted and not merely putative. The performance (sensitivity and specificity) of the annotation softwares differing a lot and consequently, the final prediction are not identically reliable. The structural annotation is generally semiautomatic because human intervention is necessary to integrate the results of the different predictions, in the final gene structure. Although a fully integrated annotation platform is still lacking, some annotation centers use an interactive method to visualize the output of the prediction tools and sequence similarity searches to help in this critical decision step.

(ii) ***Functional Annotation :*** At the present time, the functional genome annotation is based on the idea that some sequence similarities detected between two proteins means that they are homologus, i.e., that they come from the same ancestor and share the same biochemical function. Therefore, for each predicted gene, the protein is deduced from the coding region and is compared through BLASTP with the protein databases. If the similarities detected are considered relevant, the name (function of the putative homologue protein is associated with the prediction). This minimum approach allows, in the best cases, the biochemical function of the gene product to be suggested. The high-throughout annotation realized by the annotation centers is too basic and quick to extract reliable information on the biological function. Some annotators confirm and complete the BLAST results by full-length alignment between the query protein and the closet homologue detected and by looking for motifs and family signatures. This approach appears to be the best to attribute one or several biochemical functions to a predicted protein. The name attributed to the predicted genes/ proteins depends on the results of the homologus sequence research. Four categories of genes have been defined, but the associated nomenclature is not very homogenous. The tendency is nevertheless the following when a predicted gene product is 100% identical to an already characterized protein; it receives the same name, whereas sequences with stringent similarity to known proteins are called putative proteins of the same name. The sequences for which only similarities to ESTs are detected are named unknown proteins. Finally, genes without similar sequences and hence only deduced from intrinsic prediction programs are labeled hypothetical.

(iii) **Limits :** The annotation of a genomic sequence is never perfect and always inevitably incomplete. Classical errors and limits inherent to the annotation will be discussed here. The multinational and fragmented organization of genome annotation allows the scientists to follow the daily huge sequence production, but sets the problem of the heterogeneous character of the results. All annotated genes donot have the same reliability. The validity level of each prediction is rarely specified in the feature section of the sequences, making it necessary to consult the annotation centers Web site. The ideal case is when the different prediction software are in agreement with each other and with the detected conserved regions. In this too rare situation, the final prediction is very reliable. More frequently, the similarities found are too low and small to influence a choice between different predictions and the validity of the annotation is extremely difficult to estimate. The Rebuilt gene has little chance of being true. As shown by the graphical interfaces of the Web sites, the data at the origin of annotations can be very different in terms of quality and quantity, and the resulting genes have to be considered with caution. Classical errors in the structural annotation, as a result of prediction failure, are gene splitting (two genes are predicted instead of one) and gene merging (the opposite situation). Even with exon prediction tools becoming more and more efficient, it is still difficult to predict whether the exons are internal or external.

Indeed the gene extremities are not easily predicted for many reasons. The nucleotide content of the introns and intergenic regions is very similar and at least in Arabidobsis, very long introns (up to 4 kb) and very short or even rarely no intergenic regions (overlapping genes) can be found. Consequently, gene-modeling programs have difficulties in making the distinction. Furthermore, very few experimental data on plant promoter sequences and translation initiation sites are available to help the 5' Prediction. In the 3' extremity, the canonical polyadnylation may occur and hence cannot be used to predict final exons. As in the case for mammals and yeasts, some times only the detection of similarities with only one or two different proteins allows the discrimination between one or two genes. For this reason gene merging is more frequent in genomic regions that contains gene clusters. Prediction softwares evolve very rapidly but it may take sometime to recognize which is the most efficient. For example, gene mark has been evaluated as the best genome-modeling program for Arabidobsis but surprisingly not used by the AGI Annotation centres. To give an idea of the prediction efficiency, this program can find 80% of the actual exons although the modeling of perfect genes is only approximately 40%. An obvious but important limit is that prediction are based on previously known data and consequently the rare and novel gene features splice sites, overlapping genes, atypical translation start, alternative splicing, etc., cannot be found in the annotation. The systemic sequencing of full-length cDNA will probably be the unique long-term solution for structural annotation. In functional annotations, the major problem occurs when an erroneous function is attributed to a predicted gene and spread by recurring references in numerous other annotations. The automatic interpretation of a BLAST result is very dangerous because it increases the background noise of high scoring but biologically irrelevant matches. In several cases, the similarities detected by local alignments have to be more deeply analyzed to avoid giving importance to a no significant match. The additional use of full-length alignments between the predicted protein and the best hits detected by BLAST reduce the error rate but is not systematically done.

Because the databases TrEMBL andGenPep are used to find similarities with each novel predicted protein, a false function can be used as a reference and so be propagated afterwards. This kind of problem is very frequent in the case of MultiDomain Protein, to which wrong functions attributed by crossed references are spread even when the similarities detected by BLAST are significant. By a snowball effect, annotations and databases that exploit them (for instance PFam and PRODOM) are really polluted. Transitively assigning function to a series of closely related sequences appears to be a risky issue. To estimate the consequences of these different difficulties, the automatic annotation of a 400-kb region from arabidiopsis chromosome 4 has been compared to a manual annotation carried out by an expert in sequence analysis. The two annotation methods are in totally in agreement (at structural and functional levels) for only 23 genes out of 106. At present time, the fully automatic annotation methods are not satisfactory and the integrated annotation platforms managed by bioanalyst and regularly actualized seems to be the solution. The nomenclature of genes, proteins and their function is also a source of ambiguities. There is a clear lack of controlled vocabulary both in the literature and the databases. This problem linked to the sequence redundancy in the databases, which can contain several times the same genes under different names. The resulting loss in time for the search and the annotation is very serious. Further more the multi origin of the annotation amplifies the diversity of the nomenclature. For example, the AMERICAN Annotators named as putative or–like a function deduced from similarities, whereas the Japanese center and MIPS use potential and similar respectively. For the latter putative applies to unknown proteins tagged by EST the annotations of bacterial genome suffer from the same kind of problems. The ephemeral feature of some annotations, especially the number of ESTs matches and the closet homologue has to keep in mind when they are used and imposes a regular update. The last important general problem is the lack of accuracy in the annotation sources. It is not always easy to know where the reality ends and where the prediction begins.

Predicted and actual genes are considered identical for statistical analysis or definition of motifs and signature of families. The heterogeneity of the annotations can introduce a significant bias in such studies. Once more the consultation of the annotator/web sites is necessary, but is not optimized for automatic works. Biologists have to consider all these weaknesses to optimize their searches and to be capable of exploiting fruitfully genome annotations.

11.3   Analysis of Gene Functions and Metabolic Pathways From Databases

The availability of the complete genomes allows many new types of experiments and analysis. The new approaches and question that the genomes make possible are usually   referred to as functional genomics. The task is to define the function of a gene (or its protein) in the life processes of the organism, where function refers to the role it plays in a larger context. But what are these life processes? The most obvious example is the metabolism of an organism, the basic chemical system that generates essential components such as amino acids, sugars and lipids, and the energy requires to synthesize them and to use them in creating proteins and cellular structures. This system of connected chemical reactions is a metabolic network.

An important emerging field in bioinformatics is to understand metabolic and signaling networks in term of their function in the organism and in relation to the data we already have. This requires combining information from a large number of sources: classical biochemistry, genomics, functional genomics (e.g., micro array experiments), network analysis, life process descriptions, functional genomics and simulations. A theory of the cell must combine the description of the structures in it (genome, proteome, subcelular structures, etc.,) with a theoretical and computational description of the dynamic of the life process. One of the most important future challenges to the bioinformtics is to how to make all this information comprehensible in biological terms. This necessitate in order to facilitates the use of the information for predictive purposes. We want to do more than just describe what is going on in an organism : we also wish to be able to say what will happen in given some specific set of circumstances. This kind of predictive power will only be reached if the complexity of biological processes can be handled.

11.4 Computer Assisted Analysis of Transcription Control Regions

Identification of all of the genes in the genome is a major objective of the genome projects. Recently as the genome project has entered the phase of large scale sequencing, computational approaches to gene finding have begun to draw significant attention from the molecular biology and genomics community. In addition, significant advances in gene finding methodology have taken place in the past two years, and the current methods are significantly more accurate, reliable and useful than those available in the past. Gene discovery in prokaryotic genomes is a quite different problem from that encountered in eukaryotic sequences, owing to the higher gene density typical of prokaryotes and the absence of introns in their protein coding gene. These properties generally implies that most open reading frames (ORFs) encountered in a prokaryotic sequence that are longer than some reasonable threshold, such as 300 and 500 base pairs will likely corresponds to genes. The primary difficulty arising from this simple approach are that very small genes will be missed and that the occurrence of overlapping long ORFs on opposite DNA strands (genes and shadow genes) often leads to ambiguities. To resolve these problems several methods have been devised that use different types of Markov Models in order to capture the compositional differences among the coding regions, shadow coding regions (coding on the opposite DNA strand) and non-coding DNA. Some degree of caution must be exercised in using such statistically–based methods in view of the relatively high frequency of genetic transformation, the occurrence of lateral gene transfer in many bacteria, and other factors that lead to heterogeneity in gene composition.

11.5 Translational Signals

The principal translational signals that have been used in gene finding are the Kozak signal ((GCC) GCCGCCATGG), proposed by Kozak located immediately upstream of the initial ATG, and the termination codon, used primarily for its absence (in frame) in coding exons. Since these signals contains far too little information to allow discrimination in bulk genomic DNA, reliable prediction of translation start and stop sites may not be possible until more progress has been made towards predicting the sites of transcription initiation and termination, which would dramatically reduce the amount of sequence that needs to be searched. Using simple weight matrix description of the Kozak and translational termination signals in the context of the integrated gene-finding program GENSCAN, about two third (66%) of translation initiation sites and about three quarter (78%) of termination codons have been correctly predicted, with specificities of 84% and 91% respectively. Although these levels of accuracy are high enough to be useful they are significantly lower than those achieved for splicing signals, and leads to poorer prediction of initial and terminal exons that has been achieved for internal exons.

11.6 Splicing Signals

Even if one could reliably predict promoter and polyadenylation signals, and translation start and stop sites in genomic sequences, this knowledge would generally help only in predicting the location of the first and last exons of a gene. Since most vertebrates, invertebrates, and plant genes contains several exons, accurate prediction of gene structure in these organisms is much more dependent up on the ability of predictions to pin point splice signals. Nuclear Pre-mRNA introns are excised from the primary transcript by a large ribonucleoprotein complex known as the spliceosome, which recognizes sites at the 5' and 3' ends of the intron (the donar and acceptor splice sites respectively), as well as an internal site known as the branch point. With a few interesting exceptions, virtually all spliceosomal introns begins with GT and end with AG, and this nearly invariant rule is used by the majority of gene finding programs to narrow the search space of possible exon and intron boundaries. Many early gene-finding methods used simple weigh matrix independent models of the position specific compositional biases present in the 5' and 3' splice sites and of the bias towards pyrimidine nucleotides upstream of 3' splice sites. More recently several authors have observed statistically significant dependencies between positions within both the donar and acceptor splice sites. Certain observed dependencies between donor splice sites positions can be interpreted in terms of the thermodynamics of

RNA duplex formation between U1 small nuclear RNA (snRNA) and the 5' splice site region of the pre-mRNA. Of the dependencies observed for human acceptor splice sites, some appears to result simply from the compositional heterogeneity of the human genome, whereas others probably relate to the specificity of pyrimidine track binding proteins. The development of more complex splice signal models that are capable of capturing such dependencies has been a significant recent trend in the gene finding literature: example includes the Maximal dependence decomposition (MDD) and windowed weight array (WWAM) models, Hidden Markov Models, decision tree methods and multilayered neural networks. These more complex models typically yield significant but not dramatic improvements in splice site discrimination over the simpler models, which assume independence between positions. The final level of accuracy achieved depends critically on whether prediction is measured in isolation or in the context of an integrated gene finding methods.

11.7 Comparative Sequence Analysis

DNA is a very dynamic molecule that undergoes a wide variety of alterations and modifications and gene duplications occur naturally and frequently. With two copies of a gene available in a genome, one copy could provide the necessary original function while the other could accumulate mutations that may alter its function, if this altered copy evolved eventually to serve a new function, it would be retained in the genome and passed on to later generations. It is plausible that most modern genes originated from one or a few ancestral genes, but this is difficult to prove or disprove because the amount of change that would have occurred since then will have obscured any similarities among their modern descendents. Many genes and proteins of an organism are homologous are obviously the products of gene duplication. The genes of such homologus proteins in a genome are said to comprise a gene family. As the number of known protein and gene sequences increases, more and more gene families have been found. The most studied one family, and the most striking for the similarities among its polypeptide chains, is that of globins of higher organisms; this family includes single, Chain myoglobin and the various polypeptides of tetrameric Haemoglobins.

The globins have related functions in that they store oxygen; myoglobin store oxygen in muscle and haemoglobin in erythrocytes, while transporting it. The various polypeptides chains of haemoglobin function at various stages of life, and they associate to form comparable tetrameric molecules.

11.8 Eukaryotic Gene Prediction

The aim of this practical is to get hands-on experience running some Web Servers for eukaryotic gene prediction on an "unknown" sequence. We will use coding prediction programs together with promoter, splice and poly-A site prediction programs. All the information gathered has to be combined to find the coding regions of the gene. There is no time to go into the theory behind the prediction methods.

As anyone who has looked at automatically annotated genome sequence data will know, automatic gene prediction in higher eukaryotes does not work very well. Perhaps this is not surprising, considering that differential and tissue-specific splicing, genes within genes, TATA-less promoters, the rare class of U12-dependent (AT-AC) splice sites, the need for species-specific parameters, all complicate the problem.

In practice, the bench biologist is best advised to inform themselves of the species-specific signals (e.g. mammals tend to have a looser splice site consensus than the worm) that they should expect and then run several servers and synthesize the results, looking (in part) for consistency between different servers. As there is a lot of activity in gene prediction (even though much of it is "reinventing the wheel") we may hope for better predictions and better presentation in the future.

Step 1

(i) *WWW Servers used in the Gene Prediction practical*

We will use :

- NetGene2 and HMMgene to predict coding exons and splice sites in eukaryotes.

- The LBL Promoter prediction service and TSSG, TSSW from the Sanger Center.

- The POLYAH server for the prediction of the poly-A site.
- GeneWise (from the Wise2 package) for aligning protein v. spliced DNA sequence.

Note : You now have the sequence available in a form that can be cut and pasted into the query forms we are going to use. Or else get the sequence from the NCBI. How to obtain sequences from NCBI database is explained somewhere in this book. before proceeding further read that information.

1. Net gene

2. HMM gene

3. LBL promoter

4. TSSG   *For all these just type "gene prediction programs" in google search option window.*

5. TSSW

6. POLYAH

7. Genewise

Step 2

(ii) *Looking for a Promoter candidate*

Promoter prediction is heavily dependent on finding good matches to the TATAAAA motif. CCAAT-Box, CpG islands and other transcription factor binding sites may provide further clues. But if you run MatInspector with the TRANSFAC DB on our query, you will be astonished at the profusion of candidate sites throughout the sequence - so we won't bother. We will run two promoter prediction programs and tentatively assume that the best intersecting promoter is the correct one.

- Load the LBL Promoter query submission page.
- It is worth familiarizing yourself with the layout and note the on-line help.

- Cut and paste the query sequence into the sequence box and submit the job.
- When the result arrives look at the set of predicted promoters
  - *Can you see matches to the TATA box consensus* tATA$^A/_T$A$^A/_T$
  - *Which promoter has the silliest TATA-box?*
- Open a new navigator window and load this page into it.
- Load the TSSG query submission page.
- Toggle on the **TSSG** button.
- Don't use the sequence paste box. (It can't strip out numbers from the sequence).
- Type (or paste) **/home/seqanal/public_html/courses/spring99/ seq.fasta** in the load box and then perform search.
- When the result arrives look at the set of predicted promoters
  - How many TATA boxes were found?
  - Are the listed transcription factors binding sites informative?
  - How well do the two searches agree on candidate promoters?
  - How many candidates do they both find?
  - Is there a single best candidate from combining the *searches?*

Note : These outputs are rather terse to say the least. Doing this for real, you should look at the web site helps to get some idea of what is being done and be willing to go to the literature if need be.

Step 3

(iii) *Poly (A) site prediction*

In mammalian genes, polyadenylation sites are usually preceded by AATAAA or ATTAAA ~20 bases before the cleavage site and followed by a more weakly conserved GT-based motif. While these motifs are trivial to find, they only function in the right context which is harder to define and includes regulation by upstream splicing factors.

An important rule to remember is that there must not be an in-frame stop codon in an internal exon *i.e.* the true translation termination will be in the last exon. (Violations to this rule suppress mRNA production, to the cost of many experimentalists, and is occasionally used for differential mRNA regulation *e.g.* for certain Ig splice variants.)

- (As needed, open a new navigator window and load this page into it.)
- Load the POLYAH query submission page.
- Toggle on the **POLYAH** button.
- Look at the POLYAH help and note the quoted prediction accuracy.
- Don't use the sequence paste box. (It can't strip out numbers from the sequence).
- Type (or paste) **/home/seqanal/public_html/courses/spring99/ seq.fasta** in the load box and then perform search.
- When the result arrives, look at the predicted poly (A) sites.
  - *How many candidate sites were found?*
  - *If one or more of these sites are false is the prediction accuracy as good as claimed?*
  - *How might over prediction of poly(A) sites be avoided?*

We can't assess the context of these sites properly until we have the coding/splicing predictions to hand.

Note : If incase you do not get the result by typing the above mention seq file, then paste the sequence in sequence paste box.

Step 4

(iv) *Predicting Splice Sites and Coding Exons*

There are a number of servers that separately predict splice sites and coding sequence bias but this information needs to be analyzed together. We found that the CBS site in Denmark could provide all the information, though from two different servers.

The NetGene2 server provides graphical postscripts output that we could print out and mark our predictions on. From the same group, the HMMgene server (using different algorithms) provides list output including potential Start and Stop codons. Both servers over predict splice site candidates. In case you need reminding, classical splice sites look something like:

- Donor Consensus: $^c/_aAG \wedge \mathbf{GT}^A/_gAGt$
- Acceptor Consensus: $(T>C)_n N(\mathbf{C>T})\mathbf{AG} \wedge gt$

- (As needed, open a new navigator window and load this page into it.)
- Load the NetGene2 query submission page.
- Paste in the sequence and submit the job, which takes a few minutes to run.
- The output provides a list of candidate splice sites (on both strands) and a graphical coding/splicing prediction.
- However it is not clear which translation frame is supposed to be coding.
- It is worth printing this figure out and using it to summarize our prediction attempts!
  - Click on **Direct strand** and save the compressed postscript output (has a .Z suffix).
  - Open a UNIX X-window (**terminal** from the desktop)
  - Uncompress the file by typing UNIX command
    - **gunzip** *filename*.**ps.Z**
  - Print the file to the printer outside by typing
    - **lpr -Plw-v111** *filename*.**ps**
  - Now load the HMMgene query submission page.
- Paste **/home/seqanal/public_html/courses/spring99/seq.fasta** in the local file box.
- Select **5 best predictions** and toggle on **predict signals.**

- Submit the job.
- Click on the **Explanation** link to understand the output format.
- We can now begin to assemble a complete gene prediction.

Step 5

(v) *Combining the server outputs into an overall prediction*

We now have predictions for all the components needed to assemble the gene, rather inconveniently spread over many separate web outputs. We have to manually assemble all this into one prediction. This can be done on the Netgene2 and DNA sequence outputs using biro and fluorescent marker. The following guidelines may help.

- Start from a strong point such as:
- A well-predicted internal coding exon with good splice borders.
- Work forwards and backwards toward the promoter and poly(A) boundary signals.
- Reported splice site quality is not a completely robust guide to usage.
  - Context dependence is also important.
  - Splice sites tend to be over predicted.
  - Some (true) splice sites might be better predicted by the HMMgene algorithm than by NetGene2...
- The terminal exon should be partially coding, including the stop codon and the poly(A) signal.
- The initiation codon should obey the Kozak rules:
  - It is normally the first methionine from the 5' end of the mRNA.
  - At least one of the underlined residues should be present in the consensus APuXXAUGG.
- Once the prediction is completed, we can check it in the next exercise.
- Good luck!

Step 6.

(vi) *Gene prediction by homology using GeneWise*

Usually nowadays, related sequences are already present in the databases. When available these may be the fastest way to get a good gene prediction. Often this prediction will be more reliable than the coding bias predictions though one should be aware of the possibility of sequence error, differential splicing etc. and of course finding the coding exons is not a complete gene prediction. The gene wise program has an exhaustive (slow) algorithm to align a protein to a DNA sequence, allowing for splice site recognition. (In a real situation, BLAST programs would be useful for first picking up the matches in a DB search.)

- Open an *X-window* (or *terminal* on Tau's desktop).

- Type *prepare wise2* in the window.

- We've prepared files with the human DNA and a homologous chicken protein to compare.

- Now you can type or cut and paste the following command into the UNIX window:

  - **genewise /home/seqanal/public_html/courses/spring99/ kad1_chick /home/seqanal/public_html/courses/ spring99/hsak1.dna**

- The program will run with default parameters and after a couple of minutes will print out the matched exons.

- Now compare the results to the predictions so far

  - How many Exons are found?

  - Are the splice sites between or within codons?

  - Did you find all these coding regions earlier?

  - Have we now found all the coding exons (the chicken homologue has 194 AA)?

- Now lets look at the annotated genomic sequence entry for our test sequence, HSAK1

- Note that no cDNA has been sequenced for this gene: gene structure was inferred by some transcript mapping and by protein homology.

- Most of the elements of the gene are listed in the feature table.

  - Did you get the promoter?

  - Did you get the starting methionine? Does it obey Kozak's rules?

  - How many amino acids are in the first coding exon?

  - If you made any errors in the prediction, can you see where you went wrong?

  - There is a problem with the annotation of the first intron's acceptor:

    - Do you think this is -

      - An unusual splice site?

      - An annotation error made *by the authors?*

(vii) *Take Home Lessons*

There seems to be no single high quality tool for doing eukaryotic gene prediction work. The variations in the results from prediction servers indicate that there is scope for improving the algorithms. Graphical presentation of the results is patchy for example we need to know start, stop codons and which frame has the coding potential, information that we did not get from the graphical plot. To do this for real, we would need to assemble results from many servers and work with a hard copy of the DNA sequence and it would take longer than the morning we set aside today, to do the job properly. In fact the Staden package has for many years been able to produce a plot with all this information, although it was clumsy and old fashioned to use and some of the prediction methods may be more sensitive now. This package has been updated recently and we will have a look at how useful it is for gene prediction in our next edition.

Good Luck ....

Current gene-finding programs are complex integrated systems that incorporate a number of different methods for gene finding. The set of methods used and the way they are integrated vary between individual programs. It has been observed [1, 2] that these different techniques often correctly predict different elements of the gene, suggesting that programs could complement each other, yielding better predictions.

In order to test this hypothesis we explored different methods for combining predictions from two gene-finding programs. After extensive evaluation of current eukaryotic gene-finding programs, Genscan and HMMgene were chosen for their high prediction accuracy and their reliable estimates of the accuracy of the exon prediction. The predictions were combined on the exon level, using three separate techniques: decision trees, modified set operations and probabilistic networks.

Some of these methods yielded notable improvements in the prediction accuracy especially at the exon level: the sensitivity increased from 0.76 to 0.79 (4.0%) and the specificity increased from 0.77 to 0.86 (11.7%), compared to the best exon level accuracy measures achieved by any single program. The successful methods were tested on three independent datasets, each time outperforming any individual gene-finding program. The results were especially good for the dataset containing sequences with several genes, where exon accuracy measures were improved by 30% compared to Genscan's results.

Appendix A

List of Bioinformatics Course Web Pages

US List of links to Bioinformatics courses (not all links work)

http://www.wiley.com/legacy/products/subject/life/bioinformatics/courses.html

Comprehensive list of graduate programs in Bioinformatics, including international programs.

http://www.iscb.org/univ.shtml

Report on bioinformatics skills sets

http://bioinf.man.ac.uk/ember/PDF/CALreport.pdf

Birkbeck College (UK)

Principals of Protein Structure Using the Internet. This course is from 1996, but it is still a very good resource. Updated versions of the site require course enrollment.

http://www.cryst.bbk.ac.uk/PPS2/course/index.html

Carnegie Mellon

http://www.cmu.edu/bio/education/masters.html

Duke University

Center for Bioinformatics and Computational Biology including information on the certificate program

http://www.cbcb.duke.edu//

Harvard

Biophysics 101 page. Genomics and Computational Biology taught by George Church.

http://icg.harvard.edu/~bphys101/

Indiana University

Computer Sources in Chemical Information

http://www.indiana.edu/%7Echeminfo/401syl00.html

Johns Hopkins

Program in Computational Biology at Johns Hopkins

http://www.jhu.edu/~ibr/bwf.html

CS 600.439 Principles of Computational Biology Fall 1999 taught by Steven Salzberg

http://www.tigr.org/~salzberg/cs439.html

MIT

Bioinformatics and Metabolic Engineering at MIT. Includes a list of courses offered.

http://web.mit.edu/cheme/gnswebpage/links.shtml

18.417: Introduction to Computational Molecular Biology MIT course with notes and slides

http://theory.lcs.mit.edu/~bab/01-18.417-home.html

North Carolina State

Bioinformatics Masters Program

http://genomics.ncsu.edu/bioinfo.html

Functional Genomics Masters Program

http://genomics.ncsu.edu/function.html

San Diego State

BIMM 140 Introduction to Bioinformatics. This course looks very comprehensive and the homework assignments are very helpful.

http://www.sdsc.edu/~gribskov/bimm140/

Introduction to Bioinformatics Molecular Biology BGGN 220. This is a course related to BIMM140, but has a different instructor, Douglas Smith.

http://www-biology.ucsd.edu/others/dsmith/bioinformatics.html

Bioinformatics I / PHARM 201 Biological Data and Analysis Tools Course offered in Pharmacy Department by Doug Bourne. The web page is from Fall 2001.

http://www.sdsc.edu/pb/edu/pharm201/

Hands-on companion course PHARM 207 also offered by David Bourne. Nice hands-on links.

http://www.sdsc.edu/pb/edu/pharm207/pharm207.html

Stanford University

Stanford offers an on-line certificate course in Bioinformatics.

http://scpd.stanford.edu/SCPD/courses/proEd

subjList.asp?sdID=5&sdName=Bioinformatics

Syllabus for Stanford class delivered via streaming video called Representations and Algorithms for Computational Molecular Biology. This is pretty heavy-duty computation and math syllabus.

http://www.smi.stanford.edu/projects/helix/bmi214/

Syllabus for another Stanford class delivered via streaming video: Computational Molecular Biology. This is the course description and syllabus. Course materials require registration.

  http://cmgm.stanford.edu/biochem218/#Description

Syllabus for the third Stanford course: CS 262 Computational Genomics offered Spring 2002.

  http://www.stanford.edu/class/cs262/

University of Arizona

Course developed by David Mount. This elaborate course page was preceding his book. The new course link isn't as complete as the old course link.

  http://www.blc.arizona.edu/courses/bioinformatics/

University of Illinois

Bioinformatics Unit W.M. Keck Center for Comparative and Functional Genomics at the University of Illinois at Urbana-Champaign

  http://titan.biotec.uiuc.edu/

University of North Carolina, Chapel Hill

Program in Bioinformatics and Computational Biology

  http://bioinfo.med.unc.edu/Bioinformatics/index.html

University of San Diego

Bioinformatics and Computational Biology at UCSD

  http://genome.ucsd.edu/

Updated list of courses taught in Bioinformatics in San Diego, along with links to some other courses with information on-line.

  http://www.sdsc.edu/pb/Edu.html

Great course web pages from University of San Diego: They offer an interdisciplinary program in bioinformatics described at

http://bioinformatics.ucsd.edu/

BENG 202/CSE 257A Bioinformatics II: Sequence and Structure Analysis.

Instructors: Shankar Subramaniam and Pavel Pevzner Strong computer/Math focus.

http://genome.ucsd.edu/classes/be202/

Math 578 - Spring 2002 DNA and Protein Sequence Analysis

http://www-hto.usc.edu/%7Etingchen/Math578/

University of California Santa Cruz Bioinformatics Courses:

A proposed MA/PhD Program in Bioinformatics at UC Santa Cruz

http://www.cse.ucsc.edu/centers/cbe/prop-ms.html

UCSC Bioinformatics (Computational Biology) Home Page. This page covers links to all their bioinformatics and Computational Biology offerings.

http://www.soe.ucsc.edu/research/compbio/

University of Exeter

Postgraduate Programmes in Bioinformatics MSc (EPSRC-supported MRes), Certificate, Diploma Exeter is a partner school with WV State College.

http://www.dcs.ex.ac.uk/~anarayan/bioinf/msc.htm

University of Pennsylvania

University of Pennsylvania Center for Bioinformatics

http://www.pcbi.upenn.edu/education.php3

University of Virginia

Biochem 508, Spring 2002 Computer Analysis of DNA and Protein Sequences William R. Pearson. Very nice exercises. Especially for those wishing to compare FASTA and BLAST. Pearson developed FASTA.

http://www.people.virginia.edu/~wrp/bioch508/

University of Washington

Introduction to Computational Molecular Biology:

Genome and Protein Sequence Analysis (Winter/Spring Quarter 2002). This class emphasizes programming and has nice homework assignments. It is a graduate level class. It is a two-semester class, and the slides are summarized as pdf files.

http://www.phrap.org/compbio/mbt599/

Another University of Washington Course: Bioinformatics and Gene Sequence Analysis. Notes pages are very useful. This is also a graduate course. Course was offered in spring 2002.

http://courses.washington.edu/bioinfo/

University of Washington Course Genetics 570 Phylogenetic Inference offered spring, 2000. This course emphasizes Phylogenetic tree building, and one of the course faculty is working on a book. Nice list of references and some data files to use for practice.

http://depts.washington.edu/genetics/courses/genet570/2000/index.html

University of Washington Course CSE 527: Computational Biology offered in 2001. This course emphasizes the computational aspects. It is a graduate course with nice slides available. Lots of discussion of analysis of micro array data.

http://www.cs.washington.edu/education/courses/527/01au/

University of Waterloo

The Bioinformatics Research Group in the School of Computer Science at the University of Waterloo

http://monod.uwaterloo.ca//courses.php3

University of Wisconsin

Dr. Ann Palmentberg at UW teaches a Biomodules course to intro Biochemistry graduate students. She has links and tutorials available at these sites.

http://www.virology.wisc.edu/acp/pages/Classes
CommonResources_index.html

Dr. Palmenberg's great glossary

http://www.virology.wisc.edu/acp/pages/Classes/ClassMaterials/
TableofWords_711_00.html

Another syllabus from 2000.

http://www.virology.wisc.edu/acp/pages/Classes/Syllabi/Syl_711_00.html

Computation and Informatics in Biology and Medicine- an interdisciplinary program.

http://www.cibm.wisc.edu/

Virginia Tech

Courses taught by Cynthia Gibas at Virginia Tech.

Her homepage has links to her syllabus.

http://gibas.biotech.vt.edu/

http://gibas.biotech.vt.edu/methods1/methods1.html

Graduate Options in Bioinformatics at Virginia Tech.

http://graduate.bioinformatics.vt.edu/

Washington University

Bio5495/BME 537 Introduction to Computational Molecular Biology. Syllabus for a graduate class.

http://bio5495.wustl.edu/

Yale University

Bioinforatics Degrees at Yale

http://bioinfo.mbb.yale.edu/

MB&B 452a / 752a2 Fall 1999 BIOINFORMATICS MODULE. This has a great reading list, but the links don't all work. They could help your interlibrary loan quest though.

http://bioinfo.mbb.yale.edu/mbb452a/bioinformatics.htm

Appendix B

Downloadable Resources to Power Up Your Web Browser

Stuffit Expander/Aladdin Expander

Free utility program to decompress files downloaded from the web (handles many file formats)

http://www.Aladdinsys.com/expander/

Adobe Acrobat Reader

Free viewer for documents in Adobe **PDF** format

http://www.adobe.com/prodindex/acrobat/readstep.html

Macromedia Shockwave player

Free viewer/player for Shockwave and Flash animations (includes games, cartoons and music as well as academic content)

http://www.macromedia.com/shockwave/download/

RasMol

View and rotate molecular structures in 3D - particularly useful for PDB data files.

http://www.umass.edu/microbio/rasmol/getras.htm

Chime

Chime is a browser plug-in that allows you to view 3D molecular structures within a web page.

It is used for many online tutorials about structural biology

Download Chime http://www.mdli.com/support/chime/download.html

Chime Resources http://www.umass.edu/microbio/chime/index.html

QuickTime 4

Free viewer for internet video in QuickTime 4 format (Macintosh and Windows 95/97/NT)

    http://www.apple.com/quicktime/install/

Real Player

A free viewer for RealAudio/Real Video Internet audio and video formats from Real Networks (currently the most popular format on the Web) - available for all types of computers.

    http://www.real.com/products/player

    downloadrealplayer.html?wp=dl0599&src=choice_1&lang=en#form

Microsoft Media Player

A free viewer for Microsoft's own format for sending video over the Web

    http://www.microsoft.com/windows/mediaplayer/

Microsoft PowerPoint Viewer

A free viewer for Microsoft PowerPoint slide presentations

(Useful if you don't have PowerPoint, or just don't have enough RAM to run it while you browse the web)

Macintosh version

    http://www.microsoft.com/macoffice/productinfo/98dl/pptvdl.htm

Windows 3.x

    http://officeupdate.microsoft.com/downloadDetails/ppview16.htm

Windows 95/97/NT

    http://officeupdate.microsoft.com/downloadDetails/ppview97.htm

Appendix C

Background/Introductory material on Molecuar Biololgy

Access Excellence (high school biology students and teachers)

Genentech

   http://www.accessexcellence.org/index.html>

About Biotechnology

   http://www.accessexcellence.org/AB/BC/

Winding your way through DNA

   http://www.accessexcellence.org/AB/WYW/index.html

An Introduction to Nucleic Acids

Helen M. Berman and Christine Zardecki, Rutgers Univ, NJ, USA

   http://ndbserver.rutgers.edu/NDB/archives/NAintro/index.html

Beginners Guide to Molecular Biology

Nathalie Castells-Brooke

Institute of Arable Crops, Rothamsted, UK

http://www.res.bbsrc.ac.uk/molbio/guide/

Tutorials in Molecular Biology (Shockwave movies)

Steve Sobolevsky

UCLA Undergraduate Biological Sciences Education Program

http://locutus.lsic.ucla.edu/ls3/tutorials/

A collection of Shockwave movies on a number of molecular biology topics including transcription, translation, electrophoresis, sequencing, PCR, the Lac operon, and the Lambda life cycle. Very little text, very slow to download over a modem.

WWW Cell Biology Course

Mark Dalton, SGI Inc.

http://www.cbc.umn.edu/~mwd/cell.html

On-Line Biology Book (1999) - freshman biology - an awesome amount of content

Michael J. Farabee, Estrella Mountain Community College

http://gened.emc.maricopa.edu/bio/bio181/BIOBK/BioBookTOC.html

MIT Biology Hypertextbook

The Experimental Study Group, Massachusetts Institute of Technology

http://esg-www.mit.edu:8001/esgbio/

US Dept. of Energy Primer on Molecular Genetics (1992)

Denise Casey, Oak Ridge National Laboratory,

http://www.ornl.gov/TechResources/Human_Genome/publicat/primer/intro.html

Interactive Biochemistry Online

Edward K.O'Neil & Charles M. Grisham

University of Virginia, Charlottesville VA

   http://cti.itc.virginia.edu/~cmg/

Makes heavy use of Chime and VRML plugins

www.ingramcontent.com/pod-product-compliance
Lightning Source LLC
Chambersburg PA
CBHW050646190326
41458CB00008B/2443